WOMEN IN THE HOUSE OF FICTION

Women in the House of Fiction

Post-War Women Novelists

LORNA SAGE

Routledge
New York

First published 1992 by
THE MACMILLAN PRESS LTD
Houndmills, Basingstoke, Hampshire, RG21 2XS
and London
Companies and representatives
throughout the world

First published in North America 1992 by
ROUTLEDGE, CHAPMAN and HALL, INC.
29 West 35th Street
New York, N.Y. 10001

Cataloging-in-Publication data is available
from the Library of Congress

ISBN 0–415–90658–X Hb
ISBN 0–415–90659–8 Pb

Printed in Hong Kong

For my daughter Sharon

Contents

Preface

The first thing that caught my imagination about Simone de Beauvoir – back in my teens, back in the late 1950s – was that she lived in a hotel. This single fact seemed to imply all the rest: domesticity spurned, never cooking supper for Sartre, living on words and ideas. She was the woman writer as intellectual, for her the business of writing was public, shared and out of doors (she wrote in cafés). And the writing, of course, exposed the bad faith of living inside fictions about women's 'nature'. Not only *The Second Sex*, but the novels too treated the domain of character and representation as the place where the 'others' lived, playing their parts and acting out their roles – especially the female characters, who were specialists in *mauvaise foi*. Meanwhile the author herself had the freedom of no man's land.

My picture of Beauvoir, like everyone else's, has changed a lot since then. If she is the 'mother' of modern feminism, that's because she is a figure full of contradictions. Her characters' bad faith is nothing compared to hers. She still seems to me the right starting-point, though, because she sets up the right paradoxes – in her stubborn loyalty to theory (and Sartre) in the face of her experience; in her reluctance to see herself as 'just a woman', along with her self-consciousness; in her writing of realist novels that put reality in quotation marks. This book begins with pieces on the (mostly) post-war generation of novelists who, like her, find the house of fiction ramshackle and claustrophobic. Representations fix and reproduce a world of '"types" of flesh and blood human beings' (this is Nathalie Sarraute) and conspire to naturalise us in it – 'Everybody what they are. Clinging completely to themselves.' Sarraute's narrators act like domestic vampires, sucking out the spurious 'life' from their subjects:

> When . . . these 'live' persons, or these characters, condescend to come near me too, all I am able to do is to hover about them and try with fanatical eagerness to find the crack, the tiny crevice, the weak point as delicate as a baby's fontanelle . . . . [1]

This sort of writing is often elevated or relegated to the territory of the *avant garde*, but it reads more interestingly as partisan, reactive de-composing. The 'character' that's really under attack is that of the traditional woman novelist.

Not that 'woman' equals 'tradition'. After all, 'the house of fiction' is a Henry James metaphor. Nonetheless, it's striking how personally women novelists make – and take – attacks on their inheritance. Their experimentalism, and their displacements, are not to be accounted for in terms of some universal state of textuality. The best brief description of *that* no man's land is still, I think, the one Barthes conjures out of a hat in *The Pleasure of the Text*:

> . . . we are all caught up in the truth of languages, that is, in their regionality . . . . For each jargon (each fiction) fights for hegemony; if power is on its side, it spreads everywhere . . . . but even out of power, even when power is against it, the rivalry is reborn, the jargons split and struggle among themselves. A ruthless *topic* rules the life of language; language always comes from some place, it is a warrior *topos* . . . .
>
> The text itself is atopic, if not in its consumption at least in its production. It is not a jargon, a fiction, in it the system is overcome, undone . . . . From this atopia the text catches and communicates to its reader a strange condition, at once excluded and at peace . . . . [2]

The atopic text is plural, placeless. Writing is anybody's and everybody's, the text is a heterocosm. The texts I've been reading, though, aren't like that. When they envisage a no man's land, they're consciously *utopian* (Sarraute, Christina Stead, Elizabeth Smart). That is, they have satiric, didactic, speculative or combative aims. They are part of the continuing war of languages. We hide this from ourselves, I think, by speaking the language of the *avant garde*. As Marianne DeKoven wryly points out, 'Manifestoes for avant garde . . . and feminine . . . stylistic practice often sound remarkably alike without knowing that they do or taking cognisance of each other in any way.'[3] This isn't a war, perhaps, but it's certainly not a peace either. Women's writing 'comes from some place'.

So 'the house of fiction' isn't, for my purposes, only a metaphor for containment. It's a reminder that fiction isn't placeless. Thinking about the novel and novel tradition this way has caused me to read realist texts rather differently. I had been planning to talk more dismissively about nostalgia. In the event I've found myself exploring – in the work of Iris Murdoch, in particular –

a fascinating latter-day defence of what I think of as 'matriarchal realism'. Murdoch surrounds and submerges the avatars of theoretical freedom with a multitude of representations. She domesticates them, in short. And she knows just what she's doing, as her books on Sartre and Plato demonstrate. She's 'placing' metalanguages, calling into question the (seductive) power of the over-view. What she enjoys about representation (mimesis) is precisely what Plato hates – its local, partial, illusionist tricks; everything that makes the quotidian world of passion, habit, conflict and muddle seem 'real'. Quantity is a factor here too, the burgeoning detail, huge cast-lists, and so much otherness that dualism looks defeated. Murdoch has a good phrase – 'a great hall of reflection' – for what Plato thought of as the 'cave'. It's not a bad description of her kind of novel. She also helps to explain the continuing importance of the novel's mirroring function, which is by no means confined to realism.

There's been a revaluation of representation since the iconoclastic heyday of the 'new novel'. Angela Carter's *The Infernal Desire Machines of Doctor Hoffman* suggests why: reflections don't only reproduce, they breed new meanings, and multiply possibilities –

> The Minister sent the Determination Police round to break all the mirrors because of the lawless images they were disseminating. Since mirrors offer alternatives, the mirrors had all turned into fissures or crannies in the hitherto hard-edged world of here and now . . . . [4]

The women's movement, and feminist politics, have found fictional shape in narratives that explore self-division, the multiplicity of ways to be. The novelists, I want to argue, are agents of alterneity, interested – after all – in reinscribing the boundaries of fiction. They construct halls of reflection, and they take self-consciousness for granted, as one strategy amongst many. What this book tries to do is to characterise and celebrate what they've built. Of course, there's an orgy of demolition going on as well. But the novel has proved a lot more habitable than it looked to Beauvoir: uncovering its conventions has disclosed its power to define an *invented* place. Which is perhaps just another way of pointing to the utopian uses women have found for fiction. I've tried not to travesty the achievements of these writers by reducing them to sameness; or by making them all symbolise some amorphous 'difference' (hence my allergy to 'atopia'). There's no one way of placing the woman novelist –

or even of displacing her. The language of domesticity hasn't died, at all. It flourishes alongside street-wise, picaresque writing that embraces mobility and change. I know, given my old picture of Beauvoir, which I'm programmed to prefer. However, they do have this in common: they pour back into the novel conviction, mockery and partisan passion.

1
After the War

SIMONE DE BEAUVOIR

We are no longer like our partisan elders; by and large we have
won the game.

(Simone de Beauvoir, *The Second Sex*, 1949)

Feminism was over. When Simone de Beauvoir in *The Second
Sex* heaped up all the anthropological-philosophical-sociological-
psychological evidence on the dependence and Other-ness of
women, she was researching a vanishing race: ' . . . already some
of us have never had to sense in our femininity an inconvenience or
an obstacle'.[1] She stood at the end of a century and a half's romantic
enlightenment, a human individual (almost) at last. In theory, she
would have been horrified at the thought that she heralded yet
another era of self-consciousness and polemic on the part of women
writers. Actually, of course, as *The Second Sex* testifies, she found
a new world among the horrors. And it's this fertile contradiction
– between her yearning towards universality, and her fascinated
reflexiveness – that makes her the inevitable starting-point for a
study of contemporary women novelists.

She is, besides, the forerunner who makes women writers and
critics most uneasy – truly a mother-figure in this at least, that
she has been much disliked and repeatedly rejected. Deirdre Bair's
fat 1990 *Simone de Beauvoir, A Biography* confirms the impression of
a heroine with feet of clay, a woman who systematically re-wrote
her life in order to sustain a myth of moral equality. It's a long-
standing theme. Back in 1975 Jean Leighton, in *Simone de Beauvoir
on Women*, wrote, in a tight-lipped footnote: 'I'm afraid Simone
de Beauvoir . . . evinces certain attitudes typical of the "token"
woman who "made it"'.[2] Bair, who obviously has some difficulty
in restraining her disapproval of her subject, quotes a pained Anna
Boschetti:

> Simone de Beauvoir's trajectory is conditioned . . . by her rela-
> tionship to Sartre. It reflects the traditional sexist division of
> labour. Sartre develops existentialism's philosophical, aesthetic,
> ethical and political principles. His companion applies, dissemi-
> nates, clarifies, supports, and administers them.[3]

And as Bair shows, Beauvoir did worse: she more or less pimped
for Sartre, arranging for a succession of younger women to play the
womanly roles, while struggling to reserve the part of soul-mate
for herself. The offence, then, is two-fold: first, her distance from
other women; and secondly, her failure to sustain it. No wonder
she annoys.

However, there seems to be more to it than this. Beauvoir disturbs
because she faced head-on a paradox that feminism has had to live
with ever since: that the shifts in language and thinking which make
it possible to see 'woman' as a construct also, and simultaneously,
devalue women's experience. Sartre's attack on 'essences', in which
Beauvoir joined, illuminated for her the ways in which women were
made, and the fictions by which their seemingly stable natures were
supported. But the hierarchy of languages and genres remained in
place – philosophy was 'creative' in the highest sense, while novels
and autobiography (for example) were more like testimonies or
case-studies. The universalising language of 'mankind' – even when
it was attacking universals – kept its traditional prestige; just as, in
the form of structuralisms and post-structuralisms, it has continued
to do. The relations between feminism and philosophy still fall very
easily into good old-fashioned patterns – as, for instance, when a
young novelist like Leslie Dick says her first book 'enacts an Oedipal
drama, being both an appeal to and an attack on its own symbolic
mother (feminism) and its symbolic father (theory)'.[4] Beauvoir
writes like a novelist in love with a philosopher, and so she raises
again and again the spectre of 'transcendence'. Feminist critics have
worked out ways of reading which distance women's texts from the
notion of a neutral language of authority – but these strategies don't
work with Beauvoir.

One recent example: Martha Noel Evans complains of Beauvoir's
'inability to construct with pride a female model of reading and
writing'.[5] Beauvoir simply won't give Evans what she wants, which
is a refuge from 'heterosexual paradigms based on notions of opposition or even complementarity' (p. 121), 'a change from position to
positionlessness' (p. 154). Evans's own language reveals something

of the source of her irritation: she too wants to talk transcendence, but in way which eliminates rivalry, conflict, collaboration. Beauvoir's writing 'establishes a model of reading based on the dynamics of the traditional heterosexual couple with herself as the dominant male and the reader as the yielding female' (p. 90). In short, Beauvoir has a position, one she shares with Sartre.

So she remains 'the messenger who brings the bad news',[6] the one who resists assimilation to the canon, yet can't be left out. It's hard now to capture the glamour surounding her 1950s image – a woman who spent her days in cafés, lived in hotel rooms, and built a home out of words. The end of *Memoirs of a Dutiful Daughter* (1958) is one of the classic escape scenes of modern autobiography: Beauvoir at twenty, in 1929, grabbing the world and the future in Sartre ('the dream-companion I had longed for since I was fifteen . . . the double in whom I found all my burning aspirations raised to the pitch of incandescence',[7] while her adored school friend 'Zaza' dies tragically into fiction, destroyed by her family's repressive pieties and her own emotional generosity. Beauvoir chooses herself, existentialist-fashion. The autobiographies say more about passion and commitment ('the identical sign on both our brows')[8] than they do about the content of her thinking. However – and not entirely by coincidence – another woman philosopher and novelist fills the gap. Iris Murdoch wasn't in love with Sartre, but her book on him (*Sartre*, 1953, her first published book) registers his intellectual seductiveness. We are seeing the end of an era of essentialism:

> When purposes and values are knit comfortably into the great and small practical activities of life, thought and emotion move together. When this is no longer so, when action involves choosing between worlds, not moving in a world, loving and valuing, which were once the rhythm of our lives, become problems.[9]

You can catch something of the excitement of the choices Sartre and Beauvoir were involved in when Murdoch compares the very British (and behaviourist) language of Gilbert Ryle's *The Concept of Mind* with their splendidly problematic scenarios:

> The 'world' of *The Concept of Mind* is the world in which people play cricket, cook cakes, make simple decisions, remember their childhood and go to the circus, not the world in which they

commit sins, fall in love, say prayers or join the Communist
party. (pp. 50–51)

It's a contrast betweeen lives where the over-all pattern is estab-
lished, and existences in which everything is to be invented.
Murdoch coolly plays the two off against each other, but
acknowledges the force of Sartre's argument that human 'nature'
must give way to the human 'situation'; and that we must struggle to
choose ourselves continuously – even though bad faith (unreflective
acceptance of traditional codes, settling into spurious definitions
of one's 'character', 'acting' a commitment) infects almost every
choice.

Murdoch – who in the end would want to dissent in all sorts
of ways (see Chapter 3) – nonetheless saw in these existentialist
preoccupations 'a sort of myth of our condition . . . . the situation of
a being who, deprived of general truths, is tormented by an absolute
aspiration . . . . the expression of a last ditch attachment to the value
of the individual' (pp. 108–109). And she too is speaking the
language of 'mankind' ('our condition', 'a being', 'the individual').
Beauvoir had been sharing Sartre's world in a much more intimate
and problematic sense. She lived, as she later said, in 'a delectable
but chaotic stew'.[10] And one consequence was that for some time
she found it very difficult to write and think on her own account
(though, of course, her relation to Sartre symbolised just this – the
vocation of intellectual, gender transcended). The very aspirations
that led her to think of herself as an 'individual' also helped to
bamboozle her:

> To accept a secondary status . . . would have been to degrade my
> own humanity, and my entire past rose up in protest against such
> a step. Obviously, the only reason for the problem presenting
> itself to me in these terms was because I happened to be a
> woman. But it was qua individual that I attempted to resolve
> it. The idea of feminism or the sex war made no sense whatever
> to me.[11]

Her best work, when it came, wrestled with exactly this dizzying
overlap between the human situation and the woman's situation.
Not indeed 'the sex war' as previously understood, but a much
more asymmetrical struggle.

L'Invitée (*She Came to Stay*), 1943, her first novel, is all about 'happening' to be a woman, and is splendidly savage, ambiguous and autobiographical. It draws on the period when she and Sartre confided and collaborated most intensely, and reveals the particular shades their shared world took on in her imagination. To start from a very minor moment – a stranger pinned in cruelly sharp focus in a café:

> The woman with the green and blue feathers was saying in a flat voice: ' . . . I only rushed through it, but for a small town it's very picturesque.' She had decided to leave her bare arm on the table, and as it lay there, forgotten, ignored, the man's hand was stroking a piece of flesh that no longer belonged to anyone.[12]

This reflects the sport of people-watching with which she and Sartre beguiled a good deal of their time. The game, described in *The Prime of Life*, was to spot and analyse vignettes of *mauvaise foi* – 'which, according to him, embraced all those phenomena which other people attributed to the unconscious mind . . . . semantic quibbling, false recollections, fugues, compensation fantasies, sublimations and the rest.' 'We found the women,' she remarks later in the same volume, 'more interesting and amusing than the men.'[13] And indeed a version of this particular woman turns up in Sartre's *Being and Nothingness* (also published in 1943) as a prize example of bad faith. The man is taking her out to dinner for the first time, and is hinting at a more intimate relation, but in such a way that the woman can take him as merely a friend – and she enjoys the ambiguity. Eventually, he takes her hand:

> The young woman leaves her hand there, but *she does not notice* that she is leaving it. She does not notice because it so happens that she is at that moment all intellect. She draws her companion up to the most lofty heights of sentimental speculation . . . she shows herself in her essential aspect – a personality, a consciousness. And during this time the divorce of body from the soul is accomplished, the hand rests inert between the warm hands of her companion – neither consenting nor resisting – a thing.[14]

It's a memorable instance of the way in which their bifocal vision penetrated the world. But what is perhaps most extraordinary about it – as Hazel E. Barnes observed in an incredulous footnote in *The Literature of Possibility* – is that 'neither Sartre nor de Beauvoir points out that there is bad faith on the man's side as well. His choice of ambiguous words is explicitly designed to allow him to retreat rapidly to the plane of polite friendship in case he has misjudged the situation.'[15]

Barnes is right, obviously. Why are the women 'more interesting and amusing than the men'? Because, it seems, they are the specialists in bad faith. (Murdoch, discussing this incident, is irresistibly reminded of Gwendolen agreeing to marry Grandcourt in George Eliot's *Daniel Deronda*.) A few more examples from Sartre will establish the point that the feminine is associated with fake consciousness: there is the homosexual in *Being and Nothingness* whom Sartre maintains has not chosen to be one in good faith; even better, the wartime collaborator:

> The collaborator speaks in the name of force, but he is not force; he is the ruse, the guile which gets its strength from force; he is even charm and seduction since he seeks to bring into play that attraction which, according to him, French culture exercises over the Germans. It seems to me almost certain that there is in collaborationism a curious atmosphere of masochism and homosexuality.[16]

His notorious analysis of 'the slimy' (the quality in the world that would pull down consciousness) evokes an ecstasy of revulsion: 'It is a soft, yielding action, a moist and feminine sucking . . . . In some sense it is like the supreme docility of the possessed, the fidelity of a dog who *gives himself* even when one does not want him any longer . . . a surreptitious appropriation of the possessor by the possessed.' Or again, ' . . . the revenge of the In-itself, a sickly sweet, feminine revenge.'[17] Barnes is moved by this display to say sternly that 'such an implied comparison of women with either the slimy or the In-itself is inconsistent with his view of the character of *all* human consciousness and with the belief that one chooses to live one's sex just as much as any other physical characteristic.'[18] But in fact '*all* human consciousness' didn't include women; you might almost say it was defined over against them.

To get back to Beauvoir's woman with the green and blue feathers: she is a lot sadder than Sartre's (she speaks in a 'flat voice', what she says is less pretentious, to relinquish an arm is a more desperate gesture than mislaying a hand). Nonetheless her bad faith is pinned down in that small phrase 'had decided to'. And the man is hardly *there* at all to account for his part in the act. The point of view from which this is observed belongs to Françoise, the heroine of *L'Invitée*, a projection of Beauvoir herself and (unsurprisingly) wedded to the notion of self-chosen individuality. She is outside the frame, no mere 'character', and the novel's opening scenes make the satisfactions of standing back very clear:

> Each one of these men, each one of these women present here tonight was completely absorbed in living a moment of his or her insignificant existence. Xavière was dancing. Elizabeth was shaken by convulsions of anger and despair. 'And I – here I am at the heart of the dance-hall – impersonal and free. I am watching all these lives and all these faces. If I were to turn away from them, they would disintegrate at once, like a deserted landscape.'
> (p. 21)

Even those she's close to (Elizabeth, Xavière) recede comfortably into two dimensions (the juxtaposition of 'dancing' and 'shaken with convulsions' is particularly neat).

The secret of her apartness is not far to seek. The world bears looking at because she doesn't do it alone, but with Pierre:

> Their life was the same. They did not always see it from the same angle . . . . there were . . . streets, ideas, faces, that came into existence first for Pierre, and others first for Françoise; but they faithfully pieced together these scattered experiences into a single whole, in which 'yours' and 'mine' became indistinguishable.
> (p. 44)

This collusion not only gives her the world, but enables her not to have to look at herself: she is different, not one of the observables, the ones who jig about like puppets ('Neither of us can be described without the other', says Pierre, p. 17). She does try to get herself into focus, but not too hard: '"Imprisoned in happiness," she murmured. But she was conscious of a smile somewhere deep down within her' (p. 23). One way of describing the book's action would be that it's devoted to wiping that smile off her (invisible) face. But – and this is what gives *L'Invitée* its enduring *formal* interest, its furious tension –

in this novel the heroine fights back, fights to keep hold of the point of view at all costs. She will not become a woman watched. She must be a watcher.

Xavière, who came to stay, Françoise's protegee, stubbornly refuses to be assimilated into the shared world. Her youth, her intransigence, her extremism ('"I hate these compromises. If one can't have the sort of life one wants, one might as well be dead"', p. 27) amuse Françoise (eminently observable) until she finds Pierre taking them seriously. Then of course she must (despite a prophetic 'murky taste in her mouth') acknowledge Xavière's genuine existence: 'she no longer regarded Xavière's words as outbursts: they held a complete set of values that ran counter to hers' (p. 96). And sure enough the vivid, seamy, crowded world starts to slip away – 'The centre of Paris was the café where Pierre and Xavière were sitting, and Françoise was wandering about in some vague suburb' (p. 114). The game of analysing people begins to go against her. When she talks of Xavière's listlessness and refusal to commit herself, Pierre muses, infuriatingly:

> 'When you carry inertia to the point to which she carries it, the word listlessness is no longer valid; it assumes a kind of strength.'
> (p. 129)

And when she tries to share with Xavière her view of Elizabeth (a sad parody of the independent woman, and someone whom Françoise now uneasily wants to protect) she gets a savage surprise:

> 'If you study her with a little sympathy, you'll perceive in all that a clumsy attempt to give definite value to herself as a person . . . . '
> 'Elizabeth is a vain, pathetic jelly-fish,' she said. 'That's all.'
> (p. 135)

All. And the slime, one notes, has put in an ominous appearance.

Françoise sees with new pain the vulnerability of the 'well-preserved' women around her, and begins to suspect a kinship with them – 'a naked conscience in front of the world, it was thus she thought of herself . . . . And yet . . . she too was in the world . . . a woman among women' (p. 146). But no. She will not relinquish her apartness. ('She must not be like Elizabeth',

p. 153.) Initially, her heroic effort to go on sharing Pierre's and (now) Xavière's life knocks her out: she develops pneumonia and collapses in a nursing home while (so that? motivation is hard to talk about here) they get on with the love affair that's been in the offing for some time. When they come to tell her about it, she decides, in an especially absurd and desperate act of bravado, to fall in love with Xavière herself: 'For a while Françoise gazed with loving eyes at this woman Pierre loved' (p. 210). They form a three-some – parcelling out the days in an elaborate permutating timetable, speculating endlessly in different combinations about each other and the world, and nurturing intense, intricate resentments and vicious frustrations.

Once again it's Xavière who breaks the rules, and the results are even more complicated, but the basic structure of Françoise's responses doesn't change. Forced to look at herself, and recognise her dependency, she resorts to wilder and wilder stratagems to evade it – stratagems which themselves, with the very slightest change of perspective, would indeed convict her of 'sickly sweet feminine revenge', of treachery, of bad faith *so bad* it almost amounts to insanity. The obscure violence of the novel's ending, in which she actually, quite implausibly, murders Xavière in order to vindicate her point of view, makes sense only as a colossal confidence trick. There is no *evidence* any longer that she is not as hateful and sly as (she thinks) Xavière, as hollow and deluded about her independence as (she thinks) Elizabeth. Only the violence of her *will* to be different is authentic, and the novel's last words, with their copy-book reminder of the Sartrean individual – 'She had at last made a choice. She had chosen herself' (p. 409) – remain suspended in mid-air above a monstrous gulf of irony.

Authors can kill off characters without being murderers, but characters can't. Beauvoir sets Françoise 'free' by an act of bare-faced illogic, but one which exactly mirrors her dilemma about the two roles. She wants her character to be an 'author', and yet inside the novel's world Françoise becomes more and more compromised and enmeshed. In the autobiography, she says that life and fiction were indeed uncomfortably close. Olga – Xavière's real-life original, to whom both *L'Invitée* and *Being and Nothingness* were dedicated, who wasn't murdered – had 'forced me to face a truth which hitherto . . . I had been at considerable pains to avoid – that other people existed, exactly as I did.' She had to revise her sense of herself in relation to Sartre – 'it was wrong to bracket myself and another person in that equivocal and all too handy word "we" .... The agony which this produced in me went far beyond mere jealousy: at times I asked myself whether the whole of my happiness did not rest upon a gigantic lie.' The novel, she decided in retrospect, was a kind of therapy: ' . . . by releasing Françoise through the agency of a crime, from the dependant position in which her love for Pierre kept her, I regained my personal autonomy.' And again: 'Françoise . . . once asked herself angrily "Am I going to resign myself to being just a woman?" If I chose to make Françoise a murderer, that was because I found anything preferable to this kind of submission.'[19] So she produces an anti-novel of a peculiar sort – one in which the real theme is the relation between the author and the woman.

This is why it's hard to accept at face value her statement that the novel restored her sense of autonomy. Doubtless simply getting it written and published helped, but it clearly doesn't resolve the tensions implicit in her fierce individualism. Quite apart from the vertiginous ending, there is the problem of the character of Pierre. Or rather, the fact that he isn't a character, because it proved even more difficult to make over Sartre into an observable than it was to characterise herself – 'I had put too much of myself into Françoise to link her with a man who would be a stranger to me; my imagination balked at this switch of partners. But equally, I was loath to offer the public a portrait of Sartre as I knew him . . . . '[20] Pierre – compare the absent man courting the woman with the green and blue feathers – simply *is not in question*. No matter how dubious his actions, he remains eerliy immune to analysis (even, for example, when he peers through Xavière's keyhole). If he convicts himself of bad faith, he does so with a degree of insouciance impossible to the women. They have a double dose of unfreedom, they make him look, by contrast, simple.

It's clear that for Beauvoir the novelistic domain of character and representation is a world of Others – particularly, a world of women. Here, the notion of *mauvaise foi* blossomed luridly for her, and some of her most memorable figures are women corrupted by their dependent status into permanent play-acting. Elizabeth plays at being a painter:

'I'm in the very middle of a transition,' said Elizabeth, with ironic emphasis. Her pictures! Pigment spread on canvas so as to give the appearance of pictures .... She would show them her fraudulent paintings and they would bestow fraudulent praise on her.[21]

Or Paula, in *The Mandarins* (1954), gruesomely mouthing the lines of a woman who's given all for love, to a man who winces in embarrassment and distaste (one recalls Sartre's description of the dog who *'gives himself* even when one does not want him any longer'). It's Paula, brooding neglected in her love-nest, who utters what must be for Beauvoir the definitive statement of female delusion:

> ' . . . it was I who made Henri. I created him as he creates characters in his books . . . . '
> ' . . . we're one single being . . . . it's strange, you know, to lose yourself absolutely in another. But how rewarding it is when you find the other in yourself!' With an inspired look, she gazed at the ceiling. 'You can be sure of one thing: my hour will come again. Henri will be returned to me as he truly is, as I will have returned him to myself.'[22]

These characters constitute a sub-culture. Their awfulness is a measure of their unfreedom, they are not the neutral 'beings' or 'individuals' proposed by the language of 'human consciousness'. In fact they are precisely the excluded, the ones the myths about freedom define themselves against, the exemplars of bad faith.

Beauvoir recalls in the autobiography her arguments with Sartre:

> Not every situation was equally valid: what sort of transcendence could a woman shut up in a harem achieve? Sartre replied that even such a cloistered existence could be lived in several quite different ways. I stuck to my point for a long time, and in the end made only a token submission. Basically I was right. But to defend my attitude I should have had to abandon the plane of individual, and therefore idealistic, morality on which we had set ourselves.[23]

Which they both, indeed, did. Murdoch notes the enormous philosophical difficulties for Sartre in moving out from the individual. She suggests, in a footnote, that Beauvoir has found it easier because 'she belongs to a race whose liberation can still be conceived as a proper task of Reason and one which is within its power – see her book *Le Deuxième Sexe*.[24] It was not easy, though, and Murdoch's own tone suggests why. What 'race' does Murdoch herself belong to? Why such ironic obliquity? Because, clearly, Murdoch like Beauvoir shrinks from being 'just a woman'. To admit to belonging to a sub-culture feels like regression, a re-immersion in immanence. To give up the language of universality is to surrender a utopian dream. Beauvoir wants a world of writing where the traditional divisions of labour are suspended. In fact, her genres – fiction, autobiography, cultural analysis – are those in which the force of circumstance and the weight of present history predominate. *The Second Sex* was not past history – 'When I wrote it, I thought the state of women and society would evolve together . . . . No, we have not won the game; in fact we have won almost nothing since 1950.'[25] This was in 1972, in *All Said and Done*, where she also declared herself a feminist.

However, she never would agree to see women's difference as anything other than a construct, a made-up thing; she would not celebrate it: 'The fact of the matter is that culture, science, the arts and techniques were created by men, since it was men who stood for universality.'[26] It's a point of pride with her not to argue – for example – that women somehow 'really' created culture, 'really' stand for universality by living on the margins. She would have regarded that as a delusion on a par with her character Paula's ('it was I who made Henri'). Instead, she dramatises the scandalous discontinuity between 'all human consciousness' and the 'we' of women. She may have ceased to believe that everyone was free to choose themselves, but she went on believing in the waste of unfreedom, the horror of bad faith. So she writes like a realist for whom 'reality' requires quotation marks. The novel for her is a kind of specimen jar: a transparent container that exposes its characters to curious, hostile, sometimes pitying scrutiny. She herself is partly inside, partly outside. She is unhoused, self-conscious. And in this, as in so much else, she anticipates the creative dilemmas of contemporary women novelists. Few sound like her, though: her stoical pleasure in the role of 'the messemger who brings the bad news' ('we have won almost nothing', we are experts in self-deception) is almost unique. Andrea Dworkin perhaps has something of the same penchant for telling the intolerable – but she does it with a poetical fervour that is (however unreasonably) inspiriting. Whereas Beauvoir is prosaic, lucid, bleak as an unkind mirror on a brilliant morning.

DORIS LESSING

Florence Howe: Women read it because you express what they feel again and again about their –
Doris Lessing: The funny thing is that I just took that absolutely for granted.

('A Conversation with Doris Lessing', 1966)

Doris Lessing like Beauvoir was impatient with the sex war, and wanted it over. *The Golden Notebook* (1962) faces two ways, as *The Second Sex* does. In intention it's about transcending difference, exploring a shared crisis of consciousness (her heroine comments on women's anger: 'It is the disease of women in our time . . . . The unlucky ones who do not know it is impersonal, turn against their men. The lucky ones like me – fight it').[1] In practice, of course, it's a novel that turns itself inside out, a hall-of-mirrors book that multiplies images of women. Looking for a new way of writing about wholeness, Lessing lets go of the old ways, and as a consequence leaves room for her readers to sieze on fragmentary and splintered representations, and find their own meanings there. The parts, the partial, partisan voices overwhelm the whole.

By now, the narrative that pre-dates *The Golden Notebook* is well-known. Lessing had started her career with *The Grass is Singing* (written in Southern Rhodesia, published in London, where she moved in 1949), and had written three volumes of her *Children of Violence* sequence, in traditional style.[2] She had discovered as she went on that the realist formula (the heroine whose process of growing up also symbolises and synthesises the wider conflicts of her culture) would not answer. There were many reasons for this, for example (and most glaringly), that the culture in question was that of white-dominated Africa, where

> . . . each group, community, clan, colour, strove and fought away from each other, in a sickness of dissolution . . . as if the principle of separateness was bred from the very soil.[3]

The tradition she was working in stemmed from the great European realists of the nineteenth century, with a further stiffening from Marxism. She would have believed with Georg Lukács that her predecessors 'were to the bottom of their souls bound up with the movements for the liberation of the people';[4] and with Raymond

Williams that the model was 'the kind of novel which creates and judges the quality of a whole way of life in terms of the qualities of persons', in which 'society is seen in fundamentally personal terms, and persons, through relationships, in fundamentally social terms'.[5] But these classic realist definitions grew out of a society which, despite the two 'world' wars, was basically homogenous, and depended on a European and Eurocentric habit of imagination. Lessing was an exile in Africa, but she was equally an outsider in England. Her heroine Martha Quest's progress (reflecting her own, so far as personal life goes – Martha is not a portrait of the *artist*) is a story of unsettlement, displacement and reverse emigration, not an integrative plot.[6]

This is Martha surveying her image in the mirror in the third novel of the series, *A Ripple from the Storm* (1958, the action set in Salisbury in 1942–3):

> She examined the severe young face and thought: If I didn't know myself, what would I think? Well, I certainly wouldn't guess all the things that have happened to *her* in the last year, getting divorced, being a communist, getting married again, all the complications and never sleeping enough.[7]

Martha in fact much resembles the existentialist protagonist Iris Murdoch describes – the one for whom 'action involves choosing between worlds, not moving in a world'; and who lives in an atmosphere of radical fickleness where people 'commit sins, fall in love, say prayers or join the Communist party.'[8] It was at this point that Lessing turned away from *Children of Violence* to write *The Golden Notebook*, and to explore the very premises of realism, the time-honoured assumption that – as Nicole Ward Jouve puts it – 'the world of an individual could be put into correspondence with, *represent*, the world.'[9] The novel has a conventional envelope-narrative, 'Free Women', though this time, unsurprisingly, the heroine Anna is a writer. Inside the envelope are the notebooks containing the raw material that 'Free Women' edits, orders, rewrites into plausibility and censors. More: each notebook is itself an envelope, a device for compartmentalising and making sense. *The Golden Notebook* reflects itself, and reflects on itself, at every turn.

The Black notebook deals with the African experience Anna has efficiently turned into fiction in the past; the Red records her communist history; the Yellow is made up of autobiographical stories projected onto (yet another) fictional writer, 'Ella'; and the Blue is a diary that mulls over her experience of psychoanalysis. Gradually, we realise, this filing system undermines its own purpose – each notebook spells out the same message, that putting yourself in order is the problem, not the solution. Joining the Party, or finding a genial Jungian analyst, or making up stories to live inside are all strategies for denying the underlying incoherence of things. Or rather, their common ground in violence and diversity. You *represent* the world best by letting yourself fall apart, crack up, break down. Thus, Ella in the Yellow notebook, after a futile search for a 'real man', muses:

I've got to accept the patterns of self-knowledge which mean unhappiness or at least a dryness. But I can twist it into victory. A man and a woman – yes. Both at the end of their tether. Both cracking up because of a deliberate attempt to transcend their own limits. And out of the chaos, a new kind of strength. (p. 458)

This is one of several points at which the notebooks begin to inter-fere with the frame-story. Ella's imagined plot feeds back into her creator Anna's life, when she meets a crazed, lost man (Saul) and they goad each other into temporary madness, recorded in the fifth, Golden notebook – 'and I knew that the cruelty and the spite and the I, I, I, I, of Saul and Anna were part of the logic of war . . . . ' (p. 576). As they disintegrate, they become mouthpieces for the rest, the others:

. . . if there were a tape . . . of the hours and hours of talk in that room . . . it would be a record of a hundred different people living now, in various parts of the world, talking and crying out and questioning. (p. 608)

It's a calculated – if crude – parody of the conventional happy ending, in which two become one, and so symbolise the underlying orderliness of social life. Here, two become legion, and represent a world of conflict. Saul and Anna are truly children of violence.

The ending is satisfyingly disarranged in another way, too. The envelope story has Anna patching her life together, settling for irony and 'maturity'. However, she has now shrunk to a mere character, no longer a writer – or at least not the author of *this* book. She is someone who works by cutting out and denying the multiple, clamouring voices inside, a fairly exact version of what Roland Barthes had in mind when he talked of the third person in the realist novel as 'a progressive conquest over the profound darkness of the existential "I"'.[10] In the 'inside' notebook story, however, Anna and Saul – as a kind of earnest of the new collectivity of consciousness – give each other the first sentences for new novels, his gift to her being the first sentence of *The Golden Notebook*. In other words, the inside is now the outside. The conventional form has been eviscerated and the authority belongs to the cacophonous multitude within. Author and character part company in a way that's reminiscent of Beauvoir's terminal tricksiness in *L'Invitée* – a Pyrrhic victory ('I can twist it into victory'). Lessing also clings on grimly to a universalising point of view.

Hence her anger and disappointment when she found that the book was read (as she complained in her 1972 preface) 'as being about the sex war'. Closer to the event, in 1966, she'd been even more exasperated:

> Now I could mention a dozen books by male authors, but you see, I won't bother. The attitudes to women are the obverse . . . but no one would say these men are anti-women. They would say . . . this man has a problem or he's screwed up or he has a soul-problem. After all deep problems very often are expressed through sex. But I articulated the same thing from a female point of view, and this is what was interesting, it was taken as a kind of banner.[11]

What she is resenting is the world's inability to allow women to stand for universality. In the later 1950's, in her essay 'The Small Personal Voice', she had produced a kind of credo: ' . . . one is a writer at all because one represents, makes articulate, is continuously and invisibly fed by, numbers of people who are inarticulate, to whom one belongs, to whom one is responsible.'[12] She was not, though, thinking of readers, but rather of a wordless collectivity 'behind' the book. She had left the Communist Party in 1956, but certain habits of thought survived. Indeed, one way of characterising her work is that for (now) forty years she has been looking for ways of riding the 'great whirlwind of change'[13] – recognising difference but 'speaking for' it too.

So in a sense she's among the most authoritarian of contemporary authors. And yet with hindsight one can see that the real power of *The Golden Notebook* lay in its openness to 'misreadings'. Readers responded to her violent dismantling of the sensible, ironic, well-behaved realist's (well-behaved woman's) kind of book. Her new, decentred version of the author as a 'transcendent anonymity'[14] didn't police meanings in the obvious way. You could imagine her as a cultural lightening conductor, earthing the energies that were splitting things up; as an oracle or sibyl (Margaret Drabble wrote a piece that called her 'Cassandra').[15] Lessing herself took some time to accept this role, and has never accepted it completely. Her return to *Children of Violence* kept up conventional appearances in *Landlocked* (1965), though there is a 'crazy' character who's a self-appointed visionary anthropologist. However, with *The Four-Gated City* (1969), the fifth and final volume, she makes a decisive move to rewrite the sequence from the end. Her twenty years in London spill out in one monstrous chronicle, and an appendixed scenario (notes up to the year 2000) takes off into the realms of speculative fiction. Martha Quest achieves the destiny which (we are now meant to see) was lurking unrecognised in her inconclusiveness and muddle: not maturity but madness, or what's dismissed as madness. She acquires a new reading list – ' . . . books on Rosicrucianism and the old Alchemists; Buddhist books . . . Yoga . . . Zoroastrianism and esoteric Christianity . . . the I Ching; Zen, witchcraft, magic, astrology and vampirism; scholarly treatises on Sufism . . . . everything rejected by official culture and scholarship.'[16] The novel is a collage, an anthology, an offering to the spirit of the age, as though Lessing finally found herself 'at home' in England in the 1960s, where the culture was acquiring a vagrant, apocalyptic tone, and numinous 'underground' notions took root and flourished among the ruins of the old humanism. Not only has Martha the person disintegrated, but so has the author as person, and as a result the form is, as Lessing put it, 'shot to hell'.[17]

Her work since has 'belonged' to many genres of the novel, from space fiction to realism: none of them, any longer, the kind of imaginative world you can live inside. *The Memoirs of a Survivor* (1974) demonstrates something of the strength and strangeness of this writing. It begins with the death of a city – a London that has lost its name, where warmth, food, water and even oxygen drain away, until gradually people are left living off the corpse, scavenging, stealing, bartering. Almost to the end, a sense of normality persists: 'While everything, all forms of social organisation, broke up, we lived on, adjusting our lives, as if nothing fundamental was happening.'[18] Breaches in 'outside' reality are quickly matched in private perceptions – the narrator, semi-besieged in her solid, gound-floor flat, turns from watching the new 'tribes' gather on the pavement, to find the blank wall of her room dissolving into other rooms, other times. And still the matter-of-factness continues. When a complete stranger materialises in her living room, to make her the custodian of twelve-year-old Emily, the 'impossible' situation must be accepted (as if it were some kind of administrative mistake) because otherwise nothing can be trusted. So life goes on – the narrator stepping now, almost routinely, through the wall into other spaces; Emily, hungry for life, joining the tribes of the pavement, losing her identity before she achieves it:

> . . . any individual consummations were nothing beside this act of mingling constantly with others, as if some giant rite of eating were taking place, everyone tasting and licking and regurgitating everyone else, making themselves known to others and others known to them in this tasting and sampling – eyeing each other, rubbing shoulders and bodies, talking, exchanging emanations. (p. 74)

As the boundaries dissolve, it seems at first that the inner space must be a refuge, a liberation to counter this repulsiveness, but no: the experience is more anomalous than that.

For example: people seem to be turning into animals (herding, migrating), but what is it to be 'animal'? One of the novel's most quietly bizarre effects is to invent (along with Emily) an 'impossible' creature, Hugo, a cat-dog, or dog-cat, who has all the conviction (but none of the merely whimsical appeal) of an animal in a fairy tale. Since the narrative accepts Hugo's presence with only a momentary grinding of gears, and since he's several times in danger of being eaten, we accept him too, perforce, as yet another anomaly. And one contradictory image serves to support another, so that it is with little surprise that we realise that the realm behind the wall 'belongs' to both Emily and the narrator – a composite childhood. Here the 'personal' life that is so under threat in the outside world is traced to its family origins, and inner space proves problematic in its turn. In fragmentary scenes from the nursery, the drawing room, the bedroom, a small girl is formed into a person: made to know her separateness, her nuisance value, her mother's resentment and weariness, her father's furtive sexuality. These ghosts are horribly solid: 'tall, large, with a clean-china healthiness, all blue eyes, pink cheeks, and the jolly, no-nonsense mouth of a schoolgirl' (p. 59); 'a soldier . . . . conventionally handsome face . . . half-hidden by a large moustache' (p. 60). They recall the portraits of Martha Quest's parents in *Children of Violence*, and, beyond them, Lessing's images of her own parents.[19] They are 'characters', and they manufacture a character – a rebellious, guilty girl, self-repressed in her mother's image.

The climactic scene on this inner stage (where everything is gigantized by a child's perspective) traces 'character-forming' back to the denial of the animal, and the denial of hunger:

Emily, absorbed, oblivious. She was eating – chocolate. No, excrement . . . . She had smeared it on sheets and blankets . . . over her face and into her hair, and there she sat, a little monkey, thoughtfully tasting and digesting. (p. 123)

The traumatic cleansing that follows ('naughty, disgusting, filthy, dirty, dirty, dirty', p. 124) leaves an indelible sobbing on the air. And when the narrator next enters this realm, she tracks that down too:

The finding had about it, had in it as its quintessence, the banality, the tedium, the smallness, the restriction, of the 'personal' dimension. What else could I find – unexpectedly, it goes without saying . . . a blonde, blue-eyed child . . . reddened and sullen with weeping. Who else could it possibly be but Emily's mother, the large carthorse woman, her tormentor, the world's image? (p. 128)

Infinite regress . . . . Each generation has stamped its own discipline, its own wretchedly acquired boundaries, on the next. The 'personal' is not the unique: its claustrophobia derives precisely from its repetitions.

This replay of the family scenario clears the stage, little by little. Intercut with the character-acting, and with the increasingly anarchic glimpses of the city outside, are visions of the inner space depopulated, exorcised – moving pictures that take up and transform the imagery of destruction:

> . . . walking through a light screen of leaves, flowers, birds,
> blossom, the essence of woodland brought to life in the effaced
> patterns of the wallpaper, I moved through rooms that seemed to
> have aged since I saw them last. The walls had thinned, had lost
> substance to the air, to time; everywhere on the forest floor stood
> slight tall walls, all upright still and in their proper pattern of
> angles, but ghosts of walls, like the flats in a theatre. (p. 86)

The realist setting – the house of fiction itself – is becoming transparent. The emptying city and the emptying inner space correspond;
and the new barbarism without is overwritten by the transcendence of the personal within. Despite its sometimes guileless look,
The Memoirs of a Survivor is a high-tec novel, one that displays the
struts and the plumbing and the wiring ducts. In its final move, the
book crumples up its world like a sheet of paper:

> . . . that world, presenting itself in a thousand little flashes, a
> jumble of little scenes, facets of another picture, all impermanent,
> was folding up as we stepped into it, was parcelling itself up,
> was vanishing, dwindling and going – all of it, trees and streams,
> grasses and rooms and people. (p. 182)

Into this vortex the characters cram themselves, to meet an
unimaginable future.

Memoirs (which Lessing described on the dust jacket as 'an attempt
at autobiography') banishes nostalgia for personal space, at least
for the time being. In the late 1970s, she began a new sequence of
novels, *Canopus in Argos*, set in a new space, a no-man's land where
both gender and genre are merely provisional. They are 'science'
fiction in the loosest sense, allegorical, speculative and short on
machinery; and they circle back on *Children of Violence*, in that their
main concern is colonisation. Or perhaps it would be better to say,
their main metaphor: they take on the question of who appropriates
language, why and how fictional space is mapped out, and how
to handle difference in the abstract. This series also resembles the
earlier one in another respect. From around the time of the third
novel, *The Sirian Experiments* in 1981, Lessing was planning and
executing a special kind of literary hoax. She wrote and published
the two novels that now appear as *The Diaries of Jane Somers* under
the name of Jane Somers, rather as she broke *Children of Violence* after
the third book. In this case, interestingly, it's a matter of realism

(Somers) intruding on speculation, instead of the other way around. What it suggests is Lessing's need to break out of her project, even when that project might seem large enough to accomodate more or less any 'world'. Certainly, it's a reminder of her dislike of being placed and characterised.

The overview in the space-fiction series belongs to the inhabitants of Canopus, who are a species of cosmic do-gooders, experts in non-violent colonisation. From their vantage point, lesser (quarrelsome) cultures look sadly and absurdly readable. For example:

> Shedding the Rhetoric of Empire, which they are prepared to analyse with acumen and to reject with scorn and contempt, they become prisoners of the Rhetoric of oppositional groups.[20]

This is the weary voice of Canopus in *The Sentimental Agents in the Volyen Empire*, describing how yet another generation is conned and conscripted by the armies of words. Talk of, say, 'the force of history', all the rhetoric of opposition, reflects people's atavistic need to belong to the group, to herd together. In *The Sentimental Agents* Canopus pays ironic homage to the urgency of this need by listing the proliferating names we (they?) have for designating difference: 'races, kinds, types, nations, classes, sorts, genders, breeds, strains, tribes, clans, sects, castes, varieties, grades, even species.'[21] From the Canopean point of view, difference is, as it were, what all these have in common. This whole-versus-group theme shapes all the *Canopus* novels, and can be seen at work, for instance, in the larger-scale irony of *The Sirian Experiments*, where the managerial narrator Ambien becomes a 'traitor' because she realises that all along the seemingly rival Empire had included her. Or again, in *The Marriages Between Zones Three, Four and Five*, when the Zone Four women form themselves into what looks very like a women's movement, and get imaginatively lost as a result, on an untimely pilgrimage. The group turns out to be a travesty of the whole.

These plots both celebrate heterogeneity, and render it permanently provisional. My quotation from *The Sirian Experiments* above, listing 'races, kinds, types' and so forth, ends with the words 'all of them united by *waiting*.' So difference is, seemingly, depoliticised. Canopeans do not deal in debate; they pursue a gnostic, paradoxical 'silent' speech that is meant to undermine rhetoric. Speaking is superseded by listening, waiting, 'reading'. Dialogue (like Platonic dialogue, like – presumably – Sufi teaching techniques) is about turning the mind round, so that you see new dimensions in what you already know. In *The Making of the Representative for Planet 8*, the Planet 8 people are supplied with microscopes for this purpose, so that they can see their own tissues as composite, a conglomerate of groups, mostly space. One of the most characteristic structuring devices in these books is a kind of synechdoche (the part for the whole). Some examples:

> Yet most societies, cultures – empires – can be described by an underlying fact or truth, and that is nearly always physical, geographical.[22]

> 'Our Empire isn't random, or made by the decisions of self-seeking rulers or by the unplanned developments of our technologies . . . . Our growth, our existence, what we are is a unit, a unity, a whole.'[23]

This last quotation, which comes from a Canopean agent, more or less betrays the device by naming it: it is a device for pointing always towards an (unachieved) totality. Hence its ironising effect in relation to partial, party politics – 'Nearly all political people were incapable of thinking in terms of interaction, of cross-influences, of the various sects and "parties" forming *together* a whole, wholes.'[24] Lessing's Canopeans are guardians of difference (they immerse themselves in local conditions, incarnate themselves as historical individuals) and at the same time subverters of the politics of difference.

Her need to locate an authorial 'I' that is potentially 'we' is undiminished, through all the extraordinary adventures with style and genre. She often talks of 'us' as a multiple monad, as here, in the Preface to *The Sirian Experiments*:

> . . . with billions and billions and billions of us on this planet, we are still prepared to believe that each of us is unique, or that if all the others are mere dots in a swarm, then at least *I* am this self-determined thing, my mind my own. Very odd this . . . . How do we get this notion of ourselves?
>
> It seems to me that ideas must flow through humanity like tides.[25]

Like her Canopeans, Lessing employs a double-speak that appropriates the voices of others. (Thus, she wittily redescribes the concept of uniqueness as a collective delusion.) This is less a way of renouncing authorial power, than of retaining it, by identifying with difference. In other words, she too, like Beauvoir, refuses to surrender the ambition of speaking for universality – though it undergoes some very strange mutations in her work. One's tempted, looking at the demolition job she does on realism, to believe that 'ideas must flow through humanity like tides', since she is here coinciding with a general movement towards reflexiveness which she in no literal sense 'belongs' to. When Foucault, in 1969, asks 'What is an Author?', and suggests that contemporary writing 'keeps alive, in the grey light of neutralisation, the interplay of those representations that formed a particular image of the author', he describes her strategies pretty exactly, though he was thinking of figures like Samuel Beckett, or Nathalie Sarraute.[26] Lessing is not an 'experimental' novelist: she still feels free to write realistically, like a space-traveller revisiting old haunts. She's ambivalent, two-faced (as oracles often are), and cunningly refuses to 'be' herself.

NATHALIE SARRAUTE

> At the level at which the inner dramas that I try to show are produced I am convinced that there is no difference between men and women, as there is no difference in their respiratory or blood systems.
>
> (Sarraute, in answer to a questionnaire, 'Does writing have a sex?', 1974)

Nathalie Sarraute, the same age as the century, is a deliberately experimental 'artist' in a way neither Beauvoir nor Lessing ever aspires to be. Gender, she has often said, is for her as a writer an irrelevance: 'I think that these distinctions are based on prejudices, on pure convention . . . . where the feminine or masculine authors want to possess certain qualities they think are appropriate to their sex.'[1] And most anthologists and critics of women's writing seem to have taken her at her word and omitted her, as if, indeed, her assurance and skill and *avant garde* reputation disqualified her. Sarraute, it's implied, can take care of herself; deserves to, perhaps, since she has somehow, rather dishonourably, levitated out of the woman's condition. In fact, however, she's splendidly relevant on two counts: first because her kind of career (active, dedicated, self-dependent) was precisely what post-war women writers were supposed to want; and secondly because her seamless, self-conscious *oeuvre* cultivates all the relevant doubts about artistic monuments to cultural progress. For the house of fiction was becoming a precarious refuge. Its walls were wearing to transparency, and you could see the dry rot and the priest holes and the plumbing. Inhabiting it was, of course, what one wanted; but it was at the same time, as fastidious Sarraute demonstrated, no great privilege.

'She was very reticent and talked mostly about literature, but with passion.'[2] Beauvoir's first impressions of Sarraute in 1945 (described in the autobiography) have an ominous undertone in view of her later furious dismissal ('this vanishing act . . . . this escape into fantasies about the absolute').[3] To start with, however, Sarraute seemed deceptively assimilable:

> Before the war, an unknown woman had sent Sartre a copy of her little book *Tropisms*, which had gone unnoticed and whose quality struck us both; this was Nathalie Sarraute; Sartre had written to her and met her. In '41 she had worked in a Resistance group with Alfred Peron . . . . She was the daughter of Russian Jews exiled by the Czarist persecutions at the beginning of the century, and it was to these circumstances, I suppose, that she owed her restless subtlety. Her vision of the world spontaneously accorded with Sartre's own ideas: she was hostile to all essentialism, she did not believe in clearly defined characters or emotions, or, indeed, in any ready-made notions.[4]

This character-sketch reveals rather more about Beauvoir than about Sarraute. It's not just that she's condescending to an 'unknown': she's far too ready to assume that Sarraute's background and record commit her to all the right causes, including Sartre. She might, one feels, have pondered more about how Sarraute's ideas came to correspond 'spontaneously' with his – except, of course, that that would risk compromising his originality. As time was to show, Sarraute's uprooted early life (nomadic parents divorced when she was two, a childhood spent shuttling between Paris and St. Petersburg) and her cosmopolitan education (English at the Sorbonne, some history at Oxford, some sociology in Berlin, and finally a degree in law from the university of Paris) added up to a refusal to be recruited – a deliberate exile in the world of words. Her 'little book', *Tropisms* (1939, unnoticed, as Beauvoir rightly says) was the product of a long-contained and ambitious talent. Its very modesty looks in retrospect almost arrogant, touchily perfectionist.

At the same time, there was much that Sartre and Beauvoir could recognise in the series of brief sub-dramas collected in *Tropisms*. Sarraute's lucid images of the tentacular, instinctive inner 'movements . . . hidden under the commonplace, harmless appearances of every instant of our lives'[5] must have been good grist to the existentialist mill. Even the fact that some of her most striking glimpses of chronic evasion featured women confirmed their perceptions. Sartre particularly relished this portrait of a tea-room coven in Tropism X:

> ' . . . he won't marry her. What he needs is a good housewife; he doesn't realise it himself. Certainly not; I mean it. What he needs is a good housewife . . . Housewife . . . Housewife . . . ' They had always heard it said, they knew it: the sentiments, love, life; these were their domain . . . .
>
> And they talked and talked . . . continually rolling between their fingers this unsatisfactory, mean substance that they had extracted from their lives (what they called 'life', their domain), kneading it, pulling it, rolling it until it ceased to form anything between their fingers but a little pile, a little gray pellet. (pp. 32–3)

You can see how this writing eerily pre-echoes notions like 'bad faith'. Sarraute, too, is constructing consciousness and *real* life over against the domain of the feminine ('the sentiments, love', 'what they called "life"'). Sartre, delightedly, wrote: 'Here we have Heidegger's "babble", the "they", in other words, the realm of inauthenticity.'[6] He must have felt a frisson of recognition, too, in Tropism XI, where the language of slime is used to characterise a panting aesthete ('She had to have what was intellectual'): 'There were a great many like her, hungry, pitiless parasites, leeches firmly settled on the articles that appeared, slugs stuck everywhere, spreading their mucous on corners of Rimbaud, sucking on Mallarmé, lending one another *Ulysses* . . . . ' (p. 35) In his Preface to Sarraute's first novel, *Portrait of a Man Unknown* (1948), Sartre is strikingly *intimate* with her metaphors:

Nathalie Sarraute has a protoplasmic vision of our interior universe: roll away the stone of the commonplace and we find
running discharges, slobbering, mucous, hesitant, amoeba-like
movements. Her vocabulary is incomparably rich in suggesting
the slow, centrifugal creeping of these viscous, live solutions.[7]

This grey matter is the stuff of existence, the parody of essence; the
Portrait is, he announces, an 'anti-novel'.[8] However, it was not, as
he seems to have assumed, a book that could simply be conscripted
in the cause.

Instead of moving outwards from the slow-motion images of
Tropisms, Sarraute has moved further in, into more subtly disgusting and fascinating sub-dramas, and more amorphous areas
of 'character'. It's a brilliant exercise in illusionism – now you
sense these embarrassing, gluey secretions, now you don't – and
unsurprisingly her nervous narrator suffers from near-continuous
queasiness. Is he mad to detect an unkown, microscopic, seething
activity under the surfaces of the 'miser' father and aging 'spinster'
daughter whose lives obsess him? Certainly a visit to a specialist
dispels his visions, briefly. But then, on a therapeutic holiday, he's
drawn to visit a favourite painting (the portrait of the title) whose
incompleteness and mystery re-awaken his conviction, and return
him to his quest. Now he can see through the facades to where
gothic horrors breed: the squalid fear and possessiveness that bind
father and daughter together in obscene collusion . . . . But yet
again, nothing has *happened*. Or worse, from his point of view, for
when he runs into them in a restaurant they have plumped out,
become dreadfully 'natural'. She has acquired a life-size, plausible
fiancé called Louis Dumontet (the only person in the novel with a
name); her father is ready to give her away ('"After all, I'm not
going to last forever. It's high time somebody took my place"').[9]
Defeat. Happy ending.

Louis Dumontet has a house in the country, with an apple
orchard. 'The world will take on a smooth, clean, purified aspect'
(p. 222). People are sorted into roles, sexual and otherwise: the
daughter becomes 'feminine'; her father becomes, well, fatherly.
Only the reeling narrator stays shapeless, but we all know he'll
turn into an old woman:

'Believe me, it's much better like that . . . . I always hoped, poor
thing, that she would find a good husband . . . . '

> Piously, I shall mingle my voice with theirs . . . . (p. 222)

The indecent, ambivalent oozings were only metaphors, products of an unhealthy imagination working on ludicrously minor clues. When the old servant tells the miser a bathroom pipe is leaking, why project 'a funny look on her face, an air . . . of the conventional stage procuress' (p. 146)? Figures of speech breed dangerously promiscuous suggestions: 'she enjoyed that, to be able to drag him . . . to that oozing spot' (p. 148); ' . . . the crack through which something relentless and intolerable had seized hold of him . . . through which his very life . . . was ebbing away' (p. 160). It's a small step from this to seeing his whole relation with the world as an abcess, a foul wound, at which the women (the servant, his daughter) have always sucked, draining his miserly life to the dregs. Then again, though, the daughter too is wounded, poisonous . . . . Louis Dumontet – who is incidentally installing a brand-new bathroom in his country house – puts a stop to all that. There will be no more metaphors breeding like cockroaches.

As its title suggests, *Portrait of a Man Unkown* is a novel about deconstructing character. The narrator's special disability, as he realises early on, is that he cannot manage '"well-drawn", "vivid"' characters like Tolstoy's Prince Bolkonski (p. 64), though he's well aware of their picturesque advantages, in life as in literature:

> Rich ornaments, warm colours, soothing certainties, the fresh sweetness of 'life', are not for me. When, occasionally, these 'live' persons, or these characters, condescend to come near me too, all I am able to do is to hover about them and try with fanatical eagerness to find the crack, the tiny crevice, the weak point as delicate as a baby's fontanelle . . . . And all that remains of the firm, rosy, velvety flesh of these 'live' persons is a shapeless gray covering, from which all blood has been drained away. (pp. 68–9)

Sarraute sounds here like a cross between Lady Macbeth and Tristram Shandy. It's only when her narrator vampirically extracts their juices that the people are alive in *his* sense – that they seem for a moment to stop playing conventional types, and become vital organisms, tattered and ragged round the edges, palpating and stinging each other, merging and splitting. Or indeed (this is his secret hope) that they become *one* organism of which he too –

and his author, and the reader – will be a part. The novel's ending, all 'warm colours, soothing certainties' is an ironic preparation for our return to 'real life', a small rehearsal in inauthenticity before we step over the threshold: 'Even that rather strange look, as though things were petrified, that slightly lifeless look, will disappear in time. Everything will be all right . . . . It will be nothing . . . . Just one more step to be taken' (p. 223). Close the book, and look around, Sarraute is saying, and you'll find it quite easy to accustom yourself to the fake world we all live in.

Sartre saw in this self-consciousness an emanation of the spirit of the age (and, incidentally, a set of perceptions he felt a proprietorial interest in) – 'we live in a period of reflection and . . . the novel is reflecting on its own problems.'[10] Sarraute's own critical essays, particularly her subtle and influential piece 'The Age of Suspicion' (1950) seemed to share his assumption. She argued, taking up the theme of *Portrait*, that whereas in the days of Balzac's *Eugenie Grandet* (doubtless the source for her miser and daughter) 'the character occupied the place of honour between reader and novelist . . . like the Saints between the donors in primitive paintings', now we have in his place 'a being devoid of outline, indefinable, intangible and invisible, an anonymous "I" who . . . as often as not is but the reflection of the author himself.'[11] The character becomes the appropriate vehicle for our scepticism, our suspicion of what is presented to us as 'real'. In an earlier essay, she had traced this development back to Dostoevsky: 'his characters tended already to be . . . not so much "types" of flesh and blood human beings . . . as . . . carriers of occasionally still unexplored states of consciousness, which we discover within ourselves.'[12] All of which might seem to suggest that she was preoccupied with philosophical problems. Sartre certainly thought so – 'Is this psychology? Perhaps Nathalie Sarraute, who is a great admirer of Dostoevsky, would like to have us believe that it is. For my part, I believe that . . . she has achieved a technique which makes it possible to attain, over and beyond the psychological, human reality in its very *existence*.'[13] And yet, surprisingly perhaps (why refuse such a grand claim?), Sarraute utterly rejected this reading of her work. Her writing was not – like Sartre's own fiction – an aspect of existential enquiry. She continued to treat the novel *as its own place*, her deconstructive jokes were aimed in the end not against fiction's unrealities, but against the unrealities in 'life'. As Beauvoir said with disgust, for her 'literature becomes its own object . . . . a dead world . . . . an

artificial world.'[14] Sarraute set up the practising novelist's knowledge as a rival discipline.

So she found life of a kind in the 'dead world'. When we're
enmeshed in the processes of writing and reading, she felt, we
can glimpse authenticity, and escape the conventions and prejudices that give poeple in real life their excessively well-rounded,
opaque personalities. It takes skilled and sophisticated fiction to
locate our commmon humanity: anonymous, androgynous and –
yes – grey. We must be enmeshed, entangled. Her critical essays
became increasingly concerned with detailed questions of technique; schools of opinion, intellectual reputations and so on came
to seem to her – even when they were founded on philosophies of
scepticism – overlaid with authoritarian role-playing and the cult
of personality. She shrugged off the labels: 'anti-novel' because it
implied a definitive break with the past, rather than a continuous,
self-generated evolution of the form; and even the term 'new novel'
brought her out in ecstasies of scrupulosity.[15] She refused, when
fame finally arrived, to dramatise herself as a public figure, and
paid a certain price for her consistency, as her critic Gretchen
Rous Besser rather wistfully observed: 'Because she has allowed
others to assume the role of spokesmen for the New Novel and
has restricted herself to discussing her own work and intentions,
her pioneering position in the vanguard of modern literature has
often been overlooked.'[16] In her third novel, *The Planetarium* (1959)
Sarraute invented a successful woman novelist 'Germaine Lemaire',
whom she exposed as a personage and mocked as a artistic fraud.
Portrait of a Man Unknown too takes on a further meaning in this
context: it might have been, conventionally should have been,
a 'Portrait of the Artist', an autobiographical novel. Instead, its
narrator is a useless, neurasthenic male, a version of 'anon'. Hers
was, she wrote, 'a traditional struggle against tradition'.[17] In other
words: she would inhabit the palace of art, the house of fiction, even
though no-one was more aware than she of its odour of decay.

Craft is (almost) all. Yet it's still a shock to find her – in the
last essay collected in *The Age of Suspicion*, 'Conversation and
Sub-Conversation' (1956) – referring to Ivy Compton-Burnett as
'one of the greatest novelists that England has ever had'.[18] One's
surprise is all the greater since England for Sarraute (compare
Murdoch's remarks about Anglo-Saxon pragmatism, above) is usually a country where time stopped in the nineteenth century. Tropism XVIII, for instance, features an English pastoral scene of perfect

inauthenticity; and her second novel *Martereau* (1953) uses the same imagery to describe its main character – someone crying out to be deconstructed. Compton-Burnett's country house intrigues would seem on the face of it to belong in the same wax museum. But Sarraute, looking at her as a formal artist, sees something quite else: the suspicion built into her off-hand use of physical description, and the new and subversive role played by the dialogue that constitutes the real action. (She may also have enjoyed the ambivalence about sex roles, and the incestuous family situations, but she doesn't say so.) Compton-Burnett too was engaged in 'a traditional revolt against tradition', and she seems to have represented for Sarraute a decorous alternative to the atmosphere of furious theorising in France. It's rather as if – to use another English parallel – she's bent on playing Jane Austen to Beauvoir's Mary Wollstonecraft.

She was in an ideal position to observe the fluctuations of the literary stock-market throughout the 1950s. The relative success of *The Planetarium* in 1959, when she was fifty-nine, must have had a bitter-sweet flavour. At all events, her next novel, *The Golden Fruits* (1963), was a brilliantly bleak exposé of the way books are made and unmade in the world of letters. It's her wittiest novel, and it's hard not to detect signs of her alarming sophistication, and her timing, in the fact that it won the International Publishers' Prize, and was acclaimed in precisely the terms it mocked: ' . . . the finest thing that's been written in fifteen . . . in twenty years.'[19] Sarraute was 'in' (metafiction was in), but the main effect of *that* was to reveal the chronic dishonesty and insecurity behind reputation-making.

The basic joke of *The Golden Fruits* – that its main character is a novel called 'The Golden Fruits' – reflects Sarraute's desperately serious conviction that books are living things. As she follows the novel's fortunes in the world (early difficulties, success, decline, death, a doubtful chance of immortality) she puts that belief to the most acid test she can devise. She had always maintained that the novel was common ground among lives otherwise mutilated by convention and prejudice and role-playing; but now she allows herself to imagine the common ground itself as a place where opinionated armies parade up and down waving banners. 'The Golden Fruits', written by a (fictional) unknown called 'Bréhier', begins its career as an orphan oddity, taken up almost casually by a self-chosen few. Its reputation burgeons because they stake theirs on it: it is a classic; or no, perhaps (as a connoisseur of the nearly-new has it) it's a profoundly 'modernist' work? (p. 30,

p. 35) After this, readings come thick and fast, in a splendid, meanly accurate series of vignettes – it's . . . romantic, absurdist, post-modernist . . . . And 'The Golden Fruits', hardly perceptibly at first, starts to collapse under the weight of received opinion. It's a deliberate parody, it's a pastiche, it's a fake, a bore, easily classified as a member of the Blank school. It is dead. In the end, only one reader remains convinced of its life, rather in love with the book indeed, cherishing his lonely intimacy with it. Which is, of course, Sarraute means one to realise, all there ever really is: one reader – you there – and the genuineness or otherwise of your particular response. Though even here irony creeps in. Isn't this solitary reader a bit smug about his sincerity and uniqueness, isn't he about to start a revival, some sort of club. perhaps?

'Taste' is a harmless dead metaphor, but if it's woken up, you see what an obscenity it is to accept someone else's taste:

> One has only to let oneself go, not resist, not stiffen, it won't hurt . . . the way when they make a stomach probe, as they put the thick, nauseous-smelling rubber tube down your throat, they say . . . . it'll go down with no difficulty, you'll see, there . . . . (p. 96)

Yet there's rarely anything stronger than the desire for consensus. 'We' may seem clearly monstrous – 'we all belong to the same species, the same colour, the same race, the same faith and the same rank. Welded into a single block. Here there are not and there cannot be among us any pariahs' (p. 120). But the loneliness of being shut out from communion is intolerable. 'I' depend on belonging for my fabled sovereignty:

> I the centre, I the axis around which everything gathered, revolved . . . I the unique measure of all things, I the centre of gravity of the world, I am displaced, deported . . . . (p. 122)

If 'the authorities' seem to wield enormous power, it's because each of us longs to be right, because we collude. In other words, our very instinct to pool our perceptions is the main bar to its fulfilment. The babble of insinuating, bullying, pleading voices drowns the chancy, evanescent process of communication.

What Sarraute wants finally – impossibly – is to be any novelist, every novelist, anon. 'The Golden Fruits' was any novel; the central figure of *Between Life and Death* (1968) is any writer, dabbling in the messy protoplasm of creation:

> . . . it's still there, the old fascination . . . in little drops of grey gelatine mixture worlds are gravitating . . . he yields to every touch, to every sticky contact, all repulsion disappears, all instinct for self-preservation . . . . [20]

Out of context, this sounds rather like a riposte to Sartre on slime. And indeed, in context, it's something not dissimilar – a small hymn of praise to the despised *stuff* of life, the stuff of the novel, as Murdoch pointed out.[21] Sarraute's horror of type-casting and characterising drives her into ever more twilight struggles with her medium – 'words of ours, words of yours, mass-produced words, ready-to-wear words, words that are already worn to a shred . . . . '[22] And yet, these are not in the last analysis anti-novels, but rather celebrations of the genre's decomposing powers. New mirrors are needed to undo what the old ones bequeathed:

> Everybody what they are. Clinging completely to themselves. Entirely justifying their designations and qualifications. Sweet little old women. Exquisite old men walking their dogs with the look of a dog. Lovers embracing on benches . . . . [23]

The world congeals into an idyll imagined by a benevolent dictator. It's easy to agree with Susan M. Bell's summary of the critical wisdom on Sarraute: 'If there is any one unifying principle underlying the characteristic features of [her] fictional style, it is the attempt to avoid definition.'[24] However, there is one way in which Sarraute courts definition – that is, in the value she places on fictionality. Fiction is for her the discourse where suggestive hypotheses can flourish without turning into dogma; a place of intimacy, a kind of dialogue of one. In 1983, in *Enfance*, she produced a fictional autobiography which recreates a child's world on the threshold between sensation and consciousness. It's a world where people have made the rules without consulting you, and where you fight back with words:

> 'No, you're not to do that' . . . these words flow in a heavy, massive tide . . . in order to crush what is stirring in me . . . and

under this pressure, it braces itself, rises more vigorously, rises higher, grows, and violently projects out of me the words . . . . 'Yes, I'm going to do it.'[25]
What she does is plunge the scissors into a silk settee, out of which oozes 'something flabby, greyish . . . escaping from the slit' (p. 6) – the stuff of her fiction.

* * * *

For all her scorn of commitment and her elegant evasions of Sartre and the 'New Novel' school, Sarraute was as obsessed as Beauvoir or Lessing with the issue of the 'shared' or 'common' or 'universal' point of view. The fear of marginality is there in her choice of neutered males as narrators, and her decorous refusal to be a personage outside of her work. The common ground (she's very clear about this) is only habitable if you deconstruct 'character' and undo 'plot' and stop short of definition. Her special affection for protoplasm is a measure of her loathing of the whole repertoire of well-rounded roles the world offers: 'Everybody what they are. Clinging completely to themselves.' All three writers discussed in this chapter – despite their differences, indeed their differences make their concurrence on this point all the more striking – see traditional realism as a trap. Realistic representation confirms the separation of groups, genders, kinds; it reinforces the bad faith of role-playing; and reproduces a fossilized world, a realm of unfreedom. This has a relevance to their positions as women writers, for they clearly suspect that the roles offered to women are peculiarly awful. My quotations should already have made the point, but here is one more example, a group of camp-followers at a literary party in *The Golden Fruits*:

> In the general room dishevelled women with long coarse hair beat their breasts, make faces, laugh, lift their skirts, show their grey thighs, wriggle their behinds, women, arms outstretched, in the midst of all the din, remain motionless, congealed as in the game of statues, catatonia, epilepsy, hysteria, strait jacket, douches, beatings, savage keepers. . . . [26]

This bizarre and atavistic scene, glimpsed as it were in passing, shows women inhabiting a ghetto within the culture – part brothel, part lunatic asylum. (It's possible to see them as maenads misunderstood, but not at all easy.) Again and again women seem to be either not quite part of the human world, or all-too-human – experts in inauthenticity.

Beauvoir and Lessing, both more attached than Sarraute to relatively realist portrayals of 'character', find observing women deeply demoralising. The problem is most acute with those figures who to a greater or lesser extent represent the authors themselves, and so bring their universalising ambitions up against their sense of women-as-characters. Françoise in *L'Invitée* perhaps goes furthest in her refusal to be observable: 'Françoise,' said Beauvoir, 'once asked herself angrily "Am I going to resign myself to being just a woman?" If I chose to make Françoise a murderer, that was because I found anything preferable to this kind of submission.' Lessing too is inventive in pursuit of the 'merely' human point of view. Her break with Martha in the *Children of Violence* series, and her deposition of the writer-heroine of *The Golden Notebook* are only slightly less Draconian measures. Her formal solution in that novel, indeed, has interesting analogies with Sarraute's kind of fiction. The common ground cannot be reached with everybody as they are, so you cultivate a shapeless craziness and invent a shapeless crazy man to share it.

There's a strong utopian strain in all of this – a desire to find no man's land. The strength of the wish, however, is an index of the pressure of difference. 'We all belong', say Sarraute's nightmare chorus, 'to the same species, the same colour, the same faith and the same rank.' The culture is splintering along its fault-lines into groups, sub-groups, sub-cultures. Lessing's Anna Wulf in *The Golden Notebook* spells it out this way:

> . . . we read novels to find out about areas of life we don't know – Nigeria, South Africa, the American army, a coal-mining village, coteries in Chelsea etc. We read *to find out what is going on* . . . . Most novels, if they are successful at all, are original in the sense that they report the existence of an area of society, a type of person, not yet admitted to the general literate consciousness.The novel has become a function of the fragmented society, the fragmented consciousness. Human beings are so divided, are becoming more and more divided, *and more subdivided in themselves* . . . . [27]

She's thinking of the demise of the classic realist novel, but in a way it's also a description of the motives behind the rise of the anti-realist novel. Her textual strategies, like Sarraute's, assume the ubiquity of division. That neither of them mentions gender among the dividing factors indicates, I'd suggest, just how intolerable a thought *that* was, altogether too close to home. They herald – and coexist with – a world of difference in which (like Beauvoir) they strive to stand for universality. My next chapter looks at writers who constructed themselves, and were constructed, *differently* as outsiders.

2

Displaced Persons

CHRISTINA STEAD

The people I loved were Shelley and Shakespeare. Finished.
The person who is genuinely original – and I am, in the sense
that I was cut off from literature, and I was even cut off from
family life in that I was an orphan from my first family – is not
looking for patterns.

(Christina Stead in a (Sydney) *National Times* interview, 1981)

Christina Stead's exorbitant imagination makes demands we have
not yet come to terms with. Her idiom seems often as alien as it
is impressive – a tribute to her originality and power as a writer,
doubtless, but a back-handed one. It's partly because her work
was so neglected, so unassimilated, that she is hard, still, to take.
With a less ambitious writer this would matter less, but in reading
her now it's an abiding irony. Her passionate crafsmanship should
have been part of the diet post-war readers and writers grew up on.
Major writers need re-readers, a chorus of commentary, argument
and exegesis, if they are to occupy their proper space in the canon.
Stead is *difficult* in more senses than one. She herself seems to have
spent her last grouchy ten years or so (she died in 1983), back in
her native Australia, covering her tracks, refusing to stand for any
of the things hopeful interviewers and researchers wanted her to
represent: feminism, literary experiment, the old Left . . . . 'The
"Reds" have done me a disservice by claiming me as one of their
woolly sheep,' she complained in 1973, 'when in reality I am a
goat.'[1] Chris Williams's pioneering biography (*A Life of Letters*)
portrays a woman who was stubborn, unpredictable, and mean.
As her long, wandering life curved back on itself – London (1928),
Paris, the United States (1938–46), England again, then 'home' – she
was consumed with scorn and loneliness.

In her writing she had always gutted her experience ruthlessly: father and childhood in her 'Strindberg Family Robinson', *The Man Who Loved Children* (1940); her belated adolescence in her portrait of the artist, *For Love Alone* (1944); the after-life of the Left in *Cotter's England* (1967) and the posthumous *I'm Dying Laughing*. Her life together with Bill Blake (1928 until his death in 1968) seems most of the time to have engrossed her formidable powers of loving, leaving her free to imagine the rest of the world with fierce impartiality. Bill was a banker, a roving Marxist economist, an autodidact like her, and they seldom inhabited a literary world – so that her peers didn't meet her. Add to that the routine reticences about their life in and around the Communist Party, and her suspicion (noted by Williams) that women interested in her work must all be lesbians – it was ironical, from this angle, that she was to be republished by Virago – and you have a subject of almost comic recalcitrance. Is she the last great modernist? The last great realist? A female Joyce/Lawrence? An unwomanly Woolf? Simply strange or truly innovative? Biographical facts ought, perhaps, in some ideal world, to be an irrelevance, but they are not. We still 'place' writers in terms of their images.

One ingredient in that is nationality. Stead's nomadic life compounded the effects of her fragmentary, largely self-administered education: she was un-Australian, un-English, un-American, and at the same time un-literary in the sense that she inhabited no particular group, no tradition-in-the-making. She read voraciously, and since she had not been tutored by the university system into the role of *mere* reader, she could see no reason why she should not write herself into the company she'd kept when she was poring over books. Her own first published book, *The Salzburg Tales* (1934) was written, she said, with euphoric speed, written *out*, it almost seems – unpacked from the extraordinary imaginative baggage she had brought from Australia. The result is a kind of 'treasury' of stories, a heady concoction of every style of story-telling she knew or could invent, rich and strange and overflowing with energy. Strange, above all. Her childhood and young womanhood had bred a mythomane. First, there were the stories she was told as a small, motherless girl (her mother died when she was two) by her father; then the stories she told her tribe of half brothers and sisters; and then, the cosmopolitan top-dressing she'd acquired in Paris.

The format is based on Boccaccio and Chaucer, with interwoven tales told by different narrators sparking off ideas and images in each other. It is in fact a carnivalesque classic, and (Bakhtin would have been pleased) thoroughly indigestible.[2] Stead was from the first conscious of the way disparate identities and desires struggle for space, in the family and in society at large. An interview from 1935, in the *Australian Woman's Weekly*, spelled out her position:

> My purpose in making characters somewhat eloquent, is the expression of two psychological truths: first, that everyone has a wit superior to his everyday wit, when discussing his personal problems, and the most depressed housewife, for example, can talk like Medea about her troubles; second, that everyone, to a greater or lesser extent, is a fountain of passion, which is turned by circumstances of birth or upbringing into conventional channels – as, ambition, love, politics, but which could be as well applied to other objects and with less waste of energy.
>
> There are some whom this personal sentiment makes wander-ers and some who stew in their own juice and ferment. I confess that the study of personality is a private passion, with me.[3]

She had become one of the wanderers, and a writer, but she thought of her work as a shared enterprise. In the collection *Ocean of Story* there is a piece called 'A Writer's Friends', dating from 1968, in which she says she always wanted to produce 'an Encyclopedia (of Obscure People) . . . a sort of counter Who's Who'.[4] And in a sense her work does that: uses 'real' people not only as characters but as word-stringers in their own right. Obviously enough, too, such a project fitted with her politics.

Tale-tellers in *The Saltzburg Tales* belong for a while in a magical democracy, where there is difference without hierarchy. '"What a company we are!"' exclaims the swaggering lawyer from Budapest, '"We come from every corner of the earth: we have seen the world; we know Life. Let us amuse each other."'[5] They are self-consciously diverse – a banker, a broker, a schoolgirl, a music critic, a math-ematician, a doctor, a Frenchwoman, an old lady . . . . No one scheme of classification would contain their stories, either. They are of every known kind *except* the conventionally well-made sort Stead would have called 'professional' ('It isn't necessary that . . . stories should . . . follow formula or be like Chekhov', she wrote in 'Ocean of Story', ' . . . . everyone can tell one').[6] An inventory would list Gothic, romance, folk-tale, legend, fairy tale, ghost story, fable, anecdote, joke, parody, and so on and on. The nearest thing to

a master of ceremonies is the Centenarist ('a publicist, a sales-
man . . . specialising in the centenaries of famous men', p. 38),
who is the author's alter-ego, and sets an ironical tone. He is a
cosmopolitan Jew, sceptical, sad, mischievous – 'full of tales as the
poets of Persia: he unwound endlessly his fabrics, as from a spool
the silks of Arabia' (p. 38). Although he celebrates the famous ('I
sell best-sellers', p. 177), he argues that 'the eminence of a talent
is usually a pure chance and there must be many ignored talents
who have an equal right to fame, if only for a small part of their
production. I deny the unmistakeable hallmark of personality, the
unquestionable superiority of everything done by a man of genius'
(pp. 176–7). Stead was uncannily preoccupied right from the start
with *uncanonical* art.

In *The Saltzburg Tales* these issues of individuality and creativity
surface many times, but their most suggestive and frightening
articulation comes in a story called 'The Mirror'. It is told by
the Mathematician in response to the Centenarian's argument, as
an exploration of personality, and is about the dark side of 'difference'. The ability of mirrors to reproduce the image of the self
is slyly confused with procreation (children as 'reflections' of their
parents) to produce a domestic nightmare. The story's tragic heroine
Griselda is assailed from two directions at once – from the dead past
(as a child she imagines an old man who lives in the mirror, an
apish spectre) and from the future embodied in her children. She
shakes off the first threat, but the second is ineluctable. Her body
tells her, in dreams of unbearable vividness, that new life means
decay. The myth of individual integrity can't withstand the general
urge-to-live:

> She saw . . . the surface of the germinating earth: horribly
> suggestive roots and cotyledons arose waving violently and
> tossing their sensitive blinded tips as if in the grip of primitive
> and ruthless passions. (p. 195)

This is creativity as a force that grows through people. Her son is in
league with the old spook in the mirror, reflections drown her. In a
1942 letter, Stead wrote about 'the awful blind strength and cruelty
of the creative impulse' –

> . . . that is why we must have what are called 'errors', both of
> taste and style: in this it is like a love-affair (a book, I mean).

A love-affair is not delicate nor clean: but it is an eye-opener!
The sensuality, delicacy of literature does not exist for me; only
the passion, energy and struggle, the night of which no one
speaks . . . . [7]

The 'Mirror' short story is one of 'the million drops of water that
are the looking-glasses of all our lives' she talks of in 'Ocean of
Story'.[8] Such stories – such mirrors – feed our sense of difference
and diversity, and at the same time submerge us. In this sense, for
Stead, all creative impulses introduce us to the death of the self, and
all talent is a drop in the ocean.[9]

Her books were her children. For once the old cliché seems
actually to apply to a woman writer (and in any case, as she pointed
out, she'd done plenty of mothering of her little half-brothers and
sisters). Chris Williams, in her biography, looks hard for signs that
Stead regretted not being a mother, but can't find any: indeed,
the evidence of at least three abortions suggests that she had
had enough of family life at the beginning to last her for good
and all. No reader of *The Man Who Loved Children* will find this
surprising. It was described by Clifton Fadiman in his *New Yorker*
review as *'Little Women* rewritten by a demon',[10] and it portrays
the household she grew up in as indeed a site of 'passion, energy
and struggle' – a maelstrom in which she and her father emerge
as battling Titans and rival mythmakers. Stead, as the biography
reveals, wrote up her real 'originals' without compunction – 'It's
exactly word for word. And plenty of words. Of course, she didn't
try to poison her stepmother, but she thought about it, because
of the fearful unhappiness.'[11] Father, naturalist David Stead, was
an extraordinary figure: obsessive, ebullient, puritan (he loathed
dancing, the theatre, distrusted the arts altogether), a militant and
moralistic atheist overflowing with righteous self-confidence, fertile
of projects, and much married. Christina was his only child by his
first marriage; he remarried after two years, and fathered six more
children, and his second wife left him in 1931; his third wife, Thistle,
was Christina's age, and for years one of her correspondents.

There is no evidence that she communicated directly with her
father after leaving Australia in 1928, but the novel twelve years
on portrays him from the life. The biography (again) shows that
he *did* talk to his children in the grotesque, wheedling jargon she
gives him in the book ('Thoes who duz thare dutie ar luvly wuns
thay will get some frootie . . . . From DadPad the Boald').[12] He also

refused to send her to university, and he didn't, seemingly, ever read the novel that immortalised him as the most fascinating and nightmarish of her line of epic egoists. He seems, in short, to have supplied her most formative experience of the universal human struggle to invent oneself. Indeed, the very language in which she often talks about it owes something to him, since it calls on the naturalist's (and Darwinian's) vocabulary, and assimilates people to the animal and vegetable worlds. In a late interview, she said as much:

> When you're a little girl and you look in an acquarium and you see fish doing this and that, and snails and so on, you don't criticize and say they should do something else. And that's the way in which I was brought up, and in which in fact I see people.[13]

She often labelled her writing 'naturalist', referring not to the literary school deriving from Zola but to this more idiosyncratic provenance. Her narratives distribute creativity and share out eloquence; they always come from someone else as well as the author, often several someone elses. In *The Salzburg Tales* the effect, though overwhelming, is basically inclusive and benevolent – an embarrassment of riches. But in the novels conflict comes to the fore, in the form of the pressure one life exerts on another, one voice on another. They are dialogical works in Bakhtin's sense. Although he refers to 'joyful relativity', while Stead is frequently far from festive, the disruptive energies work in a similar way to destabilise the narrative.[14] She writes against the notion of the scarcity of creativity, and in this sense she writes against art.

This is why her work resists the 'modernist' label. She will not worship art, will not set the artist apart, will not separate out the struggle to invent literature from everyone's struggle. She is a hunger artist who novelises the dreams of outsiders. Her portrait of the artist in *For Love Alone* is a story of starvation and mutation. By this time (1944) she had achieved prestige, but not sales, and it's doubtless no accident that she is preoccupied with rejection. She and Bill had been in the United States since 1938, and had taken a great gamble on their capacity to live on their wits, on the saleability of their radicalism. 'There must be a star, as yet undiscovered, called Flux', she wrote to her half-sister in 1942, 'for under Flux I was born, and Bill, too, under Flux.'[15] Both wrote for the *New Masses*, he wrote a textbook, *Elements of Marxian theory and its Criticism*, taught economics at the School for Democracy, spoke at meetings of protest against the Dies Committee (McCarthy's forerunner); she taught a writing course, and landed very briefly a screen-writing job with MGM in 1942. That perhaps was a symbolic moment of hubris – certainly things went wrong shortly afterwards (Bill's FBI file starts in 1943). How far the increasingly chilly Cold War atmosphere affected her reputation is hard to judge: after all, her writing isn't overtly political; and it had already struck Fadiman, reviewing *The Man Who Loved Children*, that she was undervalued and under-read:

> Eventually, Christina Stead will impose herself upon the litera-
> ture of the English-speaking countries. I say 'impose herself'
> because her qualities are not apt to win her an immediate,
> warm acceptance. She may have to fight as long and as hard
> as did Joyce before gaining the suffrage of the majority. Her
> prose is difficult, often unnecessarily so. Her characters are like
> so many fiends . . . . Her humor is savage, her learning hard to
> cope with, her fancies too furious . . . . [16]

With *For Love Alone*, she must have been digging in her hope-chest, taking stock.

The book has a mock-naive, 'first novel' format: a young woman's entrance into the world. Those stories, though, are classically destined for settlement, marriage and happy endings, whereas this is the tale of the making of a wanderer. Rites of passage are the obsessive topic – how Teresa is to get out of Australia, out of innocence, out of lovelessness. She uses books, a raft of letters made up of the oddest bedfellows: Homer and Darwin, Ovid and Marx. '"If you think my life is real to me – it's only a passage"', she says, in scorn, '" . . . To Cytherea, perhaps . . . . night passage, isn't it? . . . a kind of Darwin's voyage of discovery, as the voyage to Cytherea."'[17] We revisit some time-honoured metaphors. Spanish philosopher Ortega y Gasset, whom Stead may or may not have read, has some parallel musings on love: 'In loving we abandon the tranquillity and permanence within ourselves and virtually migrate towards the object . . . . this constant state of migration is what it is to be in love.'[18] This is the primitive, restless motive that structures Stead's narrative. True to form, she puts in the voices of others – for instance, Aunt Bea, with her 'miraculous descriptions of weddings and feasts long past' (p. 57). Aunt Bea is a modern-day bard, who celebrates the mating customs of suburban Sydney, and her account of the trousseau given to disillusioned Malfi, whose wedding is the first major event of the novel, is an ironic commentary on dreams of bliss. The chapter (Four) is simply titled 'She Had –':

> . . . six voile nightgowns for summer, and two ninon . . . . half a dozen handmade panties, three *crêpe de Chine* and three lawn with Madeira work and hem-stitched borders . . . . six dozen handkerchiefs . . . in choice arty combinations, so to speak, of navy and leaf, lilac and rust, eau-de-Nile and salmon, chaminade and ibex, Mediterranean and coral, black and chromium . . . . (pp. 49–50)

All of this luxurious fabric – this texture – weaves its way into the text. Teresa has a mental inventory that rivals Malfi's spoils ('the disorderly loves of Ovid . . . the exorbitance of Aretino . . . the experiments of Sade, the unimaginable horrors of the Inquisition, the bestiality in the Bible . . . and what the sex-psychologists had written', p. 76); she imagines an academy of love, where the young might learn the languages of passion, and the university she didn't attend takes on the improbable guise of a love school:

> . . . a gleaming meadow, in which beautiful youths and girls strolled, untangling intellectual and moral threads, but joyfully, poignantly, and weaving them together, into a moving, living tapestry, something into which love, the mind, the soul, and living beauties like living butterflies and early summer flower-knots were blended. (pp. 122–3)

Here Stead is writing the epic that never was – the story, not of Ulysses, but of Penelope, who wove her way through years of waiting.[19] This is a spinster's adventure, a journey away from inarticulate want ('I am certain that as I lie here now,' thinks Teresa, 'frenzied with desire and want, all women have lain for centuries, since innocent times and never an ounce of bravado to throw off the servitude of timidity', p. 101).

Out of her loneliness she generates an object – Jonathan Crow, graduate and extra-mural guru to a fascinated bevy of frustrated women, shortly en route to London to take up a scholarship. Again,

it's typical of Stead that the reader is not for a moment allowed to
share Teresa's vision of him. He enters the novel to a ribald chorus
of insults from his male university contemporaries – '"Mr Master of
Arts Crow . . . back from a trip to the nearer suburbs with lectures
on free love in Croydon, contraceptives in Strathfield, and sterilising
the unfit in Balmain . . . . Or How the Modest Man Can Ravish
Women with No Cost to Himself . . . . "' (pp. 171–2) The analysis of
their relationship is a cruel and persuasive version of the fascination
of Lawrentian man. Crow lectures on men and women as 'two races
with different needs'; intellectual women 'imitate men's civilisation'
only to fail in their biological purpose; 'the elect of the race . . . are
going towards the vanishing point' (pp. 182–183). He is a frigid
flirt and he leaves Teresa to make all the running, to follow him
to England (having nearly starved herself to death to save the fare)
and then to be rejected. Asked, where does she stand, he answers
'You do not "stand" anywhere' (p. 345), and the words levitate out
of the text as a chapter-heading, a sentence of non-existence.

And he nearly kills her. Only in the nick of time does her
London boss, James Quick, divert her from her suicidal musings
by turning out to be lover and literary critic rolled into one. Teresa's
hunger-ordeal, her curious private writings, have metamorphosed
her, she has come out the other side of the world of deprivation.
And to prove it she is unfaithful to Quick, and loves another man,
almost immediately. She is a wanderer and a spendthrift, and she
spins a prodigal future out of her privations:

> . . . at present she had merely fought through that bristling black
> and sterile plain of misery . . . beyond was the real world . . . it
> was from the womb of time she was fighting her way and the
> first day lay before her . . . . there was something on the citied
> plain for all of them, the thousands like thin famished fire . . . .
> (p. 494)

This vision of a new world where creative fulfillment belongs to
'the thousands like thin famished fire' is Stead's defiant credo. It
is also about as close as she gets to spelling out her literary politics.
She doesn't subscribe to the notion that art is something separate
from living wants, nor to the convenient idea that talent is rare, and
will somehow always make its way to recognition. Teresa's story is
indiscreetly autobiographical; it is also – deliberately – *improbable*.
She stands for all the others who don't survive.

In *For Love Alone* Stead recaptured her years of hope; in the novels that followed, she wrote more and more about the experience of defeat, the other side of the same coin. Randall Jarrell, re-introducing *The Man Who Loved Children* in 1965 as a forgotten classic, speculated on the effects of literary rejection:

> When the world rejects, and then forgets, a writer's most profound and imaginative book, he may in spite of himself work in a more limited way in the books that follow it . . . . The world's incomprehension has robbed it, for twenty-five years, of *The Man Who Loved Children*; has robbed it, forever, of what could have come after . . . . [20]

Stead wrote to Jarrell, in response, 'I do not think the lack of appreciation . . . stopped me writing. I have grit . . . . '[21] Nonetheless, he seems to have been right up to a point: acquiring new readers did encourage her to finish *Cotter's England*; and even though she was devastated by Bill's death, in 1968, she salvaged *The Little Hotel* and *Miss Herbert (The Suburban Wife)*, both published in the 1970s alongside reprints of her earlier work. There's a further point, however, not just about literary neglect. She and Bill were privateers of the Left, who'd risked their all on a defeated vision, and who were, perhaps, unsurprised by the turn of events. They'd departed the United States in 1946, ahead of the investigators, were asked to leave Belgium for political reasons, and went to ground in austere, post-war England with seeming stoicism. Neither on the page, nor personally, did Stead make any convincing efforts to compromise. She did have grit, all too much of it, and in the later fiction this comes out in the cruel clarity of her portrayal of losers, all that hunger turned back on itself.

Stead didn't believe in pluralism, and she wrote as an unbeliever – about struggle, and about exclusion. In other words, she offended against one of the more cherished myths of Anglo-American (and for that matter Australian) culture, that there is a creative 'free-for-all', an endlessly expanding market-place for cultural production. Ellen Rooney, reflecting on the power of pluralist thinking, remarks that 'political pluralism, "American-style," is nothing but the exclusion of marxisms, both in domestic politics and abroad'.[22] This may seem a far-fetched reason to invoke for Stead's stubborn 'difficulty', but I don't think so: her writing calls the bluff of pluralism, in its insistence on the reality of the losers, and its refusal to levitate into art-for-art. Marxist critics – though they have shown no great interest in her work – are the ones who come closest, in theory, to describing her kind of world. Terry Eagleton, for instance, when he writes that 'art for the modernist writer was the name of that other, geographically unlocatable space where national identities crumbled' – whereas for the 'world proletariat' its name was 'exploitation', and for subjugated groups and peoples, its name was 'oppression'.[23] Stead's writing, I have argued, refuses to make 'art' into an 'other' homeland. She was ahead of cultural criticism in questioning the values attached to Literature with a capital L, and in exploring the meanings of displacement.

I'm Dying Laughing (edited by her literary executor R. G. Geering) is an appropriate legacy: a relentless anatomy of the hell which waits for defeated visionaries. American Reds Emily and Stephen, under pressure both from the Party (for individualism and deviancy) and from McCarthyite persecution, find their new 'home' in a European Bohemia. It's a world that, with romantic views of literary exile in mind, others might think of as a creative place. But Stead portrays it as a lazaret, a ghetto of the spirit where people rot and betray each other. Before leaving the States, Emily is already turning into a monster. Her frustrations tip her over the edge, into a crazed vision of the battle for survival – not only among people, but planet-wide, involving animals, birds, fishes: 'those who spoke with other tongues than ours, who hissed, chirped, rattled, scuttled, flew, slid'.[24] This is 'difference' in its most destructive aspect, the old world-picture of Stead's first book turned upside down, a world now with no room, where desires denied become paranoia. Here, underdog eats underdog, and consumerism rules:

' . . . *crêpes flamandes* for the masses! Our battle-cry! Pressed ducks for the people . . . . ' (p. 429)

In her disillusion, Emily is a devilish self-parodist, a true citizen of the night-world of Bohemia. Stead here speaks the unbearable – that co-existence is war by other means, that desire is the twin of hate, and cannot be divorced from the will-to-power. There's no special literary place, only the actual, material world where hunger isn't transcended, but perverted. The most difficult thing she has to say, in the end, is that the waste of talent in the world is real and unredeemable. It's this message that makes her books so hard to take.

JEAN RHYS

> So as soon as I could I lost myself in the immense world of
> books, and tried to blot out the real world which was so
> puzzling to me. Even then I had a vague feeling that I'd
> always be lost in it, defeated.
>
> (Jean Rhys, *Smile Please*, 1979)

Jean Rhys is the post-war writer as ghost. The oft-told tale of her
disappearance from the literary scene (missing, presumed dead)
after *Good Morning, Midnight* (1939), and her rediscovery via a radio
adaptation of that novel in the 1950s, is a twentieth century classic,
in its way. She became in the last two decades of her life (she died in
1979) a voice from the other side – not only from the past, but from
all sorts of other sides. And in her later writings – *Wide Sargasso Sea*
(1966), the short stories in *Tigers are Better-Looking* (1968) and *Sleep
it Off Lady* (1976), and the fragmentary posthumous autobiography
Smile Please (1979) – she perfected the role of the *revenant* (her first
title for *Wide Sargasso Sea*), the un-person, the returning phantom
who refuses to fit into the collective continuum. Carole Angier,
writing in the Viking 'Lives of Modern Women' series, starts by
announcing that 'Jean Rhys was not a modern woman . . . . It is,
of course, her writing that is modern'.[1] Francis Wyndham suggested
that her earlier works had vanished because 'they were ahead of
their age, both in spirit and in style'.[2] Rhys was unstuck in time.
She anticipated the recuperative moves of feminist scholars – she
had already fixed on the image of the madwoman in the attic, the
first Mrs Rochester, for *Wide Sargasso Sea* years before Sandra Gilbert
and Susan Gubar published their compendious history of nineteenth
century women writers under that title.[3] And yet, as Angier says,
'She was quite without the consolations – the shared burden, the
hope of change – which any "ism" brings.'[4] A small anecdote about
her schooldays in *Smile Please* sets the tone. She and one other girl,
she recalls, were pariahs at the convent because of their chronic
untidiness: 'She tried to make friends with me, perhaps she thought
that outcasts should stick together, but I preferred being an outcast
by myself . . . . '[5] In fact, the only place she had ever 'belonged' was
the Bohemia Stead described with such inwardness and distaste.

Rhys was a white West Indian, shipwrecked in cold England at
seventeen (in 1907); and she made her way to the wrong side of
the tracks with the somnambulistic assurance of one whose story

was foretold – 'I swear that looking out of the porthole that early morning in Southampton, looking at the dirty grey water, I knew for an instant all that would happen to me.'[6] It was in the world of dandyism and despair and ragged rebellion that she found her distinctive voice. When she was 'discovered' by Ford Madox Ford in Paris, she was already typecast as one of the lost. His Preface to her first collection of stories, *The Left Bank* (1927) spelt it out:

> . . . I should like to call attention to her profound knowledge of the Left Bank – of many of the Left Banks of the world . . . . coming from the Antilles, with a terrifying insight and a terrific – an almost lurid! – passion for stating the case of the underdog, she has let her pen loose on the Left Banks of the Old World – on its gaols, its studios, its salons, its cafés, its criminals, its midinettes – with a bias of admiration for its midinettes and of sympathy with its lawbreakers.[7]

It seems, described like this, a picturesquely shady prospect, with lots of fellow-feeling about. One imagines her as part of the world mythologised in all the memoirs. Thus, David Plante, acting as her amanuensis and listening to her reminiscences fifty years on, was to find himself picturing her among the literary exiles:

> It was as if she suddenly opened the door to the closed centre of her life, a café in Paris in the twenties, and in the café were Jean and Ford and his wife Stella at one table, and at other tables were Hemingway, Gertrude Stein and Alice B. Toklas, and half-blind James Joyce.[8]

But her life in Paris, Vienna or London was hardly *literary* at all in this sense, as she often pointed out – 'The "Paris" all these people write about, Henry Miller, even Hemingway etc. was not "Paris" at all – it was "America in Paris" or "England in Paris". The real Paris was nothing to do with that lot . . . . '[9] She was far more radically displaced than any of the literary figures imagination now obligingly supplies to surround her.

Her own café images are rather different. There is the Russian girl in her short story 'Vienne', for instance, who shoots herself at twenty-four, at a cosy corner-table: 'With her last money she had a decent meal and then bang! Out –.'[10] Even the mutual sympathy of outsiders ('Salut to you, little Russian girl', p. 234) is not to be relied upon. As Stead saw, Bohemia (*real* Bohemia, if that is not a contradiction in terms) nourishes discord and distrust. Beyond the pale, the weak savage the weak, and the most frightened are the most dangerous. Rhys's story 'Hunger' provides a grindingly nasty image:

It is like being suspended over a precipice. You cling for dear life with people walking on your fingers. Women do not only walk: they stamp. (p. 196)

Her world had little in common with the egalitarian and convivial counter-cultures Ford and Plante conjure up. In the four pre-war novels that followed *The Left Bank*, panic becomes the keynote.[11] Her heroines live on their looks and on their wits, and so expose themselves to the malice not only of conventional society, but also of their fellow drifters. The imagination of beauty – warmth, grace, colour, texture, taste – resolves itself into the apparatus of seduction and betrayal. The rouge, the khol, the powder and the scent become the mask for fear. In *Good Morning, Midnight* time passes on the hard surfaces of the mirrors in the (now dully *déjà vu*) Paris cafés, where shadows of past selves and spectres of future ones jostle with one's present image on the same glassy plane. It's as if the heroine Sasha cannot step outside these reflections. When she revisits familiar places, what she recognises is her own chronic strangeness. She cannot – realises she has never been able to – sustain any continuous conviction of her own humanity, let alone other people's.

In 1927 Rhys had returned to England, and increasingly it became a prison to her, a dreadfully solid, cold, conforming country. In a story titled 'Outside the Machine'(written, or at any rate begun in the 1940's) she gives a voice to her suspicious 'hosts': '"English, what sort of English? To which of the seven divisions, sixty-nine subdivisions, and thousand-and-three subsubdivisions do you belong? . . . My world is a stable, decent world. If you withold information, if you confuse me by jumping from one category to another, I can be extremely disagreeable . . . . I have set the machine in motion and crushed many like you."'[12] She came to believe quite seriously in the paranoid joke that 'persecution maniacs (so called) always have been and usually still are, the victims of persecution'.[13] She wrote more and more as someone who's at once excluded from the conventional culture and locked up in it like a restless spook. Another 1940s story, 'A Solid House', is told from the point of view of just such a lost soul. Teresa suffers from 'nerves' which, on the face of it, are easily explained by the bombing. She leads a quiet, contained, convalescent life in an immaculately respectable lodging house; however, it is her secret, subversive conviction that she is already dead, since the concrete three-dimensional house and its inhabitants seem thoroughly unreal to her. The stuffed birds, the china ornaments and the landlady Miss Spearman all mock her. Conversations take place entirely at cross purposes – Miss Spearman (who is anyway deaf) offering good advice, Teresa hearing threats:

> ' . . . and then of course don't be too much alone. People don't like it . . . . Write letters. And a good laugh always helps, of course.'
>
> 'Which helps more – with or at?'
>
> 'I don't quite follow you,' Miss Spearman said. 'And then a little bit of gossip.'
>
> . . . See people. Write letters. Join the noble and gallant army of witch-hunters . . . .
>
> But are you telling me the real secret, how to be exactly like everybody else? . . . Tell me how to get back; tell me what to do and I'll do it. (pp. 141–2)

As if in answer to Teresa's unspoken plea, Miss Spearman confides that she knows a spiritualist – for all the world as though she suspects Teresa is literally on the other side. Small wonder one of Teresa's problems is suppressing bouts of witch-like laughter. The secret of ordinariness slips through her shaky fingers. '"It's being adapted, that's what it is"' says another of the pariahs, in 'Tigers are Better-Looking': '"And it isn't any good *wanting* to be adapted, you've got to be born adapted"' (p. 87). Repeatedly in these stories the shadow-world and its substantial opposite achieve the grotesque coincidence of justified paranoia. Thus, in 'Outside the Machine', a ward of sick women decide in hard, vindictive voices that an attempted suicide deserves to be hanged.

It's this kind of structural pun that informs *Wide Sargasso Sea*, where Rhys pieces togther a paranoid's *apologia pro vita sua*. In writing *Jane Eyre*'s antithetical 'inside' story, the story of the crazy Creole wife in the attic, she finds a splendidly dramatic metaphor for her relations to men, to other writing women, to Englishness in general. And this time, for the first time, she gives her heroine

Antoinette/Bertha a country of her own – the Dominica she'd left so long ago, now distanced yet further as the just post-slave society of the 1830s. In place of Brontë's robust all-encompassing first person, Rhys has first persons whose narratives are partial, baffled, cross-threaded : hers vivid and lyrical at first, but faltering as the depth of her alienation from 'Rochester' begins to be revealed; his sullen and grudging at first (a younger brother sent to the West Indies to collect a rich bride), wakened into fascination by the strangeness of her territory. Brontë's Rochester shared with Jane, Othello-style, the wide world of masculine adventure she'd never known. Rhys's anti-hero, contrariwise, finds himself suffocating in a poisonous paradise of alien intensities – 'Too much blue, too much purple, too much green. The flowers too red, the mountains too high, the hills too near. And the woman is a stranger.'[14] Antoinette's loneliness has no defence against him and yet she can give him nothing (apart from her body, apart from money), since her vagrant intuitions, her patchwork of insight and superstition, her self- surrender, all spell deviousness and impenetrability to him. Her 'secret' locks him out. And so he will lock her in his reality, take her to England, and make her part of *his* past.

This Rochester is a member of the witch-hunting brigade: 'Very soon,' he thinks, 'she'll join all the others who know the secret and will not tell it. Or cannot . . . . They can be recognised. White faces, dazed eyes, aimless gestures, high-pitched laughter' (p. 172). The gulf between Rhys' protagonists is emblematised in their houses: hers, 'Granbois', looks (to him)

> like an imitation of an English summer house – four wooden posts and a thatched roof . . . . the house seemed to shrink from the forest behind it and crane eagerly out to the distant sea. It was more awkward than ugly, a little sad as if it knew it could not last. (pp. 71–2)

His is all 'thick walls . . . a long avenue of trees and inside the blazing fires and the crimson and white rooms. But above all the thick walls' (p. 178). At Granbois one knows oneself a stranger and a transient, but no more strange than the creatures and plants of the forest, for instance. (In a diary of the 1940s Rhys staged this dialogue with herself: 'I do not know "everyone". I only know myself. *And others*? I do not know them. I see them as trees walking.')[15] At Thornfield, some are strange, others are at home, like Miss Spearman among her bomb-proof ornaments in 'A Solid House'. Rhys's heroine, you realise, has never been at home: her Creole background makes her an outsider even in the place whose colours and scents and beliefs have formed her.

The final English section of the novel, where its plot converges with that of *Jane Eyre*, is a sustained feat of illusionism, with Brontë's setting hollowed out into a transient nightmare, the solid house going up in beautiful red (Dominica-coloured) flames. *Wide Sargasso Sea* has extraordinary haunting power for several reasons, one of which is that for once (courtesy of Brontë) Rhys manages an ending that is triumphantly vengeful instead of depressively wretched.[16] She also makes Rochester into more than a mere villain; she identifies with him, gives him a real 'I', by seeing him too as fearful and paranoid (this perhaps is her nearest approach to fellow-feeling, extending the realm of paranoia). Most important, though, is her complex sense of place – Antoinette grows up in a paradise already lost, conscious of her own difference, conscious of endless difference. There are real (realistic) reasons (she is white, but through her mother's one-time poverty and (later) madness an outcast from the white community, as well as from the black, and so on) but Rhys endows her with a dreamy obliquity that makes her a heroine of every elsewhere. When Antoinette says '"There is always the other side, always"' (p. 120) she carries a conviction the other post-war Rhys heroines lack. And this seems to be because she's inhabiting a special textual place, because she exists in relation to a ready-written fiction. As a result, she can symbolise (in truth it's more strategically vague) a state of indeterminacy, a volatility and a vulnerability that suggest infinite regress ('*always* the other side'), as against Brontë. Rhys finds a form for her claustrophobia by writing between the lines; and gives the whole thing an extra pungency by choosing an archetypal 'woman's book' to interleave.[17]

Wide Sargasso Sea brought her fame for the first time.[18] It also had, and continues to have, an uncanny contemporaneity. As for Rhys, her loneliness had become a prized possession. The short stories in *Sleep it Off Lady* (1976) start and end with imagery from the West Indies, and while there are no vengeful pyrotechnics, there's no sign of mellowness either. She focuses repeatedly on those experiences of blank misgiving that convince her characters of their precious (if disastrous) specialness. In the title story a dying woman is dismissed as drunk by kind Samaritans who've been counting the bottles in her dustbin. In 'The Insect World', set in London during the war, Audrey meditates on the mechanisms of acceptance: '"It's as if I'm twins" . . . . Only one of the twins accepted. The other felt lost, betrayed, forsaken, a wanderer in a very dark wood. The other told her that what she accepted so meekly was quite mad, potty.'[19] The 'other' collects evidence in unexpected places. A secondhand novel she's reading has inane comments from a previous reader in the margins:

> But it was on page 166 that Audrey had a shock. He had written 'Women are an unspeakable abomination' with such force that the pencil had driven through the paper . . . . And yet, she told herself, 'I bet if you met that man he would be awfully ordinary, just like everybody else' . . . . But it was always the most ordinary things that suddenly turned round and showed you another face, a terrifying face. That was the hidden horror, the horror everybody pretended did not exist . . . . (p. 127)

If you allow yourself to see it, you lose control, as Audrey does when her flatmate addresses her affectionately as 'old girl' – '"Damn your soul to everlasting hell, *don't call me that* . . . . "' (p. 136). 'Old girl' has two faces: it's like an arm around the shoulders, a sign of acceptance; and at the same time it reminds her that at twenty-nine, alone, unassimilated, she's threatened ('"Women are an unspeakable abomination"') with all the paranoid venom hidden in ordinariness. Then again – since every 'other' has an 'other' – even the arm around the shoulders is sinister, since it threatens her precious apartness, enlists her along with 'them'.

Rhys remained hypersensitive to the segregations and the cunning adjustments concealed in ordinary exchanges of language. Not that books were immune. The dreadful, drawn-out agonies of composition and revision which dogged her seem to have been in part to do with a fear of exposure, of being read at all:

> As a matter of fact I *hate* publicity and the public – I hate to think of them pawing at my book – Not understanding. This of course is idiotic for I long too for it to be understood and read and so on.[20]

So although there was a nightmare attached to neglect, there was a definite attraction in the role of ghost. The last story in *Sleep it Off Lady*, 'I Used to Live Here Once', takes her back again to Dominica, to a rickety white house. Things have, naturally, changed – the house has been added to, a car stands outside – but it is only when the children playing on the lawn stare through her and shiver that she realises she's not there, merely a cold shadow. This small epilogue encapsulates her sense of being cut off from 'her' country, except as a country of the mind. It also provides a neat, hallucinatory image of sudden disinheritance, the transition from the child's specialness to the old woman's alienation completed, at last, with mocking ease.

ELIZABETH SMART

> I raise my eyes to the books and say, Well, *they* were here and whirl around still all over the western world, which means that their followers-on must too, for nothing stops so suddenly. Are they hidden in veils or strait-jacketed by domestic lives or hammering at their sores in lonely rooms?
>
> (Elizabeth Smart, *The Assumption of the Rogues and Rascals*, 1978)

Like Stead's *For Love Alone*, Elizabeth Smart's *By Grand Central Station I Sat Down and Wept*, published a year later, in 1945, laid claim to a heroic literary legacy; also like Stead, and Rhys, Smart – who was born in 1913 – was a migrant (a Canadian on the run) who ended up in England, where she died in 1986. *By Grand Central Station* has been resurrected more than once (1966, 1977). Its companion-piece, *The Assumption of the Rogues and Rascals* (1978), pretty well completes Smart's fictional *oeuvre*, and together they form a passionate and witty commentary on literary displacement. The first novel was not (is not) an innocent forgotten book waiting passively to be retrieved, but a knowing dramatisation of the fate of an over-reacher. Being jilted by Lit. is Smart's theme. Or to put it more elaborately, *By Grand Central Station* is the story of a love-affair with the high style (poetry and tragedy) which came to a sticky end in the low-mimetic mode.

Brigid Brophy in her foreword to the 1966 re-issue says that 'The entire book is a wound', but if so, it is a wound as jewel-like and inevitable as those adorning lovers in Petrarchan sonnets – 'every scar', writes Smart's narrator, 'will have a satin covering and be new glitter to attack his heart.'[1] The story may lack a shell, in the sense of a protective layer of rationalisation, may be 'skinned, nerve-exposed', in Brophy's words; but it possesses instead a simple and rigid structure – the life-span of a love-affair from birth to dissolution – which shapes the writing from inside. This is literary love (love as an art, art as a passion) which begins 'when he, when he was only a word' (p. 20). ('He' is a poet; Smart may be implying that she fell in love with his writing first, or that she imagined him before he materialised, or of course both.) This love has the capacity to elevate people into legend in their own eyes, and to give even a female hierophant a right to the best lines. For like Stead's Teresa, Smart's nameless 'I' plays almost all the parts herself. He is ambivalent, bisexual, formless, and married, so that she becomes heir to the archetypes of torment and euphoria that men, as well as women, have imagined:

> . . . smoothed away from all detail, I see, not the face of a lover to arouse my coquetry or defiance, but the gentle outline of a young girl. And this, though shocking, enables me to understand, and myself rise as virile as a cobra, out of my loge, to assume control. (p. 23)

In fact, the only women writers who figure at all prominently in Smart's elaborate tissue of allusion and quotation are St. Teresa of Avila, and Emily Brontë – 'Heathcliff's look bored a hole through England which generations of heather on the wild moor have never erased' (p. 101). For the most part it is Shakespeare (*Macbeth* in particular), Milton and the metaphysical poets whom she plunders. *Macbeth* supplies blood and fatality. The following passage, for instance, combines echoes of Lady Macbeth's 'all the perfumes of Arabia will not sweeten . . . ' with her 'we fail!/ But screw your courage . . . ':

> . . . neither nunneries nor Pacific islands nor jungles nor all the jazz of America nor the frenzy of war-zones could hide any corner of consolation if this failed. (p. 72)

There is a hint, too, of Milton's *Comus* ('If this fail/ The pillar'd firmament is rottenness'); certainly in another place Smart appropriates the tears of Milton's angel from *Lycidas* – 'I look homeward and melt.' (p. 61) And Donne's sensuous hyperboles are everywhere: 'we can include the world in our love' (p. 43); 'I am empress still of a new-found land, that neither Columbus nor Cortez could have equalled . . . . ' (pp. 46–7). These particular allusions, interestingly enough, have an androgynous flavour for other women too – Millett, for example, or Carter.[2]

Smart's 'I' is the woman who fights with her destiny, not against it. She 'collaborates' with her lover's writing in a frenzy of self-consciousness – 'The typewriter is guilty with love and flowery with shame, and to me it speaks so loudly I fear it will communicate its indecency to casual visitors' (p. 27). Playing hostess Macbeth-style on holiday in California, she conspires relentlessly to break his marriage, 'breathing like a workman setting out on a job' (p. 38), and watches agonised and unrepentant as his wife suffers. And once she has him to herself she enjoys a splendid if hell-tinged bliss that seems to her to embrace the whole world, feed the hungry, end the war, melt the poles. Though the world sets obscene and absurd traps for runaway lovers (the Arizona police arrest them crossing the state line for 'immoral purposes') the 'ritual rhythms' of the *Song of Songs* and of Donne's *The Canonization* turn humiliation to triumph: 'Could we corrupt the young by gazing in each other's eyes? Would they leave their offices? Would big business suffer?' (p. 56) Love is the alchemist's formula, the phoenix in the furnace – 'With it I can repopulate all the world. I can bring forth new worlds in underground shelters while the bombs are dropping above . . . . ' (p. 72). Even when passion fails, she savours the sense of fatality and enjoys the coming end. As her lover returns to his ghostly wife, she refuses consolation – *that* comes in a quite different tradition. There is a cadence from Wordsworth's *Tintern Abbey* in 'Even in transient coffee shops and hotels, or the gloom of taverns ' (p. 45) but she's fiercely against his palliations (years that bring the philosophic mind).[3] She imagines those other derelicts, the refugees, the old who 'trudge over Europe pushing carts and enormous bloated-with-hunger bellies', not as wise through suffering, just cheated by time:

> . . . does nature walk beside them, holding their flabby forearms and whispering medicinal lies? For memory deserts them and their eyes get dimmer as the past achieves perspective. (p. 102)

She's conscious of the shame of failure ('I see it all, the poop of burnished gold', p. 84), but she'll not compromise the finality of loss.

The novel's conclusion is tragic in a double sense. Once her lover is gone, leaving her pregnant with their child, she feels herself losing the whole world of (magical, poetical) words. Her life sub-divides into fragments, the baby she is carrying takes a part, the lover another, leaving her with 'the insane loneliness of the first split amoeba' (p. 122). She is exiled from artifice, for birth, bringing forth and creation are no longer visionary metaphors to her. The imagery has come home to roost: 'that child was the naked newborn babe striding the blast. He is the one focal pinning me to my own centre' (p. 118). The lover has a tomorrow, 'Tomorrow' capitalised indeed, personified as 'an ardent boy of Socrates', with whom he'll inhabit the visionary upper world where creation is a game, and procreation is a metaphor for what male writers do.[4] Meanwhile she'll drown among 'The uninterpreted. The inarticulate' (p. 126). Words become the greasy currency of survival:

> You must adjust yourself to conditions as they are, that's all. You have to learn to be adaptable . . . . Everything's hotsy-totsy, dandy, everything's OK. It's in the bag. It can't miss. (p. 128)

This is the language of poverty, with which you scrape by 'realistically', with no miracles. And here, the story outside the novel takes over, the one on Elizabeth Smart's dust-jackets: 'They never married but Elizabeth bore George Barker four children . . . . After the war, Elizabeth Smart supported herself and her family with journalism and advertising work.' Her second novel, more than thirty years on, *The Assumption of the Rogues and Rascals*, is a wry and rueful coda. The 'poetry' is salvaged this time out of the unsanctified mess of work, and children, and the body's weariness ('*it* only wants ease and absence from shock, and comfort, and the strength to go on . . . . It is not amused by the Muse').[5] There are few literary models of the kind she respects for this experience. She shares a joke with Beckett – 'Driven to drivel, dribble . . . signs of parturition!' (p. 110) – but his acrobatics on the edge of silence seem somehow, still, more *voluntary* and more figurative than hers. 'Once upon a time there was a woman who was just like all women' (p. 89) just doesn't sound like a promising start. No fairy-tale there. Women's lives aren't even part of the time-scheme of the public world. Her 'war', for instance, only really begins when the official one ends, amid British shortages and rationing:

> Out of this weary landscape . . . you are to step through a couple of decades with your children on your back . . . . heaving your heavy rucksack full of the future . . . .
>
> I am friendless, covered in mud, cowardly, weak, untrained. But signed up for the duration. (pp. 15–16)

The army of women march to an uncertain beat that hasn't a lot to do with the past intensities of desire – 'Was it for this that so many miracles came roaring like bombers across the wilderness of America? . . . I too have chilblains and a faithless lover and trouble making ends meet, say the women in the fish and chip queues.' (p. 37) Love, if it comes, is indeed a metaphysical proposition, since it must transfigure the dead weight of things, unfocussed circumstance and 'conditions as they are'.

The central sections of the book are about recovering the desire to write, against all the grain of daily survival. She chooses once more the company of the 'rogues and rascals', the poets and pretenders, the improvident non-providers ('They raise their stolen hats and buy me a bitter with borrowed cash', p. 48), because they at least fit in with the extravagance of her suppressed wishes. Though nowadays they pose no temptation to passion, only offer an antidote to the parsimonious lessons life is bent on teaching. Her struggle to write is a solitary one, the metaphors of making and creation have to be re-invented out of the passive language of 'labour' and 'bearing':

> But where, woman wailing above your station, is it you want to go to, get to, accomplish, communicate? Can't you be amply satisfied with such pain, such babies, such balancing?
>
> No. No. There's a blood-flecked urge to go even a step further . . . . What if nobody listens? Is it all to be wasted? All blasted? What about that pricey pain? . . . .
>
> If it is all to be buried, all just lived through, life becomes a warmish sort of bath, or worse. (p. 63)

The echoes of the poets (George Herbert in 'all . . . wasted? All blasted?') are a reminder of her distance now from the writer of *By Grand Central Station*.

Returning to the idiom of the literary love-affair, she sees in it a language that can only be used *by her* at the cost of a continuous sense of displacement – 'A pen is a furious weapon. But it needs a rage of will' (p. 67); or, more jokily, 'Is ego a prick to the Muse then?' (p. 109) *The Assumption of the Rogues and Rascals* becomes the story of its own difficult conception. She must be her own Muse, fertilize her own imagination, against the rules of nature, and only precariously supported by the traditions of art:

> Lying like an immobile amoeba, gigantic, out of season, and idiotically waiting for instigation. You know this can't be. Leave the washing up and take a look around. (p. 71)

The amoeba image is picked up from the earlier novel, as is much else. In the 1970s Smart was writing in a context of feminist thinking which made the 'anxiety of authorship' a familiar topic;[6] what's striking, though, is the fact that she had canvassed it so explicit back in 1945. One of the reasons for her prescience is, it seems to me, quite simply her furious romanticism. She refused any middle way – the prose of realist fiction, for instance, or even poetry in the Wordsworthian tradition – and so dramatised the clash between the language of creation and the experience of reproduction with a kind of exemplary force. Christine Brooke-Rose, contemplating the difficulties of the experimental woman writer, sums up the mythology in question like this:

> Gender, genre, genius, genesis: all come from the same Indo-European root *gen: to beget/to be born. Only man begets, woman bears and travails: genius vs. work.[7]

There are many morals that might be drawn from Smart's twin prose-poems. In a sense, you can see her as repeating the past, discovering *yet again* what a careful reading of Emily Brontë (or Emily Dickinson) could have taught her. However, there's a different way of looking at it. Our later twentieth-century sensitivity to women writers' anxiety of authorship reflects, after all, our own time's agenda. Perhaps (for example) it's precisely in the post-war era that the question of who has 'the divine and metaphoric power of producing one thing out of another thing through the word'[8] becomes really pressing? Because (thinking of Smart's metaphors-turned-literal) it was then that women began to be able to *play around*, in all seriousness, with their own fertility.

TILLIE OLSEN

> I had said: always roused by the writing, always denied. Now,
> like a woman made frigid, I had to learn response, to trust this
> possibility for fruition that had not been before.
>
>   (Tillie Olsen, 'Silences in Literature', 1965)

With American Tillie Olsen, not writing came close to being the
whole story: there's *Yonnondio* (1974), subtitled 'From the Thirties',
when it was written, and pieced together from long-neglected
manuscripts forty years on; and a collection of stories written
in the 1950s, *Tell Me a Riddle* (1962). The stories made the near-
impossibilities of communication their theme, and *Silences* (1978)
put together some non-fiction pieces in which she explored, via
a collage of quotations, the rich variety of ways in which it's
possible to be wordless. Not because of the inner imperatives
of one's medium (she'd share something of Elizabeth Smart's
ironic distance from Beckett) but because of social and cultural
and ecomomic exclusions. Olsen is a socialist realist when it comes
to describing the conditions for literature's production – 'In the
twenty years I bore and reared my children, usually had to work
at a paid job as well, the simplest circumstances for creation did not
exist.'[1] But she's a socialist idealist when she thinks of the meaning
and value of writing:

> . . . writing, the hope of it, was 'the air I breathed, so long as I
> shall breathe at all'. In that hope, there was conscious storing,
> snatched reading, beginnings of writing, and always 'the secret
> rootlets of reconnaissance'. (p. 19)

Like Stead, Rhys, Smart, she longs to see the world of books as a
common inheritance (she quotes Virginia Woolf on literature as
'common ground'), a place where the processes of 'sorting' and
segregating can be deconstructed.[2] In fact, the radical, working-
class tradition that sustains her (compare Stead, above) also speaks
plangently of *loss* and waste – of its own loss, indeed.

Yonnondio takes on a new layer of meaning as a lost – partly
irretrievable – book. It was conceived in the crusading spirit of
nineteenth-century realism, particularly, perhaps, on the model of
Rebecca Harding Davis's once-famous *Life in the Iron Mills* (1861),
which Olsen came across in a junkshop when she was fifteen.

Though there are also many other echoes – especially of Hardy, patron saint of autodidacts. In one sense, therefore, it belonged to a robust, even 'epic' tradition. However, its unfinished state has made it into an exemplary object of a different sort, a book caught up and mangled in the defective social machinery it was seeking to expose. One can't tell how the plot about the struggles of the Holbrook family in the Depression years would have ended, but probably on a note not unlike the one it famously ends on now – baby Bess surfacing for the first time to human consciousness from under a summer heatwave and the meatpacking factory stench, banging a fruit-jar lid:

> Bang, slam, whack. Release, grab, slam, bang, bang. Centuries of human drive work in her; human ecstasy of achievement, satisfaction deep and fundamental as sex: *I can do, I use my powers; I! I!*[3]

This moment's triumph gets a lot of its polemical force from the book's sense of all that works against the realisation of more than a fraction of human potential, in individual lives, and across the generations. The 'human drive' so miraculously reborn every time is worn out in drudgery, or deformed, in very unmiraculous ways. We're always starting again.

A case in point for Olsen was that early heroine, Rebecca Harding Davis, whose novel, she wrote, had been one of the works that said to her '"Literature can be made out of the lives of despised people," and "You too must write".'[4] It was also, however, a book that had itself vanished from literary history; and its author, Olsen discovered, had spent most of her later life as a hack writer, supporting her family. As she herself began writing again, discontinuity became her hallmark. The title story in *Tell Me a Riddle* fixes on a grotesquely telling image – a dying woman reliving her (laborious, taciturn) life in an incessant babble of words that takes her back to her radical youth in Europe:

> *Lift high   banner of reason   justice   freedom   light* (tatters of an orator's voice)
> *Humankind   life worthy   heroic capacities*
> *Seeks* (blur of shudder) *belong human being*[5]

Taking the syntax out is a savagely appropriate gesture. There's no narrative filiation here, no 'line' that links the old time and place to the present. In the America of the 1950s the rhetoric of revolution is meaningless (or worse). For her husband and children, who are getting on in the approved ways, the old woman's noisiness in dying makes her a stranger, a kind of traitor almost, a spy in the family: 'it seemed . . . that for seventy years she had hidden a tape recorder . . . trapping every song, every melody, every word read, heard and spoken – and that maliciously she was playing back only what said nothing of him, of the children, of their intimate life together' (p. 120). Only her granddaughter, by virtue (ironically) of her distance, can catch a meaning from the disjointed non-sense that flows out of her as her life ebbs away - from its form, as much as from its content. As Cora Kaplan says, the disorder Olsen mimes in her character's words ('"Salt tears. For free. I forgot to shake on salt?"', p. 123) amounts to 'a concrete poetic testament'.[6] This is the woman's legacy, a bundle of unforgotten, unacted aspirations that have survived her submergence in the day-to-day domestic labour of living.

The language of comradeship and equality echoes across the gaps between generations, or genders, or (in 'Hey Sailor, What Ship?') between the wanderers and the settlers. An ageing, much-travelled, booze-soaked seaman drifts away from his landlocked friends: once they were bound together in the brotherhood of the Left, now they're snared by memories, only the past provides a common tongue. The abiding irony of these stories lies in their portrayal of the way the words of unity have been scattered to the winds ('*Humankind   life worthy   heroic capacities*'). The dividing silences speak as loudly as the words, just as *Yonnondio*'s unfinishedness testifies to what is irretrievable, the (hi)story silenced. Solidarity has lost its place, speaking of humankind you speak in splinters, in a fugitive poetry. Only literature, perhaps, offers a refuge where wandering words can find a home and a posterity. Olsen's understanding of the value and meaning of writing is that it is the place where the 'human ecstasy of achievement' is realised, preserved and passed on. Survival itself becomes a triumph, and the resurrection of lost texts is a way of handing on the torch. She thus bridges yet another gap – that between the realist ambition of documenting and describing 'new' social groups not represented in literary tradition; and the modernist emphasis on literature as a revolution *in words*.

In *Silences*, she elided the struggles of working class, modernist and women writers (among others), and so made of 'writing', by implication, an egalitarian republic, a realm of the (heroically) human. It was a position she shared by 1979 with many feminists, and one which has fuelled the retrieval and revaluation of the work of countless women. Its basic strategy might be described as a generalisation – or diffusion – of the category of the marginal. Women's writing is on the heroic edge of silence, produced against the odds, part of the ongoing process by which the oppressed wrest a right to articulacy from hegemonic culture: '*I can do. I use my powers . . .* ' The strength of such a language is clear; it speaks union and progress, and it's proleptic (utopian), looking to art as a commonwealth where words are no one's exclusive property. It's worth remembering, though, that Olsen's fiction reveals that this is a *transposition* of radical politics, not a straightforward expression of them – an act of piety towards a tradition that in social reality has been all but buried. The notion that getting words onto the page is itself a liberation and an historic act is a measure of loss. Indeed, it feels most appropriate applied to fields like nineteenth-century studies, partly because that's the period it comes from. If you look not at literature's production, but at its reception and comsumption in the present, then the picture changes. The effect of stressing, as Olsen does, that there's no scarcity of creativity, puts pressure on this very point. As Elizabeth Smart says, 'What if nobody listens? Is it all to be wasted? All blasted?'[7]

Smart's unravelling of the creative/procreative opposition is relevant here. Olsen writes of motherhood as 'the least understood, least and last explored, tormentingly complex *core* of women's oppression (and, I believe, transport as woman');[8] or again, of women's oppression as 'entangled through with human love, human needs, genuine (core) human satifactions . . . . ' (p. 258) It's not easy to decide exactly the direction she's thinking in, though it seems to be for her a matter of the sheer labour of love most societies have made women's work. Children represent time, energy, money, imagination, responsibility enough to account for women's failure to use their writerly talent. However, as Smart suggests, there's something else going on, too. Making it new in literature is bound up with (male, metaphorical) conceptions. Olsen associates women writers on the margins with the birth of the new. But the terrain of the literary *avant garde* has proved singularly inhospitable. The margins, it turns out, are already occupied. Marianne DeKoven in 'Male Signature, Female Aesthetic: The Gender Politics of Experimental Writing', puts it this way:

Manifestoes for avant-garde . . . and feminine . . . stylistic practice often sound remarkably alike *without knowing that they do or
taking cognisance of each other in any way*.[9]

Critics who claim that women's writing '"rejects mastery and domi-
nance"', and brings '"the marginal into sudden focus . . . opting for
openness and possibility"'[10] describe something indistinguishable
from experimental writing in general. However, women's work
is largely ignored by literary histories of the new. This state of
affairs is a sorry travesty of the freemasonry of writing Olsen had
in mind.

One reason for this is that in the mythology of literary invention
and originality 'the divine and metaphoric power of producing one
thing out of another thing through the word is deeply felt as a
male power.'[11] Another reason is the difficulty of accepting women
writers as distinctive voices unless they are placed and identified
as belonging in a particular world. (They have to seem married,
somehow, to a set of values: Jane Austen is the archetype here;
more recently, and much more ambiguously, there's Virgina Woolf
and 'Bloomsbury'.) It's no accident that of the writers discussed
in my first chapter it is Nathalie Sarraute who provides the most
nightmarish image of women as literary camp-followers:

> . . . dishevelled women with long coarse hair beat their breasts,
> make faces, laugh, lift their skirts, show their grey thighs . . . epi-
> lepsy, hysteria, strait jacket, douches, beatings, savage keep-
> ers . . . . [12]

Sarraute's experimentalism made her wincingly aware of the gross
constructions of Bohemia – the stereotypes that await those who
step out of conventional roles without acquiring the armour of a
vocation. It is of course an image not unlike the one Rhys took up
in re-writing 'Mrs Rochester', and not far removed either from the
self-images of her earlier heroines: exposed, painted, dishevelled.
Feminist criticism has often pushed this *demimondaine* portrait of
the (woman) artist back into the past. Indeed, Olsen in *Silences*
does so too, associating 'Parasitism, individualism, madness' with
Victorianism, and making the present sound much more rationally
organised – 'For twentieth century women: roles, discontinuities,
part-self, part-time . . . . '[13] But actually (so wierd is women's literary history) you could almost reverse these descriptions. Bohemia

hasn't gone away, the margins, limbo, no man's land have their
pariahs too.

In suggesting that displacement is almost every woman writer's
condition, Olsen hopes to disperse some of the bad magic it has
generated. However, as Rhys's Antionette says, there is always
the other side. Rhys's short story 'The Lotus' (1967) exposes the
outsider's nakedness. Ronnie and Christine live on the Bohemian
fringe, and find in their neighbour Lotus Heath (middle-aged,
over-painted, alcoholic and 'artistic') a focus for their anxieties:

> 'Garland says she's a tart.'
> 'A tart! My dear Christine, have you seen her? After all, there
> are limits.'
> 'What, round about the Portobello Road? I very much doubt
> it.'
> 'Nonsense,' Ronnie said. 'She's writing a novel. Yes, dearie
> –' he opened his eyes very wide and turned the corners of his
> mouth down – 'all about a girl who gets seduced – '[14]

To Ronnie Lotus is a reassuring joke, to Christine she's a hateful
portent. When her clownish, shameless performance – '"I wrote
it with the tears running down my face and it's the best thing
I ever wrote"' (p. 119) – culminates, later in the evening, with
her breaking down, tearing her clothes off and running into the
street, their satisfaction is clear. Now they can disown her, and
cuddle up together cosily and obscenely, their fears banished for
the moment by such a perfect scapegoat. Olsen's sheer decency and
reasonableness lead her to play down the witch-hunting that goes
on even on the Left Banks of the world. Her straightforward attack
on the issue has something of the effect of putting a railway line
through a red-light district.

To generalise displacement is to make 'writing' into a kind of
utopia, where there's always room. But that move in turn reveals
the persistence of irrational but powerful stereotypes which make
some outsiders more equal than others. A recent example: David
Plante's *Difficult Women* (1983) combines three memoirs – of Rhys,
Sonia Orwell and Germaine Greer – which very exactly police
the boundaries of Bohemia. These women have little in common
beyond being 'difficult'. That is, they are tough, exciting, abra-
sive, exorbitant . . . and dishevelled, isolated, noisy, public. Drink
figures large, so does sexual and/or emotional exhibitionism. These

difficult women, it's implied, expose themselves, so that in a sense they're actually 'easy'. This is just one way in which the displaced are in fact placed. The outsiders' club (Plante, for instance, prides himself on his sexual ambiguity) has always been good at type-casting women. Sandra Gilbert and Susan Gubar, in Volume Two of their mammoth history of 'The Place of the Woman Writer in the Twentieth Century', *Sexchanges* (1989) show how transvestite episodes in the work of founding modernists (Joyce, Eliot) actually serve to reassert gender definitions.[15] Olsen writes for potentiality – 'Remember women's silence of centuries, the silences of the rest of humanity. Not until several centuries ago do women writers appear. Sons of working people, a little more than a century ago. Then black writers . . . . '[16] Like Stead, she reveals the limits of our pluralism and openness.

FRANÇOISE SAGAN

> I have lots of blood brothers and sisters all over the world. That's why I like to talk about the night-birds and party-goers, liars and drinkers. They're the only people with any imagination.
>
> (Françoise Sagan, *Réponses*, 1974)

Outsiders are typecast. There is no clearer example of this that Françoise Sagan. Born in 1935, suddenly world-famous with *Bonjour Tristesse* in 1954, she was the other side of 1950s conformism, and her career is a nicely paradoxical reminder of how very fashionable displacement can be. The fairy-tale ease with which all the ingredients of the Sagan legend fell into place rapidly revealed, especially to her, how conventional the whole process was. As she remarked later on in *Réponses*:

> In 1954 I was faced with a choice: I could either be a shocking writer or a middle class girl. Actually, I was neither. A shocking young girl and a middle class writer might have been a more accurate description.[1]

The drink, the extravagance, the affairs, the fast cars and the night-clubs were *de rigueur* (not for nothing was her favourite uniform a little black dress worn with a string of pearls). Her success trapped her in a style of life that her eighteen-year-old self had imagined as freedom:

> I became a commodity, a thing, the Sagan myth, the Sagan phenomenon. I was ashamed of myself. I hung my head when I went into restaurants . . . . I was being trapped into a role and I couldn't get out of it. A life sentence of going to bed with sordid drunken characters . . . . (p. 40)

Réponses (an 'imaginary interview' based on actual interviews she gave over twenty years) invites the reader to picture her on a plateau of time – 'I adopted the legend as my mask' (p. 41) – where gambling, alcohol, lovers, friends, novels, even the car crash that nearly killed her, even the birth of her cherished son, seem just aspects of her loneliness. Also, of course, of her special brand of bad faith, which consists in a kind of sentimental tough-mindedness. She took to mingling *in propria persona* with the beautiful shop-soiled, irresponsible characters of her fiction, unable to allow them full reality, and unable to claim it for herself.

This characteristic Sagan manoeuvre is doubly ironic. She grew up, imaginatively, on a precocious diet of Sartre, Beauvoir and Camus, and was thus splendidly equipped to recognise bad faith in herself, as in others. *Bonjour Tristesse* was a 'shocking' novel because its characters, including its first-person narrator, were treated as existences, not essences. It's easy now to catch the echoes of the author's anti-creed. At the book's crisis-point, Cecile defies her would-be step-mother Anne: she refuses to give up her boyfriend Cyril and spend her summer studying Bergson for her philosophy exam. As she plots to undermine her father's love for (orderly, intelligent, moral) Anne, Cecile is, as it turns out, putting herself through an impromptu vacation course in existentialist ethics:

> I took stock. She wanted my father; she had got him. She would gradually make of us the husband and step-daughter of Anne Larsen; that is to say, she would turn us into two civilized, well-behaved and happy people. For she would certainly make us happy . . . .
> How infinitely desirable . . . the liberty to think, even to think wrongly or not at all, the freedom to choose my own life, to choose myself. I cannot say 'to be myself', for I was only soft clay, but still I could refuse to be moulded.

I realise that one might find complicated motives for
this . . . spectacular complexes . . . but I know the true reasons
were the heat, Bergson, and Cyril, or at least his absence.[2]

It's rather like a replay of Beauvoir's *L'Invitée*, told from Xavière's
point of view. The guiding motive ('to choose myself') and the
sideswipes at Freudianism ('spectacular complexes') are impeccably
'free' from conventional guilt. You can already detect, however,
signs that the freedom is itself a little 'tarnished' (a favourite Sagan
epithet), a little ritualised. When Sagan kills off Anne, by having her
commit suicide, there's none of the sense of desperation you feel
with the ending of *L'Invitée*.[3] The plot about choosing oneself has
become, almost, a matter of choosing a 'lifestyle'. Cecile chooses a
Bohemianism which – as she's quite aware, since it's her father's
style – is easy, ready-made. She, of course, unlike father, thinks that
she's 'only' role-playing.

In a sense, most of Sagan's writing since *Bonjour Tristesse* has
been about that book's reception. She was taken at her word, as
though she'd uttered a fatal spell against herself. True, in her
second novel, *A Certain Smile* (1956), her heroine Dominique is
still celebrating the pleasures of living outside the pale – 'I felt
absolutely light-hearted. Paris belonged to me: Paris belonged to
the unscrupulous, to the irresponsible . . . . '[4] – and still satirising
the explanations of psychology:

I didn't believe in revealing slips of the tongue, intercepted
glances, and swift intuitions. There was a phrase that always
surprised me in novels: 'And suddenly she knew that he lied.'
(p. 32)

Sagan characters know better, they are acting in bad faith *knowingly*.
However, the elation Dominique feels at being ahead of the game,
experimenting with her identity (she whiles away an afternoon kissing a stranger in the cinema, and goes home to curl up with Sartre's
L'Age de Raison) is denied to later Sagan heroines. The novels become
increasingly obsessed with themes of boredom and loneliness. Her
characters carry on a mirror-dialogue with their images, and she
carries on one with hers. It's as though the role she finds herself with
has blocked off the world for her, so that she has acquired almost no
new mental furnitures since 1954. She is doomed 'to choose myself'
over and over again. The disastrous bitter-sweet love affairs that she

writes about resolve themselves into quizzical self-interrogations: Sagan the prisoner of freedom inspecting the ritual scars she has acquired over the years of gallantly acting her part.

In *Réponses* she quotes the heroine of her play *La Robe Mauve de Valentine* – "'I always end up looking as people want me to look'".[5] She deliberately reads back intimations of her fate into her earliest years:

> On my way to school for seven o'clock mass on Fridays, I used to see all the party-goers, the people who'd been up all night in clubs. They were all in evening dress and waving bottles of champagne, just like the characters in Scott Fitzgerald. (p. 30)

The fact that she is, in every sense, the luxury edition of the Bohemian woman serves to spice her ironies. For her insecurity is something that has to be stage-managed by gambling too recklessly, driving too fast, and so on:

> I love those fleeting moments when people have had a few drinks and begin to be a bit unsteady. They let themselves go, stop acting and take their clothes off. They take off their masks and begin to say something real. (p. 141)

The moments when you stop acting are themselves rapidly recouped as part of the act, however. One way of describing Sagan's distinctive tone is just this: she shows how the ad libs were all along part of the script ('I didn't believe in revealing slips of the tongue'). Her success *as* the outsider vividly demonstrates the collusion that can spring up between ousiders and insiders. It's not merely that she was secretly bourgeois (though she was, not very secretly) but that she offered a deeply satisfying version of the woman artist as public property, and 'chose' the role that was ready for her. People used, at the height of her fame, to have a confused impression that she was a film star, perhaps because she was so thoroughly what she was *seen as*.

*   *   *   *

As love affairs with literature go, Sagan's was a dream of consummation – fame at eighteen with her first novel. Following her career since seems tasteless, like asking what happens after the happy ending. Her later novels provide a dusty answer. To quote one of her (admittedly more desperate) characters from *Wonderful*

Clouds (1961) – '"It's as though we'd been invited to spend the weekend in a country house full of rotten planks and treacherous staircases . . . . "'[6] The house of fiction, which seems so spacious, corners you and categorises you. Sagan, for instance becomes the poor little rich girl of letters: in her sadness and excesses (and celebrity) she confirms the notion that real literary adventurers are hard-working, serious, full-time and almost certainly not women.

She provides a kind of coda to this chapter because she demonstrates that Bohemia needn't spell unsuccess or neglect: simply, that it has a tendency to turn the woman writer into a *demimondaine*. However, she differs from the other writers discussed here, since she belongs to a very recognisable place and idiom (Paris, fashionable existentialism). Stead, Rhys and Smart are all 'post-colonial'; Olsen speaks for an American working-class tradition. And although they are members of an earlier generation, they represent types of displacement that are in many ways more contemporary. The pattern that emerges, post-war, is not one of 'exile' in the modernist mode. Paris, despite Sartre, Beauvoir, Beckett, Sarraute, the 'new novel' . . . was no longer *the* centre of literary life. There wasn't such a centre. The wanderers, male or female, had no very convincing spiritual home – certainly women writers like these would have been hard put to it to find the kind of cultural refuge Shari Benstock describes in *Women of the Left Bank*.[7] In any case, the utopian sense of Art as an alternative homeland doesn't stand too much scrutiny. Stead and Olsen, both brought up on radical asumptions, do indeed imagine utopia, but they also understand and portray a world of struggle and exclusion. An uncanonical literature, a literature where stories are drops in an ocean, remains a visionary prospect.

This is why generalising displacement as a feature of all *avant garde* writing, or all women's writing, or 'ecriture feminine', seems wrong. These aren't texts without signatures. (Foucault in 'What is an Author?' quoted Beckett: '"What does it matter who is speaking," someone said, "what does it matter who is speaking?"'[8] As one of my students wittily pointed out, you would recognise that anywhere as a quotation from Beckett.) Literature, so far, has not contrived to return to the state of radical anonymity. Rather the reverse: anonymity has become the thing writing cannot do, the thing *theory* wants of it, and (ironically) a reason for devaluing women's work.[9] The writers noticed this process a lot earlier and felt it more intimately that the critics. Displacement *enters into* the writing of all the women in this chapter, not as a by-product of some state of textuality, more like iron into the soul. This is not surprising, since it is precisely on the margins that claims to originality are laid and disputed. Smart suggested back in 1945 that the very metaphors of creativity kept turning out to be a male preserve; certainly, if you look at the ideas of 'movement' and change that form the background to 1970s 'liberation' writing in America, you can see that the image of the writer, and the mythology of mobility, have become thoroughly male. Tomorrow, as Smart put it, is an ardent boy out of Socrates; or at least a recognisable avatar, in the form of a Ginsberg or a Kerouac (see Chapter 4).

All of which helps to explain why, despite its theoretical anachronism, realist writing goes on. Alongside the anti-realist pressures, and the writing from 'the other side', a new – revisionist – realism takes shape. Perhaps after all the traditional novel was *rightly* anti-utopian? Density, detail, particularity, local truths, all the paraphernalia of representation acquire a new urgency and poignancy now that they have lost a large part of their prestige. This revaluation of realism has something nostalgic about it, of course. But it also reflects dissent: a protest on behalf of fiction-as-family, as the middle ground where genders and generations can be pinned in focus together. We arrive back home, but home has changed.

3

The Middle Ground

IRIS MURDOCH

> Freedom is not choosing; that is merely the move we make when all is already lost. Freedom is knowing and understanding things quite other than ourselves.
>
> (Iris Murdoch, 'The Sublime and the Beautiful Revisited', 1959)

This chapter's title is borrowed from a Margaret Drabble novel of 1980, but its obvious starting-point is Iris Murdoch. She inhabits 'the middle ground' – what she calls 'ordinary human jumble', the realist territory of nineteenth century novel tradition – more authoritatively than any of her contemporaries.[1] Indeed she swarms over it at the head of an army of words: she has published twenty-three novels in thirty-six years of fiction-writing, and the sheer bulk and variousness of her *oeuvre* have become a major part of her meaning. She stands for continuity and for belonging, for the circumstantial life crowded with personal relationships and personal 'things'. Her plots are those of a moralist and a match-maker. One of her favourite quotations, echoing through the novels, comes from the medieval woman mystic Julian of Norwich, and proclaims 'all shall be well and all shall be well and all manner of thing shall be well.'

The implications are, of course, often savagely ironic. Her people are dismissed to disaster or violent death as well as to marriage, and the two opposite fates are, anyway, not so far apart as they might seem. Nonetheless there's always an implicit celebration of the plenitude of existences ('all manner of thing'). The novelist's art, for her, 'goes on existing for better and for worse'.[2] She has been openly nostalgic for the densely-populated worlds of Sir Walter Scott or George Eliot. The fact is, though, that she began in the 1950s (she was born in 1919) as a much more abstract writer, akin (distantly) to Sarraute and (more closely) to Beauvoir. Her pre-fiction life had involved a Marxist period in her twenties, and work with Displaced Persons at the end of the war, as well as academic training in classics and philosophy. Her first published book, on Sartre (1953, she'd been a philosophy fellow at Oxford since 1948), is in a sense a revaluation of that early experience. She's clearing the way for the novels, working out a place for herself.

She questions, in particular, the left-over idealism of Sartre's account of 'the individual', and of the meanings of 'freedom' (compare Beauvoir's comment on 'the plane of individual, and therefore idealistic morality on which we had set ourselves', above). According to Sartre, Murdoch argues, '"The act of will" . . . is already framed in my unreflective and self-prolonging conception of how things lie. Liberty lies deeper than will.'[3] To paraphrase: one's freedom – one's degree of freedom, one's unfreedom – depends on the quality of one's awareness of the surrounding world, of 'how things lie'. Yet Sartre's novels, she points out, picture the individual in isolation, as a monologuist. There is only one self in focus at any particular time, so that a vital link (between persons, and between the novel and the reader) is missing:

> If we are to be either touched or terrified there must be the concrete realisation of what George Eliot called 'an equivalent centre of self from which the shadows fall with a difference' – and this . . . Sartre does not give us in the novels. (p. 60)

The traditional novel of character is, she suggests, a better medium for 'picturing consciousness' than the monological form Sartre employs both as philosopher and novelist. George Eliot located the problem of freedom in the fabric of our relations with the world, whereas Sartre 'has an impatience, which is fatal to the novelist proper, with the *stuff* of human life' (p. 118). His novels reveal that he lacks 'an apprehension of the absurd irreducible otherness of people, and of their relations with each other.' (p. 118)

'Otherness' has for Murdoch here none of the sinister significance it had acquired for Beauvoir in *The Second Sex*. It is the otherness 'of people', not of women, that Murdoch stresses. A contrast between their positions is revealing. Beauvoir came to see women as inhabitants of a kind of ghetto, doomed to 'bad faith' (conventionality, spurious self-definition, dependence). Murdoch argues that, since 'will' and 'choice' are metaphysical hypotheses, and since we cannot divorce our selves from the surrounding stuff of human life, we *all* live in that ghetto, even (most of the time, anyway) philosophers. 'Freedom,' she wrote in a 1959 essay, 'is knowing and understanding and respecting things other than ourselves.'[4] It's a statement her nineteenth century predecessors (Elizabeth Gaskell, and of course George Eliot) would have agreed with. And like them, Murdoch puts the woman question to one side. At the same time, however – again, as they did – she is feminizing the whole human condition. The individual is pictured enmeshed in 'relations', surrounded by fixtures and fittings (compare Eliot's insistence on portraying and judging public men amid the exigencies of personal and domestic life). No-one can levitate for long out of the condition of being a 'character', on this view. We are all relative beings, Murdoch argues, and the novel in its traditional form, therefore, rightly reflects us.

In her book on Plato, *The Fire and the Sun* (1977), she describes art ('especially literature') as 'a great hall of reflection where we can all meet and where everything under the sun can be examined and considered.'[5] Again, as with Sartre, she's inserting a space for fiction into a philosophical system that squeezes it out, or diminishes it. Plato, the father of western philosophy, and scourge of mimetic artists, is persuaded to provide a role for realism. The myth of the cave from *The Republic* (where ordinary, unphilosophical humans are trapped, benighted, in illusion) turns into a justification of living in the house of fiction. Since, according to Plato, 'we are limited, specialised animals', we know ourselves best in an art form that is ambiguous, mortal, imperfect and provisional (p. 84). Her image of the 'great hall of reflection' – where reflection implies thinking and mirrors – converts the claustrophobic cave into a rather stately communal space. The 'dialogue' of the philosophers (all too likely to drift into monologue) is opened up once you have *'hypothetical* hierarchies and *intermediate* images' (p. 86, my italics). She writes admiringly of 'the pierced nature of the work of art, its limitless connection with ordinary life' (p. 86). Realist conventions, in particular, place a saving distance between characters and authors. In the 'hall of reflection' everyone shares in limitation, so that it's a most instructive model of the world. As J. P. Stern put it, (in *On Realism*), 'what [realism] implicitly denies is that in this world there is more than one reality'; the realist writer 'has no doubt about the singularity of the world in which realism lives, in which we all live'.[6] He also has a brush with Plato, and concludes that 'even if we accept that the Reality outside the cave' (ie. the world of Forms or Ideas) 'acts upon life in the cave, and is therefore intimated in it, what realism is concerned with is precisely that life inside the cave as it is acted upon and reacts to the intimations of the Reality outside . . . . ' (p. 46). This is roughly Murdoch's position, too.

However, as should be clear by now, it is a position she has to argue herself into. Her realism is polemical, a way of keeping abstract speculation and radical deconstruction at bay.[7] One favourite plot-device is to mete out violent comic punishment to those characters who have ambitions to write 'great books' of philosophy – or even novels of the wrong sort.[8] Here she echoes George Eliot's treatment of Casaubon, with his Key to All Mythologies; and reflects on the dubious example of the great modernists (Proust, Joyce) for whom 'The human task has become a literary task, and literature a total enterprise, wherein what is attempted might be called reconciliation by appropriation'.[9] Novels shouldn't try for finality, their 'limitless connection with ordinary life' dooms them to imperfection. Or to put it another way, their imperfection is a continuous critique of totalising ambitions. (This, in the end, is why Plato needed to banish the artists.) The writers in her books are not allowed to get away with metafictional gestures, they are inside the cave, levelled with other characters. At the same time, of course, the very process of drawing them in, laughing at them, cutting them down (a few are murdered) reveals her self-consciousness. She presents the paradox of the realist under siege. She is writing against utopia, which is not at all the same thing as simply writing about 'this world'.

Indeed it took a long while for her to find a form that looks realistic. Her first eight novels (1954–64) all, in different ways, reiterate the arguments of the Sartre book. *Under the Net* (1954) and *A Severed Head* (1961) are the liveliest of these perverse novels of ideas, and it's no accident that they both feature male monologuists. Jake in *Under the Net*, in particular, is a wittily conceived composite contemporary 'hero', with echoes of Sartre, Beckett and Raymond Queneau (the whimsical author of *Pierrot mon Ami*, to whom Murdoch dedicated the novel). But though he begins as an alienated 'voice' he ends by seeing himself, after all, as having a character and a context. All along he has had two possible role-models: Hugo Belfounder, whom he reveres as a sceptical moralist, a mind unpolluted by worldliness or word-mongering; and Jean-Pierre Breteuil, a prolific French novelist whose 'bad best-selling stuff'[10] he translates and despises. Murdoch's plot ingeniously reverses these valuations, so that philosophic Hugo comes to sound like a bad novelist - '"It's like life isn't it? I love Sadie, who's keen on you, and you love Anna, who's keen on me"' (p. 227) – while Jean-Pierre, to Jake's chagrin, at long last writes an unmistakeably good novel:

> The style had hardened, the manner was confident, the pace long and slow . . . . Starting a novel is like opening a door on a misty landscape, you can still see very little, but you can smell the earth and feel the wind blowing . . . . (p. 246)

And so Jake is naturalised in his life, made to pay attention to the ways its possibilities shift and change and falsify his expectations.

Of course he realises that he too means to be a novelist. In effect, *Under the Net* is a fable about writing 'a novel proper' which would be elaborate, illusionist, unselfconscious . . . ('you can smell the earth'). It *isn't* that kind of novel though, nor is *A Severed Head*, which again entraps its monological narrator in a cruel and scandalously funny plot that forces him to recognise the unpredictability of the lives around him, and – eventually – his own. This narrator, Martin Lynch-Gibbon, is deliberately distanced from Murdoch's own writerly preoccupations (she makes him a wine merchant and part-time military historian), and the shocks she applies to his ego are more violent. Nonetheless, the effect is, again, strikingly schematic. You don't smell the earth, you smell midnight oil and mental sweat – especially with the advent of Martin's improbable lover, Honor Klein, Cambridge anthropologist and avatar of the dark gods, ugly, visionary and dangerous. She is the 'severed head' of the title: the Medusa who symbolised castration fears for Freud, and the fear of being observed for Sartre, and who for Murdoch encodes 'otherness'. Honor is the sheer fact of others' difference, which the self-preserving ego mythologises into a figure of dread. Potent (and funny) as she is, though, she is generated out of a footnote in *Sartre*.[11]

It was not until *The Red and the Green* (1965) – ironically, a much less successful book – that Murdoch arrived at the more sprawling structure, more securely rooted in time and place, that was to make her truly the laureate of 'ordinary human jumble'. It's surely significant that this, her only historical novel, takes her back to her family's roots in Ireland. She'd been born there, of Anglo-Irish parents (though she'd been brought up in England), and her return in imagination to the violent events of 1916 is an act of reverence and curiosity. A sign, too, that she was turning away from the European scene that has claimed so many Irish writers as permanent exiles. *The Red and the Green* places her in a new sense, though there is nothing autobiographical about it, by acknowledging the importance of 'background'. The descriptions of Dublin are among the best things in the book:

> Blessington Street . . . . had, under the pale bright sky, its own quiet air of dereliction, a street leading nowhere, always full of idling dogs and open doorways . . . . Looked at closely, the bricks of these houses showed in fact a variety of colours, some purplish red, some yellowish grey, all glued together by a jelly of filth to form a uniform organic surface rather like the scales of a fish, the basic material of Dublin, a city conjured from the earth all in one piece by some tousled Dido.[12]

This kind of writing is a comic riposte to the nausea with which fastidious Sartrean heroes respond to the slimy otherness of things.[13] Murdoch comes out politically, too, in defence of the (grubby, imperfect) workings of English 'liberal' values, as opposed to the fanaticism of the abstract man – here, heroic, puritan Pat Dumay, who wishes he was bodiless, hates women ('muddled and unclean, representative of the frailty and incompleteness of human life', p. 91), and dies in a fervour of idealism.

She had exorcised a certain absolutist ghost. The rich, repeatable formula of the later novels – their shameless dedication to 'muddle' – is here in sight. *The Nice and the Good* (1968), *A Fairly Honourable Defeat* (1970) and *An Accidental Man* (1971) establish it as a formula, a set of conventions designed to highlight the circumstantial or (a favourite Murdoch word) 'contingent' pressures that confine people for better and for worse to the middle ground they share with each other. One of the central techniques, I've already suggested, is to generate whole ranges of 'difference', so that the isolation of the individual comes to seem not a metaphysical problem, but a continuous local truth. Murdoch, now, takes to inventing enormous numbers of characters, Victorian-fashion, a huge cast linked by family ties, marriage, friendship, lust, exploitation and so forth. From now on, you can identify a Murdoch novel from its cast list. What's distinctive is the over-precision of the naming, which both suggests the endless strangeness of people, and acknowledges how nearly impossible it is to keep them in focus. Their inter-relations (again, a mutated version of nineteenth century fictional mores) allow plots and sub-plots to breed with an abandon that makes the perverse erotic permutations of *A Severed Head* look over-tidy. Thus for example Gracie Tisbourne, halfway through *An Accidental Man*, sums up a typical state of affairs:

> It appears that Ralph loves Ann Colindale who loves Richard Pargeter who (currently, he never does anything for long) loves Karen who (although she denies it) loves Sebastian who loves me who loves Ludwig who loves me.[14]

'So that's *that* situation tied up', she concludes, though she could hardly be more wrong. There are more moves to be made, always. Even the seating arrangements for a Sunday lunch have (for readers who recognise the conventions) ominous and absurd undertones, as in this passage from *The Nice and the Good*:

> Mary was sitting next to Uncle Theo who was sitting next to Edward who was sitting next to Pierce who was sitting next to Kate who was sitting next to Henrietta who was sitting next to Octavian who was sitting next to Paula who was sitting next to Barbara who was sitting next to Ducane who was sitting next to Mary.[15]

These are confessedly quantitative, and in a sense mechanical devices, but they produce qualitative changes. Any one character, however central – or marginal – moves in a dense network of other lives. Freedom comes dowm to paying attention, and so finding room to manoeuvre.

Except that attention is too neutral and altruistic a word. Murdoch's people are inveigled into 'seeing' each other by atavistic urges – desire, fear, passions of all kinds. Mary, for instance, in *The Nice and the Good* cannot help Uncle Theo because she means too well:

> She felt compassion for him and willed to help him, but her relationship to him remained abstract. The sad truth was that Mary did not love him enough to see him clearly. (p. 91)

'Love' here means something disconcertingly close to sexual chemistry. The cave we all live in is foggy with feeling, our common context is made up of a kind of ectoplasm, extruded by everyone (at such moments Murdoch sounds a little like Sarraute):

> Each human being swims within a sea of faint suggestive imagery. It is this web of pressures, currents and suggestions, something often so much less definite than pictures, which ties our fugitive present to our past and future, composing the globe of consciousness. We think with our body . . . . (p. 342)

Hence of course her sinister fascination with married love as an emblem of (possible) fulfilment and (likely) failure. Marriages in these novels are the locus for thinking about the limits of freedom. Tallis and Morgan in *A Fairly Honourable Defeat* are, as is fitting for a quarrelsome and separated couple, given some uncompromising things to say on this topic:

> ' . . . Marriage is a symbolic blood-relationship, it's the creation of a new family bond.'
> 'Well, I don't care for bonds, family or otherwise.'
> 'I don't mean constraint. I mean real connection.'
> 'Don't be sentimental, Tallis, I can't bear it. And don't talk about marriage as if it were a *condition*.'
> 'It is a condition. All sorts of things are conditions and it's one. It relates the past to the present.'[16]

Murdoch here is letting one of the secrets of traditional realism out of the bag: that marriage is 'really' a piece of invented human nature, the place where will loses itself.

So she agrees with Tallis, and – as author – plays the role of pandar and go-between. Even the sexual 'happenings' she sets up – chancy unrepeated encounters between improbable partners (for example, 'impotent' wandering Jew Willie Kost and hero Ducane's ex-girlfriend Jessica in *The Nice and the Good*) – are, for her, momentary symbolic marriages. The more surprising a coupling, the more tellingly it illustrates the limits of the will, and the delightful and/or grotesque potentialities of being contained by a human context. Straight, spinster Charlotte in *An Accidental Man* is made to reflect 'how astonished they'll all be when it turns out I'm living in a cottage in Sussex with an Amazon and a big dog'.[17] This improbable scenario not only materialises, but turns into a 'real' marriage, a 'condition', a kind of tragi-comic trap. Charlotte weeps over her lot, but, we're told, 'her tears were already those of married people who love each other, cannot stand each other, and know that they can never now have any other destiny' (p. 425).

One way of describing the action of the Murdoch novel that emerged in the early 1970s is as a mechanism for transmuting abstract issues into concrete ones, principles into (compromised) practice, individuals into persons. Personal relations form the texture – the fabric – of her text, as well as its foreground motifs. Her people, astonishingly, if you think about it, do nearly nothing but inter-relate: the maintenance, analysis and scrutiny of the socio-sexual culture is their collective vocation. A 1980 novel, *Nuns and Soldiers*, jokes rather wickedly about this: '"But what do you do if you're not a writer or a painter or a homosexual or a housewife?"' asks one character of another with genuine puzzlement; and the answer comes pat – '"Until lately I've been a nun . . . ."'[18] There's a serious point here: unless you remove yourself from the world altogether, you're committed to the arts and crafts of living. All tasks are thus in a sense feminised, and men are pulled by the text's gravitational field into a domestic orbit. They tend, often, to be on some kind of sabbatical from the world of outside work for the novel's duration; or they have jobs (in the civil service, or academe, or welfare) which leave them a good deal of domestic leisure, and are anyway professionally concerned with personal life; or they have private incomes; or they are artists. In any case, like the women, they exist in a world where 'work' is an aspect of the quality of one's sensibility, and where it's very hard to draw lines between educational and/or therapeutic motives and ordinary human contacts – or between (say) writing and the higher forms of gossip.

This novel of the middle-ground is the scene of sexual collusion and gender confusion. Murdoch treats sexual difference as a curious continuum, as if there might be one sex, or three (or more) but never two.[19] A lot of her talk about 'character' is a way of restating the problem of difference so as to avoid dualism. She creates so many and such shifting relations that the great divides (sex, but also class, race) are confronted locally, as particular comic horrors. In effect, her progress is almost diametrically opposed to Doris Lessing's: whereas Lessing during the 1960s was moving away from the tradition of personal relations, and finding it less and less plausible, or indeed possible, to keep the boundaries of the person intact, Murdoch was cultivating line-drawing, character-sketching, and all the crafts for keeping fictive persons distinct from each other and from their author. She was – again, most unlike Lessing, and unlike the other writers so far considered – refusing to think in terms of discontinuity, or disinheritance. She treats discontinuity as itself a continuous fact of life.

The density of local detail she manages each time is predicated on its disposability. No one novel sums things up. However, *The Sea, the Sea* (1978, winner of the Booker Prize) may serve to represent her 'middle period' and – since its hero is a monologuist – to suggest contrasts and continuities with her early fictions. Charles Arrowby is, naturally enough, an older and more substantial figure than Jake or Martin Lynch-Gibbon; indeed he is flamboyantly a 'character' – a retired and celebrated theatre-director, a sentimental cynic, a monster of egotism – and lives in a world dense with illusion and role-playing. Now, writing his memoirs, re-meeting the people who've been forced to play parts in his life, he begins to get the queasy feeling that his personal magic is failing. As he struggles to keep control, he works himself unwittingly towards the point where for the first time he sees around the edge of his own fantasising ego, beyond the picturesque delusions that have been the stuff of his personal and professional life.

The main agents of this transformation are the setting in which he retires (the lonely house, the rocky promontory, the treacherous sea) and his first and lost adolescent love, Hartley, throughout his life his excuse for not committing himself to anyone, now a shy, lumpy sixty-year-old who turns out to be living in a twee bungalow round the corner with her equally substantial husband. Re-meeting Hartley, Charles comes up against a level of existence, of sheer, mysterious *ordinariness* he knows nothing about. Her marriage may be stuffy, changeless, tasteless, even wretched, but it's real, and he can only eavesdrop on it obscenely, like a peeping Tom. He realises, almost too late, that life is a matter of immersion in one's surrounding element, and that if you separate yourself off – the manipulative, inviolate 'I' – you're more likely to sink than swim. The metaphor takes one back to Jake's realisation in *Under the Net*:

Like a fish which swims calmly in deep water, I felt all about me the secure supporting pressure of my own life . . . . [20]

But in *The Sea. the Sea* the paradoxical implications of 'my own life' come to the foreground: particularly in the person of Hartley with her quite *other* life, with its banal domestic interiors that resist Charles's acquisitive imagination:

> I took in the brown and yellow floral design on the carpet, the light brown wallpaper, the shiny ochre tiles round the electric fire which was set in the wall. Two round bas-reliefs representing churches hung on either side of the fire. A funny-looking shaggy rug upon the carpet was making extra difficulties for one of the table legs. There was a large television set with more roses on top of it. No books . . . .
>
> At the table Hartley and Fitch were sitting stiff and upright, like a married pair rendered by a primitive painter . . . . [21]

The pathos and the necessity of possessions ('my own . . . ') are here lucidly exposed. The things that mark out the boundaries of Hartley's marriage are the means by which ordinary life goes on. As another Murdoch character reflected in *The Black Prince*: '– They are poor substitutes for art, thought and holiness, but they are substitutes . . . . '[22]

This is the sad middle of the middle ground. For Murdoch, the novel is the art-form that best (most embarrassingly) symbolises the affinities between art and the muddle of living. And her own unfastidious, robust productiveness stresses defiantly all that's routine, consumable, untidy about novels (always plural for her). The fears associated with seeming dishevelled or Bohemian can turn into boasts (almost) from this point of view. Imperfection and incompleteness become evidences of humanity, signs of the limits of everyone's freedom. Her consequent slatternliness in the matter of minor points of style and structure (slips with naming, redundant and mannered formulae) is by now notorious. However, her larger-scale argument that the novel's traditional illusions should be accepted and indulged commands respect. In part, perhaps, because – as a professional philosopher – she has always produced theoretical justifications; but also because she appeals to a folk-belief in women's shocking practicality.

In other words, she's a matriarchal realist, writing under the sign of that 'tousled Dido' from *The Red and the Green*. Or she was in the 1970s. Her novels of the 1980s, in particular *The Philosopher's Pupil* (1983) and *The Book and the Brotherhood* (1987), allow a lot more space to the Reality outside the cave: metaphysics, utopianism, abstract passion and violence.[23] Gerard in *The Book and the Brotherhood* elegaically echoes Jake in her first novel:

> It's gone, he thought, the past, it is irrevocable and beyond mending and far away, and yet it is here, blowing at one like a wind, I can feel it, I can smell it, and it's so sad . . . . [24]

In this book, for once, the would-be author of a Key to all Mythologies, the intellectual terrorist Crimond, is allowed to finish his magnum opus – an indication, I think, that Murdoch's dialogue with deconstruction is entering a new phase. Plato looms large again, too: one of the main plot-engines in these novels is the teacher-pupil relationship, the addiction to 'turning the mind round'.[25] And yet, of course, it's characteristic of Murdoch that she stresses always the erotic base of this seeming-pure intellectual intercourse. The love-affair with theory, when you see it as a seduction, becomes part of the story of living in the world – ideas, as in Plato, are brain-children. The father of western philosophy, of course, thought these progeny were conceived outside the cave, free from illusion. Murdoch, conversely, sees thinking as rooted in body-language, saved by the 'stuff' the utopians take for mere metaphors.

EDNA O'BRIEN

> Goodbye to the ragwort, the chicken run, the dozy hens, goodbye to the tillage, goodbye to the green gate with its intractable hasp . . . . Goodbye to the ineradicable past.
>
> (Edna O'Brien, *Mother Ireland*, 1976)

Edna O'Brien's idiom too is splendidly untidy. Again and again, she'll veer dangerously from irony to dewy sentiment, only to rise dripping from her sorrrows with a fey smile. She might perhaps more plausibly be cast as a 'straight' Bohemian. The heroines of *August is a Wicked Month* (1965) and of the filmscript *Zee & Co* (1971) seem natural successors to Rhys's ghostly lost women, close cousins to Sagan's glamourous outsiders. Zee's memorably bitchy line on her husband – '"he likes a woman to be a mess, can't you see. That's why he's with me, he hates women"'[1] – vividly recalls the double-bind of finding oneself classified as a barbarian *within* the culture. Nonetheless, partly by virtue of the Irishness that lends her an earthy, oddly matriarchal air, she also stands for continuity and the 'feminising' tradition. Irishness may not, on the misogynistic face of it, suggest middle-ground collusions between the sexes. She contrives from the first, though to find secret allies, most particularly Joyce. Thus, best friend Baba in her first novel *The Country Girls* (1960) exasperatedly exhorts our heroine – '"Will you for Chrisake stop asking fellas if they read James Joyce's *Dubliners*?"'[2] And almost twenty years on, in her anthology *Some Irish Loving*, O'Brien remarks bitterly in her own editorial person:

> Instead of pilgrimages to Mary and Joseph, and Jude, Bridget and Ita, the women of Ireland ought to be down on their kness to Mister James Joyce who not only made their sexuality more patent to the world at large but who stripped from them the shackles of their own bound souls.[3]

Her characters cultivate a Molly Bloom rakishness. Even the young heroine of *Girl with Green Eyes* (1962) describes losing her virginity in a comic monologue that meditates on the levelling absurdity of sex:

> It was strange, being part of something so odd, so comic . . . . I felt no pleasure, just some strange satisfaction that I had done what I was born to do. My mind dwelt on foolish, incidental things. I thought to myself, so this is it; the secret I dreaded and longed for . . . . All the perfume, and sighs, and purple brassieres, and curling pins in bed, and gin-and-it, and necklaces, had all been for this.[4]

And in *Night* (1972) ageing Mary Hooligan is yet closer to Joyce's greedy, accomodating heroine – 'I can't cavil. I've had my share, even a lumberman from Scandia with a very radical thrust. A motley screw, all shades, dimensions, breeds, ilks . . . . '[5] It's this recurrent ribald note of acceptance that establishes O'Brien, despite sad and alienated gestures, on the middle ground.

She makes ironic comedy out of the romantic necessity of escaping one's roots. Her heroines are always getting away – from the farm to Dublin, from Dublin to London, and so on – as she did herself; but they remain haunted and contained by their origins. Or to put it another way: however far-travelled in desire, they're still comic characters. Thus Caithleen describes herself in *The Country Girls* as 'tall and gawky, with a bewildered look, and a mass of bewildered auburn hair' (p. 155). In *Girl with Green Eyes* she's 'the literary fat girl' (p. 13). Her loves, by contrast, have the insubstantiality of romantic archetypes: mummified Mr Gentleman in the first novel ('his carved, pale face was the face of an old, old man', p. 199) is a spookily vivid embodiment of male mystery; and even Eugene Gaillard in the second, though he's altogether more prosaically accounted for, retains an air of unreality. When he describes his work in documentary films, Caithleen (a comic Jane hanging on the words of a media-man Rochester) hears only the glamourous sub-text of a world elsewhere:

> . . . he had just finished a script for a picture on the world's starving people. He had travelled all over the world, to India, China, Sicily, Africa – gathering information for it. On his desk were photographs of tumbledown cities and slums with hungry children in doorways. It made me hungry just to look at them. 'Bengal, Honolulu, Tanganyika,' I repeated after him in a dreamy voice . . . . (p. 50)

Her longing for glitter and sophistication clashes gruesomely with his style of altruistic concern. His role, for her, is to purvey the romance of 'experience', not information. As she says later, letting the cat out of the bag, '"Some girls wouldn't take it, but I don't mind you telling me about the ice age and evolution and auto-suggestion and the profit motive . . . . "' (p. 193). Naive and clownish as she is, she's in certain senses more of a realist, a student of hunger, than he is:

> 'My mother is dead,' I said to him. . . . I wanted to say something else, something that would convey the commonplace sacrifice of her life: of her with one shoulder permanently drooping from carrying buckets of hen food, of her keeping bars of chocolate under the bolster so that I could eat them in bed if I got frightened of Dada or of the wind. (p. 33)

Caithleen is rooted in the parish of the past. She'll leave, of course, but she'll never acquire his respect for abstract 'fact'. Instead, her life – like her mother's – will be spent in yearning and passionate muddle.

In *Mother Ireland* (1976), a kind of guidebook to the country of her

own memories, O'Brien recalls 'the books we read' – 'we' being
the women and girls – as the literary equivalents of that cache of
chocolate under the pillow:

> Life was so tame beside that. The fields, the bog where the lilies
> grew, the parish of a thousand souls, the old canon delivering
> long sermons interrupted by coughs and phlegm, the pails of
> milk, the conversations were as dishwater compared with the
> nectar in these star-crossed tales. Miss Annie M. P. Smithson or
> Mrs Henry Moore or some other enchanted creature was saying
> that the moon swam high in the heavens . . . . Reality was a dull
> second. And sex the forbidden fruit was the glass coach in which
> to do a flit.[6]

She isn't so much scornful of the splendid clichés of romance,
as observant of their function as luxury goods in a puritan and
sensuously impoverished culture. In retrospect (hence her sense
of an affinity with Joyce) it's the comic co-existence of the pails
of milk and the forbidden fruit that strike her as the important
thing. Her most cosmopolitan and 'liberated' heroines are secretly
naive, bumpkins at heart, at once too dreamy and too earthy for
the sophisticated company they keep. Thus, the heroine of her
short story 'Paradise' finds herself symbolically drowning in a
Mediterranean idyll. Floating free in life is unnatural to her – her
companions, her much-loved and wealthy lover included, come to
seem meaningless because they travel light, while she's ballasted
with memories. At any moment, thoughts of 'home . . . . where
the cattle grazed . . . . The earth around the water tank always
churned up' can sink her into nausea and panic.[7] Her inner life is
landlocked, she knows that one's dreams can't be acted.

Except, momentarily, possibly, as sex. For O'Brien, the advent of
sexual freedom – the freedom to recognise and pursue one's lusts –
is the only event that divides the present from the past of 'Mother
Ireland'. And even then, I've suggested, although her characters are
often acrobatically eloquent in praise of pleasure, a rueful humour
creeps in. 'Paradise' again:

> With her head upside down and close to the tiled floor she saw
> all the oils and ointments on his bathroom ledge and tried reading
> their labels backwards. Do I like all this love-making? she asked
> herself. (p. 154)

The self-mocking tone hints at affinities between 1960s freedoms and the repressions of the past. Sex is the glass coach that turns into a pumpkin, and so serves, as often as not, to deepen one's sense of unfulfilment. Thus, while she'll pay tribute to Joyce's portrayal of women's sexuality, she doesn't see it as a radical break with the past. Indeed her reading of her great modernist predecessor is determinedly traditional in several senses. She tends – rather as Murdoch does with Sartre or Beckett – to 'domesticate' his techniques, and return his characters to realist settings and circumstances. She sees him, in other words, as bound by his inheritance: less an experimenter and exile than a co-sufferer from the 'parish' mentality, a sharer in what's still un-freedom, one of Mother Ireland's children.

This kind of implicit assertion that 'life goes on' – that neither inside nor outside literature are there revolutions that really 'take' – is as near as O'Brien ever gets to theory. Like many women 'realists', and unlike Murdoch (who's in the paradoxical position of self-consciously conserving atavistic urges) she takes the line that the business of writing is largely instinctive, and that – like the exigencies of domestic life – the rules change, if at all, very slowly. Not that she's innocent of more anomalous possibilities. *Johnny I Hardly Knew You* (1977), for instance, deliberately does violence to the notion of a shareable world, with its heroine who takes a boy young enough to be her son as her lover, and murders him to strike a blow in the sex war:

> Have I not lived day and night wanting to kill the father who sired me, the father, scion of all fathers, who soiled my mother's bed, tore her apart, crushed her and made her vassal. Was I not sucked down into her darkest chambers, the witness and nursemaid of her mental and physical haemorrhaging.[8]

However, this bloodthirsty rhetoric, rather in the style of the prehistorical queens of Ireland, gives way in the course of the novel to her characteristic comic tone - 'I had the breeches now, the upper hand. Gangsters, all would get their goriest comeuppance' (p. 138). It's hard to believe in an O'Brien protagonist as an 'instant murderer' (p. 139), the text more or less admits: they are feckless rather than tragic, careless rather than vindictive.

More convincing is the wry conclusion of her short story 'Mrs Reinhardt', where a wronged wife's vengeful adventure with a gigolo ends in tears and marital reconciliation:

... what then does a Mrs Reinhardt do? One reaches out to the face that is opposite, that one loves, that one hates . . . at least for the duration of a windy night. And by morning who knows? Who knows anything anyhow.[9]

It's in the stories. perhaps, that O'Brien's strength as a writer (feck-lessness as a fine art) is most consistently displayed. Her domestic interiors and inventories, in particular, marvellously evoke the emotional squalor of settling for survival. The woman sorting her dead mother's things in 'A Rose in the Heart', for instance, releases the precise odour of stale dreams:

There were so many hats. Hats with flowers, hats with veiling, all of pastel colour, hats conceived for summer outings and meant for rainless climes. Ah the garden parties she must have conceived. Never having had the money for real style her mother had invested in imitation things – an imitation crocodile handbag and an imitation fur bolero. It felt light as if made of hair.[10]

Or again, in her 1982 collection *Returning*, harking back to a 1940s Irish girlhood, the story 'The Bachelor' dwells hypnotically on the imagery of neglect:

A few hens had come in from the yard and were picking at a colander in which there had been cold cabbage but was now almost picked clean. They were very intent on this. A spring of faded palm was stuck beside the globe of the Sacred Heart Lamp and I reckoned that it had been there since Easter.[11]

Two other pieces in the same volume tragi-comically celebrate the parish's changelessness. In 'Savages' the neighbourhood is roused to an orgy of conjecture by the return of Mabel after ten years in Australia; when she fails to demonstrate her worldliness, gossip assigns her a phantom pregnancy to prove she's 'fast', and poor Mabel believes and swells, thus revealing – beyond any conjecture – how very intact her Irishness has stayed. 'Ghosts', on the other hand, recalls the cramped, fantasy-swamped lives of three women, a crazy spinster, a sensual girl and a drudging, lonely wife ('her husband was moody and talked only to the sheep and never kept his money anywhere but under his mattress') (p. 133), as somehow more real and, even, more glamourous than anything the 'free' world offers. As in Murdoch's fictional territory – though O'Brien's parish is clearly much smaller, closer to the stuff of autobiography – the *representative* life is lived in a kind of ghetto, where people are hobbled by circumstance.

MARGARET DRABBLE

And let us leave her there, pondering the choice between various garments . . . . The long all-faults-concealing pink cheesecloth . . . . The too-revealing dress . . . . The old black one . . . . Let us leave her there, in an attitude of indecision, confronted by choice. Not, of course, a very serious choice, unless you wish to read it symbolically; but not, you will agree, an uncommon one.

(Margaret Drabble, *The Middle Ground*, 1980)

It's not by accident that Margaret Drabble supplies the title for this chapter. For she is self-consciously a 'representative' figure, quite explicitly the mediator of circumstantial and 'common' plots. Kate, the self-made journalist heroine of *The Middle Ground*, who 'can never decide whether she is a special case . . . or . . . an almost abnormally normal woman, a typical woman of our time'[1] is a fairly transparent disguise for her author. In fact, Kate is neither special nor typical (though she veers towards the latter). She is deliberately – untidily – stationed by Drabble betwixt and between, 'free' to articulate and generalise her condition, but not otherwise odd. Fifteen years earlier the narrator-heroine of *The Garrick Year*, Emma, makes much the same point – that her difference and her freedom consist mainly in articulacy:

And do not underestimate me; although I choose to lose, I also choose that same word loss to describe my choice.[2]

The Middle Ground indeed intentionally takes up Kate's story not with her struggles to educate herself and make a career, but *in medias res*, in middle life. She is 'caught between children and parents, free of neither: the past stretches back too densely . . . the future has not yet thinned out' (p. 165). Like earlier Drabble heroines, in short, Kate is surrounded by exemplary, traditional muddle. Nothing else, we're meant to conclude, would be 'real'.

Drabble's first novel, *A Summer Birdcage*, published in 1963 (when she was twenty-four) mapped out her course more or less precisely. Like Murdoch, she is in reaction against the notion of the abstract individual; however she's disposed – a literary generation on – to treat the matter lightly. Sarah Bennett has a friend and alter-ego who conveniently embodies all that's free-floating, separate, indeterminate – Simone:

> She was most purely personal in her life. In most people, and in myself, I am vaguely aware of a hinterland of non-personal action, where the pulls of sex and blood and society seem to drag me into unwilled motion, where the race takes over . . . . With her I sensed a wholly willed, a wholly undetermined life. And how could such a person live? The French believe they can, but one has only to read their books to mark some heroic dislocation from the pulse of continuous life. She lacked an instinct for kitchens and gas meters and draughts under the door . . . . [3]

Should one detect an allusion to Beauvoir's *L'Invitée*? Probably. At any rate, Simone is no sooner invented than she's consigned to the realm of unreality – at once undomesticated, un-English and unlikely. She may give the impression of existence (she's clearly an existentialist), but she's outside the gravitational field of the novel, sentenced to an alien, romantic doom ('Simone will run down, in a train or a gutter or a hotel bedroom, like those *fin de siècle* poets she so much admires', p. 71). Drabble is making very much the same point as Murdoch had in her dialogue with Sartre – that 'Liberty lies deeper than will', and that for 'the novelist proper' it is 'the *stuff* of human life' that counts. Their closeness would be clearer if it wasn't for Drabble's use of the word 'personal' here to mean individual and autonomous (she's thinking of the opposition between 'personal' and 'social'). In the event the material she's concerned with is thoroughly personal in other senses of the word – that is, defined by concrete conditions and possessions and limitations.

And she goes much further than Murdoch here, further back into Englishness and traditionalism. The text's reminiscences of Jane Austen (in Sarah's tone, and indeed the Bennett name) and of Wordsworth (in this quotation, 'the pulse of continuous life') lend it a provincial, even a parochial air. Her heroines too usually have their roots in the English provinces, like Drabble herself, who was born in Yorkshire, and questions of people's relations with places from the past are, surprisingly perhaps, quite as important to her as Irishness is to O'Brien. This too, though, is an aspect of Drabble's deliberate traditionalism, an echo of the anti-urbanism of her literary forebears: Austen and Wordsworth, obviously, but also Elizabeth Gaskell, George Eliot and E. M. Forster. Though her characters' present and future lives may be led perforce in the city, it's only their contriving to import habits, objects and values from a more country past that makes them at all at home. They furnish their imaginative lives with reminiscent bric-a-brac, rather as their author collects verbal snippets from literary tradition. And all this 'stuff' symbolises continuity and the limits of freedom – 'the pulls of sex and blood and society'.

The novels come to share a characteristic shape, a didactic sub-text most elegantly realised in *Jerusalem the Golden* (1967). Romantic intrigue into family plot is the formula. The main device is to entangle the protagonist (who is searching for an exclusive, individual destiny) in an extended, inclusive set of relationships. The underlying model is familial rather than sexual. Indeed *Jerusalem the Golden* probably strikes one as particularly effective because it makes this so clear. Clara falls in love with the whole Denham household, and her adulterous affair with Gabriel acts mostly as a way of highlighting the contrasts between her new chosen family and the old unchosen one in the background. The cosmopolitan Denhams – stylish, civilised, loving, discriminating – exactly answer to Clara's hungers. They seem utterly, marvellously foreign to the kind of provincial, lower-middle-class world she comes from, with its emotional penny-pinching, its inarticulacy, and its tasteless puritanism. She's uneasily aware, however, quite early on – though the thought is only admitted in parenthesis '(. . . that there is no such thing as severance, that connexions endure until death, that blood is after all blood)'.[4] And when her mother's fatal illness calls her home, she discovers that the ambitions and appetites she thought of as dividing her from her past are, in fact, rooted there. Going through her mother's things, she finds evidence of 'her true descent' (p. 197):

> . . . she started . . . to open all the little pots and boxes, gazing earnestly at rings and hairpins, at bits of cotten wool and old bus tickets . . . looking anxiously for she knew not what, for some small white powdery bones, for some ghost of departed life. And in the bottom drawer, beneath a bundle of underwear, she found

> it . . . . some old exercise books, and some photographs done up
> with a rubber band. (p. 195)

The notebooks contain stilted, starveling poems and stories that
record her cold mother's warm, long-buried dreams. Reading them,
and gazing at the image that goes with them, of a yearning, hopeful
young woman, Clara is shocked into recognition. Her act of 'choice'
turns out to have been part of her inheritance. And so the novel's
balance of power shifts. Not that she rejects the Denhams, but they
recede into a middle-distance focus, and her affair with Gabriel is
transposed into a new key, becoming 'a nostalgic connection, more
precious, more close, more intimate than any simple love' (p. 206).
Life proceeds, we realise, not by violent dislocations but by gradual,
wasteful accretion. Clara is allowed, at the last, a tragi-comic vision
of multiple human lives scattered like 'constellations', engaged in
'an eternal vast incessant rearrangement' (p. 206).

The pull of such 'family' ties supplies a narrative force as inevitable as gravity in Drabble's fictional world, and is the occasion for
many didactic reveries. Emma in *The Garrick Year* for instance, 'who
had seemed cut out for some extremity or other' (p. 108) settles
for the prosaic business of maintaining life. When Julian, an actor
friend, romantically kills himself she reflects:

> I used to be like Julian myself, but now I have two children, and
> you will not find me at the bottom of any river. I have grown into
> the earth, I am terrestrial. (p. 170)

She has grown into the compost of literary tradition, too, as usual
– 'I read Wordsworth, and Hume, and Victorian novels . . . . the
phrase "of considerable duration" rolls round my mind' (p. 171).
It's a phrase from Hume's analysis of the need for stable marriage
to nurture children; Drabble is also echoing one of Wordsworth's
most famous 'Lucy' poems, where he imagines his dead love
'Rolled round in earth's diurnal course,/ With rocks and stones
and trees'. What this small cluster of allusions establishes is the
association of people with *things*. Those relations (as of blood) that
have a thing-like, given quality are most real, most compelling.

Inventories and lists thus play a paradoxically active part in
the plot. *The Needle's Eye* simultaneously questions the value of
(mobile, impersonal) money, and insists on the sanctity of (stable, personal) possessions. Simon, meeting Rose for the first time,

is not truly entangled until he steps into her scruffy Victorian parlour:

> . . . it reminded him, this room, of his grandmother's house. The tea-cosy, the bundle of knitting, the ticking clock, the armchairs, the round tin tray, they were all objects that he had not seen for years, and here they all were, well worn, well used, lived with.[5]

Simon, who is, in sociologists' jargon, upwardly socially mobile, here begins to feel how much the roots he has severed continue to ache. Just as Rose – who has tried quixotically to come down in the world, by giving away her inherited wealth – comes to acknowledge that she cannot free herself of compromising connections, like those with her divorced husband Christopher: 'she would never cast him off, she would never be single, and simple, and separate, by any processes known to courts and lawyers . . . . ' (p. 199). The novel's emotional economy works on the model of the messily extended family and its 'moth-eaten modest satisfactions' (p. 239), Rose and Simon each with marital ties elsewhere sharing an ambience of connectedness. The residual Bohemianism implied in all this is held at bay by stressing the more or less asexual nature of their relationship. They become part of a chaste 'constellation', as Gabriel and Clara were about to do at the end of *Jerusalem the Golden*.

In fact, of 'the pulls of sex and blood and society' Drabble had early invoked, it's the two last that seem to exert the force in the novels so far mentioned. *The Waterfall* (1969) goes some way to explain why. Here Jane (her name of course suggesting wildly contradictory kinds of forebear) allows the pull of sex to take her out of the orbit of class and kin:

> Reader, I loved him: as Charlotte Brontë said . . . . I had James, oh God, I had him, but I can't describe the conditions of that possession; the world that I lived in with him – the dusty Victorian house, the fast car, the race tracks, the garages, the wide bed – it was some foreign country to me, some Brussels of the mind . . . . [6]

The world of adulterous passion has a neurotic alien flavour ('some Brussels of the mind'); indeed Drabble describes sexual obsession as a special, perverse variation on mother-love. Jane's lover James, in arousing her for the first time, is performing a Frankensteinish operation:

And he had done it: he had made her, in his own image. The
throes, the cries, the pains were his . . . . but by having her he had
made himself hers . . . . A woman delivered. She was his offspring, as he, lying there between her legs, had been hers. (p. 151)

The self-conscious violence of this idiom anticipates the destructive
course of the plot – the car-crash, the break-up. However, Drabble
finds Brontë-land increasingly implausible and uninhabitable: 'I
could have maimed James so badly, in this narrative, that I would
have been allowed to have him, as Jane had her blinded Rochester.
But I hadn't the heart to do it . . . . ' (p. 231) *The Waterfall* is rather
like O'Brien's *Johnny I Hardly Knew You* – an excursion into foreign
territory which serves in the end to mark out the boundaries of
the middle ground more firmly. It's not coincidental, either, that
both novels should – in different ways – present sexual desire
as a deformation of maternal yearnings. For the pull of sex is
real enough, it's simply that it takes on a particular form in the
context of the 'feminisation' of the whole scene. Not the dangerous
exclusivity of passion, but the more diffuse, cumulative language of
ties, involvements, responsibilities.

There is, though, a cosiness about Drabble's world that
distinguishes it from Murdoch's, and indeed from O'Brien's Ireland.
The scruffy, cluttered, comfortable households her heroines create
around themselves are very different from the alien settings that
symbolise people's 'otherness' for Murdoch (see Hartley's home,
above). Drabble's house of fiction is motherly – grandmotherly,
even – like Rose's living-room in *The Needle's Eye*, a version of
nostalgic pastoral. A more worldly heroine, Frances Wingate, the
much-travelled archaeologist in *The Realms of Gold* (1975) still calls
on her memories of her grandparents' house as a touchstone:

. . . the potted plants, the old books, the plates with faded
pansies, the ditch, the yellow dog. Yes, it had been a
gloomy dump . . . . both cramped and draughty, cluttered
yet bare . . . full of cheap memories and meaningless sou-
venirs . . . . But it had been the real thing . . . . there was no
escape.[7]

The insistence on discomfort ('gloomy', 'cramped' and so on) is
on another level comforting, a kind of guarantee of authenticity.
What's distinctively Drabble is the consciousness of virtue, and the

pressure of persuasion. And as with setting, so with character: the range of difference that operates in characterisation is narrower than at first appears. Even more obviously than in Murdoch, inhabitants of the Drabble world are required to pursue personal and domestic life as a vocation. They are students of family mores, eager amateurs of social anthropology.

It is a mannerism most conspicuous with the men. Lawyer Simon in *The Needle's Eye* is caught at exactly the point in his career when he's starting to run out of steam and look for roots: 'he was no historian, but it did seem to him that he . . . had travelled rather too far too quickly . . . . Where would he have been if his mother had not fed him pelican-like with her own blood?' (p. 31). Similarly Anthony Keating, the property-speculator hero of *The Ice Age* (1977) has, at the book's beginning, suffered near-bankruptcy and a heart attack, which have put him as it were under house arrest for the duration. When at the end he's dismissed to a different future, it's implied that *that* would require a novel of a quite different genre – a spy-thriller, perhaps, or a story of metaphysical quest. This narrative cannot follow him:

. . . one cannot enter the camp, with Anthony Keating. It is not for us; it is not, anyway, now, yet, for us . . . . [8]

The end of *The Ice Age*, in fact, is staged on the very edges of the middle ground. Anthony levitates beyond our conventions – 'There, we leave Anthony' – while his lover Alison, trapped with Molly her brain-damaged daughter, sinks into terminal domesticity: 'Alison, there is no leaving. Alison can neither live nor die. Alison has Molly. Her life is beyond imagining . . . . ' (p. 287). *The Realms of Gold* had made a similar, though more light-hearted move, half way through, placing the heroine's cousin David (her alter-ego, a geologist inhabiting an inorganic, impersonal world) at the outer limits of the real – 'The truth is that David was intended to play a much larger role in this narrative, but the more I looked at him, the more incomprehensible he became' (p. 163). David is thus edged out of the picture:

Imagine him, David Ollerenshaw, standing there . . . indefinably English, indefinably odd, with the oddness of one who spends much time alone, thinking about inhuman things . . . . Tomorrow he sets sail for Africa. And we can leave him there . . . and return home to Frances Wingate;she is a more familiar figure, a more manageable figure, in every way. (p. 167)

Such ritual desertions, mock-rueful, actually celebratory – 'we can leave him there' – have become a hallmark of Drabble's narrative strategy.

'So there you are. Invent a more suitable ending if you can.'[9] The verbal shrugs, slapdash authorial confidences, gossipy asides and impulsive disclaimers are signs that she is at home with her conventions – that they fit a bit loosely even, like a down-at-heel pair of shoes. She's much given to mocking her own writerly vices, the tripartite constructions she favours, for instance:

A pretentious sentence, a sentence without verbs, a sprightly precis.[10]

Self-mockery in its turn becomes an enjoyable indulgence. This doesn't however disguise the fact that – for all the talk of 'constellations' – her kind of novel is in love with limitation. There is, as she's well aware, a flavour of cosy masochism in her self-limiting choices. The ending of *The Middle Ground* spells it out: Kate the weary feminist, running out of conviction, finds herself reassimilated to a much more time-honoured role. She is 'really' a go-between, a mediator, a hostess even (shades of Woolf's Mrs Dalloway), the individual whose life is the meeting-place of other lives:

. . . feeling as she sat there a sense of immense calm, strength, centrality, as though she were indeed the centre of a circle, in the most old-fashioned of ways, a moving circle – oh, there is no language left to describe such things, we have called it all so much in question. (pp. 246–7)

Hence the closing joke about 'choice' – a matter of choosing what to wear, no more. The larger questions are cheerfully transposed into entirely local speculations:

. . . will Stuart be civil to Ted, will Ted make a pass at Rosamund Stacey, will Evelyn find the whole thing too exhausting, will Hugo's mother find it too much of a squash, will the neighbours object to the noise? (p. 248)

So concrete circumstance closes in, claustrophobic and reassuring.

The 1980s, however, proved a testing time for Drabble. *The Radiant Way* (1987) and even more its sequels *A Natural Curiosity* (1989) and *The Gates of Ivory* (1991) are narratives that reflect on a world of loose ends. There's a larger cast, the plotting is fragmentary, episodic, almost picaresque. Mobility and *anomie* are no longer confined to the margins, but have moved into closer focus.[11] In *A Natural Curiosity* , for example, some of the strongest writing concerns Shirley Harper, whose husband Cliff commits suicide under the combined pressures of business failure and the fear that he may have contracted AIDS. Cliff is placed outside the novel's territory, in familiar fashion – 'This could have been the story of Cliff Harper, but it is not.'[12] But then Shirley herself, who goes on the run instead of reporting his death, is tracked through a wilderness of outsiders. She stops at a motorway restaurant:

> The room is full of waifs, witches, grotesques. Shirley has never seen such a miserable collection of people, such a gallery of unfortunates. What has gone wrong? Is this some outing for the disadvantaged, the disabled? No, it is Britain, round about Budget Day, March 1987 . . . . Their faces are white, pink, grey, chapped, washed out, ill nourished, unhealthy, sickly, sickening. Shirley takes a bite out of one of her sandwiches. It is dry, grey, it tastes of nothing. Shirley does not know whether she feels sorry for these tramps, these refugees, these motorway wanderers, or whether she feels she has nothing to do with them at all. Is she still part of the human race? (pp. 128–9)

Her adventure has, if not a happy ending, at least a happy middle – a Parisian affair with a stranger met on the ferry (a less portentous version of Jane's excursion into 'some foreign country . . . some Brussels of the mind' in *The Waterfall*). Nonetheless her time on the road is what counts, since it epitomises the book's fascinated, vertiginous sense of finding oneself in an alien landscape. The people Shirley surveys are almost as strange as those glimpsed in the later scenes of Doris Lessing's *The Four-Gated City*. It's as though Drabble, having warded off the threats to the language of continuity represented by the 1960s, has finally encountered them twenty years on.[13]

Stunned Shirley is playing the eye-witness, the displaced observer, and so she illuminates by contrast the familiarising perspective of

Drabble's realism. 'The subplots fester, break out, infect strangers. Dark blotches spread' (p. 141). *A Natural Curiosity* comments even more collusively than usual on its own processes ('Shirley has stepped out of plausibility', p. 141), and a good deal of the cosiness has evaporated. Still, the continuities with the earlier fiction are striking. Alix, the book's maternal eye, thinks in threes – 'a bond, a connection, a continuation of that curious relation' (p. 67); and even when the contents of her musings change, the form remains stable: 'Ah, the poverty of moral language, the poverty of discourse, the thin vagueness of words' (p. 124). This is how Drabble's matriarchal realists sound, and interestingly enough the novel's climactic revelations are all to do with motherhood. Shirley discovers a long lost half-sister (her dead mother's secret legacy); and Alix confronts a sadistic madwoman, a bad, vicious mother who 'explains' why at least some of the horrors that litter the landscape have come about. As the threats to realism multiply like a virus, its underpinnings are laid bare. Home, the past, mother are the indwelling presences that hold the whole together.

MARY MCARTHY

> It has never been like that for me; events have never waited, like extras, while I toiled to make up my mind between good and evil . . . . The 'great' decisions – those I can look back on pensively and say, 'That was a turning-point' – have been made without my awareness. Too late to do anything about it, I discover that I have chosen.
>
>   (Mary McCarthy, 'My Confession', 1953)

No nineteenth century American woman novelist ever shared the middle ground as persuasively as Gaskell or Eliot did in Victorian England. Edith Wharton (1862–1937) comes closest but she is 'social' in a rather more camp sense, her style is neither earnest nor earthy enough to suggest the rootedness of a tradition. It is, perhaps, partly for this reason that Mary McCarthy's fiction strikes one as less securely *located* than the work of her British contemporaries. She is of course dedicated to the detail of personal relations, and of the world of things and possessions – witness, for example, this memorably 'ugly cartoon of middle-class life' from her first, episodic 'novel' *The Company She Keeps* (1942):

And the more stylish you tried to make it, smearing it over with culture and good taste, Swedish modern and Paul Klee, the more repellent it became: the cuspidors and the silk lampshades in the funny papers did not stab the heart half so cruelly as her own glass shelves with the pots of ivy, her venetian blinds, her open copy of a novel by Kafka, all the objects that were waiting for her at home, each in his own patina of social anxiety.[1]

It's clear even from this one quotation, however, that the realist in McCarthy has to co-exist with a savage and dead-pan satirist. The 'middle ground' in American culture is, in theory, (almost) everywhere; at the same time it is ominously and absurdly difficult to find.

McCarthy's fictional worlds are threatened by a creeping (and unwelcomed) sensation of what she calls in a 1960 essay ('The Fact in Fiction') irreality:

. . . the novel, with its common sense, is of all forms the least adapted to encompass the modern world, whose leading characteristic is irreality. And that, so far as I can see, is why the novel is dying . . . . [2]

The main sources of non-sense, at least initially, were the witch-hunting dramas of the Cold War – the Communist-chases whose real casualty was not, for McCarthy, so much the left, as the language of reason and mediation, drowned out by the clamour of accusations, betrayals, confessions, excommunications and conversions. It was in the midst of collective paranoia that she forged her style and became (almost perforce, though she relished and embellished the role) the 'woman of letters': 'our saint, our umpire, our Lit arbiter', to quote an ironic Norman Mailer.[3] That she was quite as much the literary journalist as the novelist was (again) a sign of the times. Her essays are a series of extraordinary and almost exotic balancing acts, in which she argues and cajoles, derides and persuades by turns, in an effort to insert a 'cool' tone into the Babel of Cold War rhetorics. The trick is to expose the inauthenticity and implausibility of – for example – the 'true life confessions' of repentent Communists:

When Whittaker Chambers is mounted on his tractor, or Elizabeth Bentley, alone, is meditating her decision in a white New England church, I have the sense that they are on location and that, at any moment, the Director will call 'Cut'. It has never been like that for me; events have never waited, like extras, while I toiled to make up my mind between good and evil. In fact, I have never known these mental convulsions, which appear quite strange to me when I read about them, even when I do not question the author's sincerity . . . . [4]

This kind of self-dramatisation is elicited, she suggests, in answer to the vivid hunger of the witch-hunter. The whole thing is like a bad movie, a vulgar and untruthful projection of private grey areas into public technicolour.

Perhaps the worst thing about this scenario, for her, is the way every aspect of living gets enlisted in the service of the political code:

In order to perform or work for the Columbia Broadcasting system you have to sign a loyalty oath which is presented with your contract . . . . In other circles, approval of progressive education or a belief in cultural anthropology . . . or in the abstract school of American painting is mandatory if you do not wish to admit that you are a reactionary.[5]

So you walk the tightrope. This is where her special satiric emphasis comes in – the tone of someone expert at the business of decoding, but nauseated by its necessity: 'the liberal's only problem', she remarks impatiently in another piece, 'The Contagion of Ideas' (1952) 'is to avoid succumbing to the illusion of "having to choose"'.[6] But the climate of universal suspicion nurtures illusions. One of her more daunting fictional monsters, Henry Mulcahy in *The Groves of Academe* (1953) is splendidly a creature of his moment in his exploitation of himself as a public cause. Authoritarian, egotistical, devious Henry is able to avoid losing his teaching post by confessing – falsely – to having been a Communist Party member (a move which shocks his liberal colleagues into seeing him as a victim of prejudice). In framing himself, Henry trades on the power of stock responses to trap people into taking sides and making stands and – incidentally – removing themselves from his path. '*Dramatise, Dramatise*' he tells himself; and reflects that, in any case, he runs small risk of being found out, since in these days 'it would be a work of supererogation to show that one had been a Communist; the rub was to show one had not been.'[7]

The Groves of Academe is a moral fable about the defeat of what Henry patronisingly calls 'the ordinary liberal imagination' (p. 77). McCarthy, in inventing him and getting inside his head, is practising what she elsewhere preaches: that the liberal imagination must entertain a whole range of extraordinary and duplicitous possibilities if it's to defend itself against illusion. Even though it may have to sacrifice something of its own sanity to do so. As she herself later wrote, *The Groves of Academe* is not in the full sense a novel, it's too tricksy and deliberate, too dominated by its 'element of the private game'.[8] The game's daring and satiric amusement is, obviously, deepened by the fact that she's a woman writer impersonating a particularly aggressive male. Henry, true to type and his times, is a convinced 'separate spheres' man, and the relations between himself and his wife ('Catherine Mulcahy . . . had a womanly, Irish way with her') (p. 24) exemplify cartoonishly the dignities of differentiation. At dismal college dances, the Mulcahys are popular chaperones:

> The division of labour between husband and wife provided reassurance both to the boys who danced badly and the girls whose feet they stepped on; it gave an authoritative precedent for the differences between the sexes. With Dr. Mulcahy as a model, appearances lost their terrors. A stammer, a cast in the eye invested a cheese-faced boy with clerkly functions – he squinted on his partner from a knot-hole of male assurance. (p. 24)

There's a good deal of 'private' fun for McCarthy and the reader in this. At the same time, however, it points to a further problem for the (female) liberal imagination: that along with the Cold War, the America of the 1940s and 1950s saw a new phase in the sex war.

It wasn't, of course, during these years, a matter of conscious feminism, rather of ritual in-fighting. The contradictions Simone de Beauvoir was exploring in *The Second Sex* – between the theoretical freedom of the individual and the actual impotence of women – were more savagely on display in America than elsewhere. One sympton of this was the internationally notorious caricature of the great American Bitch: the 'dominating' or 'castrating' woman (in the language of sub-Freudian orthodoxy). Norman Mailer, who was a kind of barometer of male reaction, bemoaned 'the womanisation of America'⁹. Beauvoir herself, on her first visit to the States, notes sourly that the American woman's sinister reputation actually reflected her lack of power:

> . . . . even if it is true that the spirit of revenge in her has been exasperated to the point of making her a 'praying mantis', she still remains a dependent and relative being; America is a masculine world.[10]

McCarthy's perception of the state of affairs was characteristically cool and tough-minded, a balancing act again. Her piece on the 'Vassar Girl' (1951) describes the delusions of freedom with which her college endowed its girl graduates:

> 'Lost now in the wide, wide world', we sang fervently, but actually almost all of us were joyous to be leaving college, precisely because we had loved it, for Vassar had inspired us with the notion that the wide, wide world was our oyster.
>
> A few years later, a census was taken, and it was discovered that the average Vassar graduate had two-plus children and was married to a Republican lawyer.[11]

The irony here is directed mostly against Vassar idealism. The 'world' that turns out to be such a narrow place after all is, by implication, something to be faced up to rather than complained about (Republican lawyers are also unfree). An early short story, 'The Friend of the Family', provides a yet clearer example of her strategy:

> Will the dubious reader acknowledge that his wife and her friends possess in common some quality that is absent from his own nature? It is this quality that attracted him to her in the first place, though by now he has probably succeeded in obliterating all traces of it from her character, just as the wife who marries a young poet . . . . will soon succeed in getting him to go into the advertising business . . . . What passes for love in our competitive society is frequently envy . . . . We cannot, in the end, possess anything that is not ourselves.[12]

The sex-switch (' . . . . just as the wife') is the signature of McCarthy the umpire. She takes (mutual) sexual violence rather shockingly for granted, and places herself at a common-sensical remove.

The explicit manoeuvering, however, serves to reveal just how hard it was to play the role of mediator in McCarthy's 'competitive society'. She makes the English tradition look very comfortable by comparison – especially in its capacity to, as it were, kidnap men onto the middle ground and domesticate them. A Margaret Drabble novel will blithely dismiss any uncooperative characters as alien to the book's 'family'. In McCarthy's *A Source of Embarrassment* (1950), about a Utopian experiment in community living, it's the *representative* man who slips out of the frame:

> Haines could not be held: equivocal, slippery, indeterminate, the citizen of open opinions evaded the theoretician's grasp and returned stealthily to his habits, as if to a gentleman's club. On the wide canvas of the meadow, crowded with bright, grotesque types, the apostles of a Breughelesque vision, eating. drinking, disputing, elongated or vastly swollen, she saw the average man stealing out of one corner of the picture, a guilty finger to his lips.[13]

The surface satire is against the idealistic communitarians; at the same time, though, 'the average' evades McCarthy the author.

In her essay 'Characters in Fiction' (1961) she sees contemporary writing, her own included, as mysteriously lacking in representative figures: the 'modern American woman', or man for that matter, doesn't live in the house of fiction: not that there aren't 'characters' aplenty, but, rather like those in *A Source of Embarrassment*, they're 'bright, grotesque types', even when (like Henry Mulcahy in the *Groves of Academe*) they're seen from the inside:

> What has been lost . . . . is the power of the author to speak in his own voice or through the undisguised voice of an alter ego, the hero, at once a known and an unknown, a bearer of human freedom.[14]

The hero/heroine provides the middle ground of identification author and reader may share – 'when we identify ourselves with the hero . . . we are following him with all our hopes, i.e., with our subjective conviction of human freedom'. Once upon a time, 'In the old novels, there was a continual fluctuating play between the hero and the "characters" . . . . ' (p. 291). McCarthy's nostalgia is patent, but so is her awareness that we can't tell ourselves stories the way we used to. The satirist is bound to win. Her most idiosyncratic and aggressive novel, *The Group*, is structured around *absences*; the absentee hero/heroine, the (unwritable) novel of the common ground.

The Group starts explosively, with a dazzle of colours and a babble of voices, like a complicated, illicit cocktail: this is the era of prohibition, the class of '33, we're at Kay's wedding, and the focus of the narrative shifts restlessly from one college friend to the next, as if trying to single out the girl who'll dispose of herself significantly, whose story is only *now* beginning. Romantic convention guarantees it can't be Kay. Or can it? McCarthy sets up a teasing moving picture. Her group won't stand still for the camera, they're not that kind ('They were a different breed . . . . from the languid buds of the last decade')[15], they regard themselves with all the ominous confidence she'd identified as the Vassar girl's hallmark ('the wide, wide world was our oyster') and more, since among the Vassar chosen they've chosen each other. And they watch each other with that exaggerated awareness of their personal roles that members of a peer-group (or sisters in a large family) develop, in order not to tread on each other's toes, in order to complement each other rather than compete. Priss is the do-gooder, Lakey the beautiful bluestocking, Pokey Protheroe the hearty rich girl, Dottie the sentimental one . . . . And yet, of course, as candidates for the part of heroine, they have the faintly meretricious air of a line-up. McCarthy's authorial guile puts her reader in the embarrassing position of simultaneously trying for identification with one of them and sizing them up as rivals.

Lakey is the one we want to chose, but curiously her very superiority seems to disqualify her – she is too much the looker-on, wincing with 'vicarious mortification' (p. 9); and anyway, she's off to Europe. The only available man at the wedding-party, dissipated Dick Brown, seems to realise as much, and after catching Lakey's eye and giving her a would-be collusive wink, he settles for Dottie ('Dottie gamely winked back', p. 23) and so sets the plot on course. Unlike Lakey, Dottie's in no danger of eluding Dick Brown's attentions, or ours: 'The girls found the fact funny, but D. H. Lawrence was one of her favourite authors: he had such a true feeling for animals and for the natural side of life' (p. 24). Chapter 2, with malicious briskness, conducts her 'to this attic room that smelled of cooking-fat, with a man she hardly knew'

(p. 30) – an alien, male environment where, instead of becoming promisingly enmeshed in the 'natural side of life', she finds herself expertly, unembarrassingly (and safely) deflowered, presented with not just one orgasm, but two, and succinctly lectured on Dick's world-picture. His ex-wife Betty sums up woman:

> ' . . . . I won't change my life for her, and so Betty lit out. I don't blame her; I'd have done the same if I were made like Betty. Betty is all woman. She likes money, change, excitement, things, clothes, possessions.' (p. 46)

And he himself is the eternally boyish Bohemian:

> 'I like a man's life, ' he said. 'A bar. The outdoors. Fishing and hunting. I like men's talk, that's never driving to get anywhere but just circles and circles. That's why I drink. Paris suited me . . . . ' (p. 47)

So much for the spiritual heirs of D. H. Lawrence. This first narrative 'climax' (McCarthy is punning cruelly on the rhythms of romantic fiction) is an object-lesson on the separation of the worlds: of sex from love, of 'I' from 'you', of men from women. The passage that most readers remember most vividly must be the one that encapsulates Dottie's discovery of the loneliness of modern love – when, two days later, having bravely equipped herself with a diaphram on Dick's orders, she calls him only to find he's not there, simply out, away, vanished. She's left clutching her compromising, contraceptive package in her lap, on a bench in Washington Square, as dusk falls – a horribly pathetic and comic figure, the woman who's discovered her sexuality and has no-one to bestow it on, nowhere to go.

Dottie's humiliating come-uppance – no heroine she – establishes some of the rules of the game. For instance, that this is a world in which the 'natural' is itself packaged and produced. Thus pathetic Priss, married to a pediatrician, will find motherhood (from birth to breast-feeding to potty-training) refined into torture by fashionable medical doctrine. And Kay, driven to distraction by husband Harald's egotism and infidelity, will be committed to a psychiatric hospital where her bruises will be diagnosed as self-inflicted, and her anger as incipient schizophrenia . . . . This, though, is to make the process of cutting the hopeful members of the group down to size sound too clinical. Their successive failures to hold the centre-stage are brought about, like Dottie's, very largely through rhetoric and myth-making. Any act or choice is convertible into the currency of 'positions', stamped out into 'type' by pervasive habits of either/or thimking which affect people and possessions alike. Whether you choose a Georgian silver creamer or a Russell Wright cocktail shaker, the role of earth-mother or career-woman, you're caught up in the packaging-and-marketing process. The group itself, in its anxious collective desire to be distinctive, is passing on the same pressure in a slightly more subtle form. As we move from Dottie to Helena to Norine to Pokey to Libby and so on, we approach their choices of life with a kind of comic dread. They are, collectively, 'representative'. And what they represent is the impossibility of any way of life that seems convincingly unselfconscious, central, obvious, 'real'.

This is especially striking when – as in the case of Helena – one of them has a style that in some other contexts might make her the author's mouth-piece. Helena is ironic, observant, sensible and funny. Norine and Putnam Blake's apartment, seen through Helena's eyes (in Chapter 6) is indeed classic McCarthy:

> The kitchen was part of the living room, and the sink was full of unwashed dishes. Above it was a long shelf with cottage cheese glasses, jelly glasses, plates, and cans of food, chiefly soups and evaporated milk . . . . Along one wall . . . . were bookcases made of orange crates lined with folded black oilcloth and containing pamphlets, small magazines, and thin volumes of poetry. There were few full-size books, except for Marx's *Capital*, Paretto, Spengler, *Ten Days That Shook the World*, *Axel's Castle*, and Lincoln Steffens . . . . (p. 115)

And Helena's alternative list of recommended reading for Norine ('"real books"') is solidly in the great tradition, though it does begin to sound rather satirically desperate towards the end: 'Jane Austen. George Eliot. Flaubert. Lady Muraski. Dickens. Shakespeare. Sophocles. Aristophanes. Swift' (p. 131). However (compare Lakey's disappearance at the beginning) Helena's very qualities of irony and observation put her *hors de combat*. She is insufficiently involved in living on her own account (she's neuter, and described as a 'mule') to test her powers; and her fastidious good sense is made to seem already a dry, eccentric mannerism. The same authorial scepticism, much more obviously, 'places' Norine, whose 'earthiness' is cynically attributed to too many courses in folk lore and anthropology. And Polly Andrews (Chapters 11 and 12), who might have been a convincingly 'rooted' Margaret Drabble heroine, given her concern for others and her determined loyalty to family ties, is likewise cocooned in her own worthiness, as if caring itself had become a profession (which it has). McCarthy refuses, as author, to collude with any of her characters for long. There's a sense of arbitrariness about even the most practical and right-minded lives. Polly's closeness to her father, for instance, is turned into a period 'issue' by the question of his craziness (is it hereditary? should she marry?) and her no-nonsense marriage to Doctor Jim, who's given up psychiatry to specialise in drug therapy, can hardly be thought of as hopeful.

Nothing is merely a 'condition' in (say) Iris Murdoch's sense: "' . . . don't talk about marriage as if it were a condition." "It is a condition. All sorts of things are conditions and it's one. It relates the past to the present"'.[14] Indeed Polly is made ruefully to meditate on how marriage, to her contemporaries, has become a lonely, speculative enterprise: 'You did not have your relations to live with you if you wanted your marriage to succeed . . . . Hearing her friends hammer at her about making a success of marriage summoned up a picture of failure . . . . the class of '33 seemed to feel that you could not relax for a minute in your drive to make your marriage "go"' (p. 28). 'Success', 'drive', and '"go"' are the key words – the present is detached from the past, and *in* the present all conditions are manipulable, open to speculation, specialisation and will. The members of the group are, of course, entering the 'competitive society', though they are mostly well-heeled enough to conceal the fact from themselves, initially, by doing 'voluntary' work of various kinds. When they try for more, they find themselves abruptly confronted by the business ethic, and the separation of roles – as does Libby (Chapter 8) when she aspires to a job in publishing:

He sighed. 'Miss MacAusland . . . . Have you ever thought of trying for a job with a literary agent? Or on one of the women's magazines? . . . You're not cut out for straight publishing. You're not hard-boiled enough. You're essentially a sympathiser . . . . Publishing's a man's business. Book publishing, that is. Name me a woman, outside of Blanche Knopf, who married

Alfred, who's come to the top in book publishing. Or you find them copy editing or reading proof . . . . We've got a cracker-jack here, Miss Chambers, who's been with us twenty years. I think she was Vassar too . . . a very smart, decent, underpaid, fine woman. Our galley slave; pardon the pun.' (pp. 184–5)

Libby, it turns out, will get on as a literary agent: she has 'drive', and one of the signs of that is her ready surrender to her own fantasising ego - 'One of the big features of living alone was that you could talk to yourself all you wanted and address imaginary audiences, running the gamut of emotion' (p. 181). This trashy 'histrionic' style marks Libby out as a competitor; that is – in McCarthy's satiric version of how the world works – as an echo or distorted mirror-image of the men.

The men are notable – like Dick Brown – for their elusiveness, (or, indeed, absence). However, it's they who make the rules and set the tone. McCarthy's is a 'masculinised' world: the stage, we gradually realise, is theirs; we are in the wings with the understudies, the chorus, the bit-part players. It's no accident that Kay's husband Harald '(that was the way he spelled it – the old Scandinavian way)' is a would-be playwright and director. Like monstrous Henry Mulcahy in *The Groves of Academe*, Harald is a dramatiser who is playing, this time, the role of the unrecognised genius (held back by hacks and 'nances'); and who has turned stage-struck Kay into his toady and mouthpiece. Their marriage is, in one of his favourite (borrowed) phrases, 'a machine for living':

When Kay started at Macy's in September, Harald would get their breakfast every morning and then sweep and clean and do the marketing, so that everything would be ready for Kay to get the dinner when she came home from work . . . . (p. 60)

He contrives, simultaneously, to oust Kay from any domestic role, to live on her (boring) labour, and to blame his continued unsuccesses (and convert infidelity) on her 'castrating' tendencies. As Norine, one of his lovers, and another mouthpiece, earnestly explains to Helena:

'It undercuts Harald that she works to support him. He has to assert his masculinity. You saw what happened last night – when he burned his play. That was a sort of immolation rite, to propitiate her; he was making a burnt offering of his seed, the offspring of his mind and balls . . . . ' (p. 124)

Harald's sacrifice of his manuscript is all theatre – there are several copies, as Kay knows. However, even when her increasing resistance to his myth-making goads him into beating and hospitalising her, she clings to the habits of hero-worship:

> 'He said that as usual I'd got everything twisted . . . . "You should have seen your face, my dear . . . . I met murder on the way. It had a face like my wife Kay."' 'Did he really quote Shelley?' Polly marvelled. 'Was that what it was? Yes, he did,' Kay replied, rather proudly. 'Harald is awfully well read. Anyway, he said that if I didn't remember lunging at him with the knife, I was suffering from amnesia and ought to have psychiatric treatment.' (pp. 289–90)

Kay is the book's most cartoonish figure, but she is also, for the same reasons, its centre – or rather, its non-centre. Her maiden name was 'Strong', and she's all energy and eager conformity; when she is given a metabolic test in hospital she's almost abnormally normal ('Her organism was in absolute balance') (p. 294); and her demoralisation by Harald is a violent demonstration of the absence of common ground. Kay, in her own estimation, *is* Harald – 'She had despised failures, but if Harald had left her she was one' (p. 298) – and their separation destroys her: 'having to be "nobody" instead of the wife of a genius' (p. 338). Her death, whether by accident or suicide, is almost an afterthought, the blackly comic logical conclusion to her absorption in 'the Harald-That Never-Was' (p. 298).

That Kay's funeral should ceremonially end the book, as her wedding began it, produces an impression of unnatural neatness which exactly suits McCarthy's purposes. Her heroine is truly 'nobody' now, and irreality triumphs in the book's last act, when long-absent Lakey, returned from Europe serious, sophisticated – and lesbian – beats histrionic Harald at his own game. He is all set to steal Kay's last scene – '"She killed herself of course . . . . Sheer competitiveness . . . . For years I've been trying to kill myself . . . ."' (p. 345). And he chooses for the purpose the role he has, we realise, always coveted: Harald is (who else?) Hamlet, and poor Kay ('"living with a woman is like living with an echo"') was the virginal neglected Ophelia who '"never wanted

anyone else. Or anybody else's ideas"' (p. 347). By the simple
expedient of allowing Harald/Hamlet to follow through his fantasy
of competition – "'Let's duel on her grave, shall we?'" he suggests
coyly – Lakey contrives to insinuate that she herself was his 'real'
rival, Kay's first seducer: "'What a filthy Lesbian trick," he said.
"Not to fight openly but to poison the rapiers." Lakey did not
point out to him that he had poisoned them himself . . . . ' (p. 349).
So Harald/Hamlet is finally cheated of the godlike glamour of
having been Kay's creator-and-destroyer. And yet, of course, it's a
bitter-sweet revenge, for Lakey (alas) didn't love 'poor normal Kay',
nor for that matter did the author (nor did the reader). At the end
there are only loose ends, disconnected destinies. The war in Europe,
in the background, adds a rumble of stage thunder, reminding us
that mediation and diplomacy have failed us on other fronts too.

The Group demands space because it is not one novel, but many: a
kind of satiric compendium of the 'bright, grotesque types' thrown
up by competition and social anxiety. Any one of the characters
(with the possible exception of Pokey who's so mindlessly grand
that the telling of her story is delegated to the family butler) could
have had a novel to herself. And, indeed, in a sense *has*, since each
is isolated in her own 'life-style' and her own sexual tangle. This
is a culture dedicated to the manipulative 'I', McCarthy is saying,
and that means that the traditional arts and crafts of living are
professionalised, abstracted, denatured. Or to put it another way, all
tasks are becoming 'masculinised', so that to focus on women's lives
is to focus on an absence, an echo, a lost vocation (Dottie waiting in
Washington Square, Helena the observant 'mule'). From this angle,
The Group is a special kind of anti-novel, a sardonic salute to all
that's most wilfully unreal in America's cultural mythology. It's
instructive to compare McCarthy's ending with Iris Murdoch's in
The Sea, The Sea, where theatre-director Charles suffers an almost
mystical illumination concerning the continuity, outside himself
and his projects, of ordinary, undramatic, living muddle. In *The
Group* Harald/Hamlet is foiled by a trick, and by his own jealous
imagination, and exits monstrously deluded. Like Lakey, McCarthy
the author stands ironically aside, and invites the reader to follow
suit. The common sense they're assumed to share is a quality of dis-
embodied awareness – sceptical, vagrant, unrooted. (Un-American,
Harald hints darkly.)

McCarthy's fiction after *The Group* was – as she foresaw in
those 1950s essays – itself essayistic and self-conscious. *The Birds*

of America and *Cannibals and Missionaries* are a kind of reluctant
metafiction. The novel of the middle ground lived on (for her) in
memory and hypothesis. It would connect past with present, Europe
with America, one generation with another, women with men . . . if
it was writable.[16] She was characteristically cool and fastidious in
her refusal to settle for nostalgia. She would not be taken in by
a sweet old-fashioned girl like Polly, for example, but jumped
in with a memorably malicious aside: 'She was partial to extinct
and extirpated species, like the passenger pigeon, on which she
had done a paper for Zoology' (p. 234). McCarthy patently rather
dreaded being caught out in the matriarchal attitudes the novelists
of the old world allow themselves. There is no match-making, no
collusive warmth, only a kind of bleak community of spirit. As a
measure of the fiction's bleakness, one can turn to her description
of her grandmother in *Memoirs of a Catholic Girlhood*, where looking
back is allowed. Grandmother belongs to a lost world of closeness:

> No other woman has ever been known to me in such a wealth of
> fleshy, material detail; everything she touched became imbued
> for me with her presence, as though it were a relic. I still see her
> clothes, plumped to her shape, hanging on their velvet-covered
> hangers in her closet, which was permeated with the faint scents
> of powder and perfume, and the salty smell of her perspiration;
> she comes back to me in dress shields, in darned service-sheer
> stockings (for mornings), in fagoting and hem-stitching, in voile
> and batiste, in bouclé and monkey fur, in lace dyed ecru with
> tea.[17]

Grandmother's textures, colours and smells are a rich, surrounding,
element. In the 'irreal' consumer world no-one (and *nothing*) has
such solidity, such claustrophobic presence. She has style to excess,
but it's not 'life-style'. The difference is easy to intuit, though hard
to pin down: a matter of accumulation, of taking full possession of
one's possession's (the sweat and darns, but also the lace dyed ecru).
By contrast the well-heeled members of *The Group* are impoverished,
unable to feel natural in their lives.

*   *   *   *

In the end, perhaps, it's the relation between generations that
counts most for the novelists of the middle ground – the past as
construction, as context. In refusing nostalgia, McCarthy refused

herself (almost) anywhere to stand. She was always on the move, and made her contemporaries on this side of the Atlantic look sluggish by comparison – or at least (in Murdoch's case, say) indulgent. Nonetheless, the *notion* of continuity survives. Lakey may be mostly absent, but she's absent visiting Europe, hence by implication the old world, the past, though it's not clear whether her lesbianism means she's learned ambiguity, or is merely upping the stakes in the 'life-style' game. 'Common sense', in McCarthy's sense, does seem to mean acknowledging a common heritage of unfreedom – much as it does for Murdoch. The human condition. Except that her people are much more expert at denying it, thanks to collective paranoia and collective amnesia. And they in turn are denied the dignity of ordinariness.

Perhaps, like Lakey, one needs to take a kind of sabbatical from contemporary American reality to connect with this chapter's traditions.[18] The middle ground for American writers often seems to be somewhere mid-Atlantic: witness Alison Lurie's knowing novel *Foreign Affairs* (1984), about Ivy League academics on leave in London. The narrative plays on the possibility that English Literature will let them down. Vinnie Miner in particular (middle-aged, long-divorced, lots of life before her) reflects that 'In the world of classic British fiction . . . . People over fifty who aren't relatives are pushed into minor parts, character parts . . . . The literary convention is that nothing major can happen to them . . . . '[19] However it's precisely in the language of 'classic British fiction' that she meets and loves Chuck Mumpson, who's the kind of American ('semi-literate', a lugubrious, redundant sanitary engineer from Tulsa) she would never have 'seen', in the moral or the social sense, back home. Chuck, who has been looking for Wessex ancestors, is made to talk in Thomas Hardy tones about the reality of unhistoric lives:

> 'all those names, and every goddam one of them was a person . . . . they grew up and plowed and milked and cut the hay and ate dinner and drank the local beer at the Cock and Hen; and they fell in love and got married and had children and were sick and well and lived and died.' (pp. 173–4)

And Vinnie herself starts thinking in George Eliot's metaphors – 'each of us is always a central point round which the entire world whirls in radiating perspective'. The plot takes her back to America and Americanness, laden with imaginative baggage: 'Why shouldn't she imagine herself as an explorer standing on the edge of some landscape as yet unmapped by literature . . . ?' (p. 207).

The intimate, conspiratorial tone is much more flattering to the reader than McCarthy's – eerily close to Drabble, in fact. *The Group*'s particular power lay in its coolness towards its characters and its reader. It was the novel that set the scene – the theatrical metaphor is appropriate – for the novels of protest and Liberation in the next decade, when it was as if poor Kay, back from the grave, rose up to yell 'I' on her own account, and 'The Group' was resurrected in a whole set of women writers (Jong, Millett, Rossner, Alther, French, Johnson) bent on revenge. This meant abandoning the mediating role – the 'motherly' role – of umpire, overseer, context-maker, continuity-provider . . . . Or in some cases re-writing it solely in self-referring terms. '*Homesick for myself*' writes Adrienne Rich in a 1977 poem called, with irony, *Transcendental Étude*; and though her 'position' is deliberately disinherited ('the whole chorus . . . told us nothing, nothing of origins') her language lays claim in familiar fashion to the patchwork art of the real:

> . . . as if a woman quietly walked away
> from the argument and jargon in a room
> and sitting down in the kitchen, began turning in her lap
> bits of yarn, calico and velvet scraps
> laying them out absently . . . .
> Such a composition has nothing to do with eternity
> the striving for greatness, brilliance –
> only with the musing of a mind . . .
> pulling the tenets of a life together
> with no mere will to mastery,
> only care for the many-lived, unending
> forms in which she finds herself . . . .

This frankly woman-to-woman writing uncovers one of the any-way open secrets of the tradition, that men were always *childish* somehow, a comforting implication that survives, incongruously, alongside the literature of protest against Patriarchy.

4
The Movement

Fly, stay high, living it . . . . But is it a private thing finally?
And you lose it by writing even if writing helps you find it.

(Kate Millett, *Flying*, 1975)

The women's movement in the United States produced a best-selling genre of its own – a new novel of the first person (Erica Jong's *Fear of Flying*, 1973, Lisa Alther's *Kinflicks*, 1976) which tried for a special kind of transgression, and became instead (or as well) a voyeuristic spectacle, a Liberation striptease. In a way these books exemplify very exactly the workings of the packaging-and-marketing process satirised in Mary McCarthy's *The Group* – a commodification of 'difference' that undermines the authors' claims to be speaking something new. Indeed the very confusion the confessional 'I' invites between author and character, the suggestion of nakedness, added to their commodity-value. On the one hand these were novels all about rejecting the available roles, the 'self' in the script, in the name of real and repressed desires; on the other, they exhibited the authors themselves as objects, comforting and titillating 'representative types' to add to the gallery of unrealities. This announces itself as a writing of the body – 'Until women started writing books,' writes Jong's heroine, 'there was only one side of the story. Throughout all of history, books were written with sperm, not menstrual blood'[1] – but it's as though the female body has been written about so thoroughly and repetitiously that it can't be reclaimed. To put it more crudely: instead of the classic (male) pornographer's trick of impersonating women wanting (Cleland's *Fanny Hill*), we now have women doing it (Erica Jong's *Fanny*). Think further along these lines, and you begin to suspect that what the Liberation novel spawned was Shirley Conran's *Lace*, the apotheosis of designer sex (women turn out to want exactly what is on offer, and always better and more).

This is the way Stephen Heath, for example, charts the absorption

114

of 'difference' by the discourse of sexuality in *The Sexual Fix* (1982). He acknowledges that 'in a given situation the appeal to difference can be a powerful and necessary mode of struggle and action, can take the force of an alternative representation . . . . ';[2] but remains unconvinced, because (I think) he sees representation itself as on the side of 'the dominant order'. However, you can turn this argument on its head and arrive at a rather different conclusion – that it is only when 'minorities', the spoken-for (the represented) get in on the act that *we see what the act is*. In particular, that we glimpse the fact that representation is the battleground of 'I' and 'we'. Partisan writing involves the necessary naivety of saying 'Me too . . . ', disputing over again the category of the human. Andrea Dworkin, for example, is as conscious as Heath of the 'fix' of sexuality –

> In Amerika there is the nearly universal conviction – or so it appears – that sex (fucking) is good and that liking it is right . . . . we like it, we enjoy it, we want it, we are cheerful about it . . . .[3]

But her use of 'we' is inflected in a way that acknowledges writing as a real battleground: 'Women, deprived of words, are deprived of life'.[4] Dworkin utterly rejects the version of 'women' Jong invoked; nonetheless, she is arguing from the position of the woman writer ('Had I been the user not the used, my sensitivity probably would have approximated Henry Miller's', p. 63). Her savage, sermonising ironies – 'Trivial and decadent; proud; foolish; liars; we are free'[5] – depend on that. It is not a question of 'an alternative representation', rather a continuous process of expropriation (and being expropriated). The definiteness and fixity of the images, of the new woman, the new new woman, hide something else. Their claim to represent 'us' generates divisions that, without them, would stay invisible ('I, the author, insist that I stand in for us, women').[6] These divisions are not , as Heath assumes, built on 'the old identities, "male" and "female"' (p. 135), but on differences among women.

The nightmares of exposure are real, the euphoria was very brief. This is Kate Millett, in *Flying*, on her representative status:

> I can't be Kate Millett any more. It's an object, a thing. A joke at cocktail parties . . . . Just let me watch it from the sidelines. Like other women can. Enjoy the luxury of looking on while someone else does it for us.[7]

The move from 'I' to 'us' here is instructive, on the topic of alienation. What she calls 'the brave new chatter' – 'liberation music laughter meetings marches shouts changes' – starts to look like 'a thin veneer to hide our essential despair' (p. 317). To say this, to write it, becomes the next project of difference. With the movement women join themselves to the world in a new way, a way that brings the representativeness of the woman *writer* into question. Or better, the persona of the writer. The part the author plays in the I/we game changes – sometimes there's a naive appeal to gender solidarity, sometimes a more complex exploration of the writer's possible roles. Either way, women as writers and readers develop a new self-consciousness. The arguments from modernism which assume that 'an important tradition of modern writing that includes work by both women and men authors, Virginia Woolf and James Joyce'[8] has already dealt with the fixity of sexual identity, don't really work. One aspect of the sexual fix is that anonymity, nakedness, androgyne (the trans-sexual signs of the modern) turn out to be less universal than they claim.[9] It's helpful here to take a step back, and look at a couple of 'period' memoirs that dwell on the boundaries of fiction. The first, by Joyce Johnson, demonstrates amongst other things how very gendered 'art' can seem – and therefore, since seeming is its business, how gendered it can be.

JOYCE JOHNSON

> There are books that serve as mirrors in which one catches reflections of oneself.
>
> (Joyce Johnson, *Minor Characters*)

Joyce Johnson's *Minor Characters* (1983) is about a media 'fix' in the 1950s. This one applied to male writers, and to women only by default. Johnson looks back at her 1950s self, a footnote nowadays in the story of 'the Beat Generation', Jack Kerouac's girlfriend. She sees that self twice over, in a kind of double vision: there's the conviction and camaraderie of then, and the lonely ironic distance of now:

> I see the girl Joyce Glassman, twenty-two, with her hair hanging down below her shoulders, all in black like Masha in *The Seagull* – black stockings, black skirt, black sweater – but, unlike Masha, she's not in mourning for her life. How could she have been,

with her seat at the table in the exact center of the universe, that midnight place where so much is converging, the only place in America that's alive? As a female, she's not quite part of this convergence. A fact she ignores, sitting by in her excitement as the voices of the men, always the men, passionately rise and fall and their beer glasses collect and the smoke of their cigarettes rises towards the ceiling and the dead culture is surely being wakened.[1]

The moment is split in two ('If time were like a passage of music, you could keep going back to it till you got it right') between those whose property it became – that capitalised Generation – and those who were simply there: 'Merely being there, she tells herself, is enough' (p. 262).

Minor Characters is a reticent book, controlled and ambivalent. The experience Johnson's writing about is hers, yet not. She has been (was always?) dispossessed. In the books about the Beats, in the pictures, the histories, she and the other women become generic and interchangeable. John Clellon Holmes, for example, 'in 1977, after years of a stable and sustaining second marriage, after all the messages of Women's Liberation', writing a preface to his 1950s *roman à clef*, *Go* asks '"Did we really resemble these feverish young men, these centerless young women . . . ?"' Male characters are matched to their originals. But

. . . the 'girls' are variously 'amalgams of several people'; 'accurate to the young women of the time'; 'a type rather than an individual.' He can't quite remember them – they were mere anonymous passengers on the big Greyhound bus of experience. Lacking centers, how could they burn with the fever that infected his young men? What they did, I guess, was fill up the seats. (p. 79)

Did we really resemble . . . ? The ironies have several layers, at odds with each other; what comes out is the realisation that you cannot separate the representation from the reality. By getting it wrong Holmes gets it right: the women's selves, identities, characters, had been differently constructed.

For example: 'I'd learned myself by the age of sixteen that just as girls guarded their virginity, boys guarded something less tangible which they called Themselves. They seemed to believe they had a mission in life . . . . ' (p. 56). What breakaway Bohemia did was to reinforce this pragmatic teenage observation:

> Thousands were waiting for a prophet to liberate them from the cautious middle-class lives they had been reared to inherit. *On the Road* would bring them . . . visions of a life lived at dizzying speed beyond all safety barriers, pure exhilarating energy. (p. 137)

Among the thousands, though a lot more intimately involved with the prophet, is the young Joyce, who sees herself in Kerouac and company – 'as a writer, I would live life to the hilt as my unacceptable self, just as Jack and Allen had done' (p. 148). She also, now, sees something else: that Beat liberation, with its rejection of place and property, marriage and money, exposed the pattern of distribution of psychic 'goods' along sexual lines with a new clarity. Beat visions didn't exactly exclude women; rather, they defined themselves in relation to them, over against them, and (in several senses) lived off them. For instance, 'it was all right for women to go out and earn wages, since they had no important creative endeavors to be distracted from' (p. 207). Her own life 'with' Kerouac seems mostly a matter of waiting, waving goodbye, being left behind:

> Could he ever include a woman in his journeys . . . ? Whenever I tried to raise the question, he'd stop me by saying that what I really wanted were babies. That was what all women wanted and what I wanted too, even though I said I didn't. Even more than I wanted to be a great woman writer, I wanted to bring life into the world, become a link in the chain of suffering and death. (p. 136)

Kerouac's philosophical cocktail of vulgar Freudianism and Beat Buddhism is a topical ('visionary') way of keeping the women at home, even though they may go out to work. One's 'old lady', in hipster parlance ('Even a very young woman can achieve old-ladyhood, become the mainstay of someone else's self-destructive genius' p. 170), is cast in the role of continuity girl in the movie of one's life. Women are by definition unchanging, the enemies and the measure of change. Nature rules them (what they say doesn't count). A baby is what she wants, because women are generic, they think *species*, survival. The old ladies can't make it new.

The figure who emerges most hauntingly from this ruck of bit-part players is Johnson's long-dead friend Elise, Allen Ginsberg's lover, briefly, while he was still trying to please his analyst and play heterosexual, and thereafter his shadowy, self-appointed other self, 'her waiting . . . vast and unpeopled.' Elise, already alone and scared of madness, recognises herself in Ginsberg. She's already read about him, read him:

> There must have been for Elise a deceptive elimination of that first necessary distance between people – a kind of jet lag of the spirit. Hurtled somewhere too quickly, you can lose your bearings.
> Allen Ginsberg believed in nakedness as the best defence against the world. A self-exposure so pure and indiscriminate, so total, that no room would be left for interpretation. No legend but in the passing moment's reality.
> Thus Elise was a moment in Allen's life. In Elise's life, Allen was an eternity. (p. 78)

For Elise, much more cruelly and clearly even than for Johnson, recognising yourself in the mirror of the writing is also losing yourself. Elise throws herself on the tide of the time, and is cast up as flotsam. For her, the ambiguity of the men's sexual roles, Allen's 'beatific' homosexuality setting the tone, means that her body too becomes an irrelevance – '*naked*, that angelic and androgynising word' (p. 82) signals her exclusion. Put her back into the story and the notion that women are about survival becomes nonsense, not only or even mainly because of her eventual suicide. There was not (when is there?) enough freedom to go around: the moment had been hijacked, described, defined. And not only by repressing women, but by representing men as the prophets, martyrs and androgynous angels of change. The women's stories – their abortions, their breakdowns, their children, their writing – had to wait for another time.

Minor Characters is in the end a book about silence and its lies, chief among them the assumption that the mute are naturally that way. The Beat Generation was a tacky media event that 'sold books, sold black turtleneck sweaters and bongos, berets and dark glasses' (p. 187); it also 'sold' an idea about articulacy and freedom which merged the author's self (and sex) with the writing with a new thoroughness. As did Cleaver and Baldwin; as did Millett, Jong,

Alther, French; as did Walker and Morrison . . . . The Beats were in this sense truly figures for the times. They represent a renewed politicising of writing that gets the person onto the page. James Baldwin, writing in 1961, describes his own version of this strategy: ' . . . to become a Negro man, let alone a Negro artist, one had to make oneself up as one went along . . . . The world had prepared no place for you, and if the world had its way, no place would ever exist. Now, this is true for everyone, but in the case of a Negro, this truth is absolutely naked . . . . '[2] The naked truth becomes the stock in trade of the writing of protest. Baldwin, of course, resented the Beats, Kerouac in particular, for appropriating the rhetoric of the disinherited. However, it's easy enough with hindsight to see that he himself thinks of the artist as male (the quotation above is from an *Esquire* article addressed to Norman Mailer, 'The Black Boy Looks at the White Boy'). The point about the claim to nakedness and the unmediated expression of self, as Baldwin's remark about having 'to make oneself up' reveals, is that this is a battle over fictions, a frontier dispute over the territory of *invented* truth. Johnson recreates vividly the euphoria of the Beats' invented time, but her later self is deeply sceptical of the very notion of visionary wholeness on which it depends.

The men, she suggests, were battling for 'the right to remain children' (p. 261), trying to inhabit the heightened, conscious moment with such thoroughness that it would detach itself from America's temporal mainland, and float away. They seem fixed in their present tense, as in their photographs, advertisements for themselves, an image of 'change', 'liberation', 'movement'. She quotes John Clellon Holmes – 'The social organisation which is most true of itself to the artist is the boy gang' (p. 79) – and tries it the other way around: ' . . . *the girl gang*. Why, everyone would agree, that's absolutely absurd!' (p. 81) And in a sense, she would agree too. The gang image is regressive, profoundly 'masculine' (p. 170), and moreover constructed as against the old ladies. Yet gang thinking is also a way of sustaining the fiction of common ground, and making change seem possible. Without such a context will the women stay minor characters, their separate selves and identities subsumed in a myth that fixes them as minders? Johnson implies (as does Baldwin) that while everyone makes him/herself up, those who do it from a less privileged position are blessed – and cursed – with an extra awareness of the effort of invention involved. The world had prepared no place for them, except (naturally) as symbolising 'nature' in opposition to the dizzying acrobatics of culture. Baldwin quotes with particular distaste this passage from Kerouac: 'wishing I were a Negro. . . . I passed the dark porches of Mexican and Negro homes; soft voices were there, occasionally the dusky knee of some mysterious sensuous gal . . . . '3 To stand before someone else's mirror is to find yourself travestied and distorted. To step through the looking-glass into the space of illusion is to become exposed, unstable, inventing yourself *and knowing it.*

Johnson's writing is tense with the strain of not simply opposing a 'liberated' female culture to the old 'boy gang'. The question of the women's wants and talents remains unresolved. She's too conscious of the past injustice of having been typecast to want to lose her characters to a cause. Her feminism is as much about loneliness as solidarity, and while she gives back to the women who were once dismissed as types their names and what she knows of their aspirations, she cannot give them different lives. 'If time were like a passage of music . . . ', but that's fictive time, and this book stays on the hither side of fiction. Joyce Johnson's characters as a writer is not the one she once envisaged, in the image of Jack and Allen; hers is an understated, wry, rather private voice, self-conscious and reflective even in her novels. The euphoria of then gives way to the caution of now. Analysing 'the feeling . . . that I've always had in periods when I've been happiest', she tracks it down to ' a sense of being part of an endless family whose individual members only needed to be discovered one by one' (p. 243). It's a characteristically wary sentence: she's registering both the desire to belong and the contradictions it involves ('an endless family', for example). *Minor Characters* is bleak but also (therefore?) suggestive. There seems no alternative to the looking-glass world of representation. Yet there's no easy togetherness to be found there.

KATE MILLETT

> I cannot write that book. It would have to say that I'm what?
> And what am I anyway? I hate confessionals.
>
> (Kate Millett, *Flying*, 1975)

It's no accident that 'the girl gang' surfaces as an image in Kate Millett's *Flying*:

> 'Kerouac and his buddies lived like this and it was important,'
> Rhoda says. Can we achieve such validity ourselves, could I
> give my friends life on paper? Not unless I can listen harder,
> remember exactly what people say. So far I am trapped in self,
> trying to find me. Rhoda encourages me to write in the first
> person, a friend of hers left husband and child for the solitude
> of a cabin where her whole life poured out suddenly upon paper.
> 'This is our time. We will see our fantasies take place before our
> eyes, we have magic now.'[1]

And part of the magic lies simply in the dangerous charm of 'we'.
We are at the centre of things, and in the present tense. Millett's
memoir strays deliberately over the boundary of fiction. 'Life on
paper', eliding fictive time and lived time, seems to close the gap
between the artist and the others, and to become a code for change:
the plots of our lives are malleable, suddenly.

So the book has a quite different sense of time. Millett is of
course writing about a different time (the early 1970s), about her
own notoriety ('Unknown sculptor to media nut in a matter of
weeks, all because of a doctoral thesis' (p. 346) – *Sexual Politics*
was published in 1970), and about life in and around the women's
movement. But she's also writing on the road, on the run, with the
kind of urgency that, for Johnson, belongs to a lost moment and
to somebody else. Johnson's memoir, written later and set earlier,
is here mirror-reversed. The old Bohemia occurs in flashbacks, as
when Millett recalls being cast in the role of old lady and artist's
minder – 'I must stay back because I'm only a girl friend and I do
not want to be a pushy woman. Everyone writes articles and makes
remarks about the bitchy American female these days . . . . It
is so hard to be two artists living together. People expect one'
(p. 177). The book's 'real' present, the present of self-exposure

and androgynous visions is a function of group-grammar – 'This is our time'. The women in the girl gang have made a film together (as did 'Kerouac and his buddies'), film being the medium that symbolises most powerfully the American dream-industry, so that its counter-cultural appropriations carry a special charge. And the writing of the book itself deliberately jettisons distance, hindsight, discretion:

> . . . resorting to the outrageous publicity of being one's actual self on paper. There's a possibility of it working if one chooses the terms, to wit: outshouting image-gimmick America through a quietly desperate search for self. (p. 83)

Once again, nakedness is the stategy. Compare Johnson on Ginsberg – 'the best defence against the world. A self-exposure so pure and indiscriminate, so total, that no room would be left for interpretation.'

The characteristic narrative moves are lateral and integrationist. Millett appeals to a gay group to share in the 'patterning' of her friends' brain-damaged son ('We are creating a child' p. 319), or tries to make her friend and sometime lover Vita a partner in her writing life, as secretary, editor, critic. Her own bisexuality and her marriage to Japanese Fumio are part of the same aesthetic ('Why either or? Why not both', p. 514) and so too is her pacifism. However, the book's honesty, which is also its theatricality, its consciousness of being on stage, discovers schisms and separations on all sides. Reclaiming a self from the media people is one thing; merging your identity into the group is quite another. The utopian promise of the movement nastily resembles Warhol's crack about everyone having the chance to be famous for fifteen minutes. The 'stars' who make the speeches and write the books generate a furious anger because they block that dream by realising it. 'Paranoia lives' (p. 317) and thrives wonderfully in an environment where the elementary business of representation is being reinvented. Or, perhaps, ditched altogether. A radical democracy, where everyone spoke for themselves, would invent a different kind of communal culture, wouldn't need names.

The group-grammar, in fact, reveals the author as a kind of traitor. This comes out tragi-comically with the question of credits for the film: who 'directed', 'edited', 'produced', indeed who 'made' the film? Millett finds herself unwilling to renounce her authorial role.

She tries to see herself, over and over again, as merely a scribe, but when she apologises for her vocation by portraying it as a drudge's service, a humble recording – 'the only one watching the stove, trying to photograph things' (p. 484) – it's clearly a lie in this context. This 'I' is not self-effacing; the writing subject is the book's subject. Millett and the other movement 'names' find themselves guilty of the original sin of articulacy:

> Yes, we have done what they wanted to. Talked. Written. Got it together. And they will never forgive us for it. And why should they? But yet how odd . . . . It was for their right to express themselves that we expressed ourselves. But it is not the same. . . . You do your thing, I'll do mine. But they cannot do their thing. Why? Money. Time which is money which buys freedom. Or just the confidence to do it. That furthest beyond, that above all because if you have it really together in your head you could write *War and Peace* on the subway. Confidence. Believing in yourself. It is another kind of opportunity lost. Which we must find together . . . . Deluded into believing that there is a limited supply of paper in the world, of art, of achievement, of recognition. But there's the rub. (p. 514)

The tone of this passage is very much of the 1960s – particu-larly the line about writing *War and Peace* on the subway 'if you have it really together in your head'. It belongs, though, to the same stable as much more respectable-sounding theories of the same moment about the death of the author, with their nostalgia for anonymity; and it has something in common too with those ways of thinking about writing which turn readers into heroic protagonists.[2] This theoretical democracy exists simultaneously, and in cruel counterpoint with the idolatry, mystification and scapegoating of the writer which dates back to romanticism, but has become a favourite twentieth century sport. Maybe both the adulation and the efforts of demystification are responses to the decay of representation, its disintegration under the pressure of voices denied. As Johnson's book makes clear, those who don't speak for themselves tend to be generalised out of (cultural) exist-ence, identified with nature and mere continuity, minor characters who populate the human background. But those who do, speak for others too, each representation is also a sneaky exclusion. So, for example, on a political level Millett ricochets from anxiety about whether revealing her lesbianism will harm the public image of the women's movement, to anxiety about refusing to identify with lesbian separatists – '"gay chauvinism,"' prophesies her friendly guru Nell,'"which will come because it's inevitable, will make it very hard for you futuristic bisexual types to win out . . . . Nothing so unsettles us . . . as our own precarious sexual identity"' (p. 288). Millett wants to write (and live) ambivalence, refusing a position, yet insisting on an 'actual self'. As a result, the writing becomes an art of evasion, keeping on the move, one breathless step ahead of the moment when ambivalence turns into contradiction.

It's easiest in the dark, where group images can form and dissolve like mirages. A party where the women separate from the men mutates into a world of touch with the lights out:

> I do not have to worry about who is pretty, the tyranny of my own eyes, the continual tyranny of looks. Mine. Theirs. My hand is gentle to a shoulder, or is it a leg? A woman's cheek touches my cheek softly. It is lovely. It is different from sex but it is sex . . . . But we cannot do this. The movement cannot be queer . . . . How can we have this pleasure, it must be wrong, must not be. Afraid, my body alive with it and how curious that it doesn't matter that I cannot recognise faces, a woman, just a woman is touching me, touching woman itself. (p. 153)

This anonymity, in which they're gently disintegrated ('a shoulder, or is it a leg?') gives birth to a phantom essence – 'woman itself' – and then they reassemble themselves into their daily differences, climb back into their faces and names and rejoin the men. It's a moment when all the threats seem to come from the outside; though Millett's lesbian self adds its own tension by leaping to the guilty thought, 'the movement cannot be queeer'. Her awareness of other women as potential lovers in fact underlines for her their otherness – the frontier of the skin, and the loneliness that's assuaged or redoubled in sex. The anonymous wordless women in the dark are, in any case, uncomfortably close to the changeless generic woman – mute and excluded (even if self-excluded).

The more directly erotic descriptions keep their distance. They are all about looks and looking – 'That long full look, the look of the eyes in sex. Tonight I will ask this of her' – and possessiveness: 'The beauty of her foot on the sheet. Devour it' (p. 536). Her final and most risky demand of her lover Claire is that she allow herself to be *written* about, that she conspire with Millett the writer, be a Muse ("'Help me . . . . I can't live in this book any more'", p. 537) and 'guarantee' that writing it all out is alright, not just a lonely betrayal. Millett celebrates their love-making (as well she may) as a triumph over mutual mistrust, risking rejection on her part and invasion on Claire's:

> Being in love is saying the same name over and over . . . . Here I am, she whispers, moving within me. You are home. Flesh in my flesh. In this act we are married. How can I give you joy? Her mouth drinks in my throat. Look at me. Eyes searching for. Commanding. Here I am. You are inside me, the voice coming as if softly. Only the two of us. (p. 536)

What she finds with Claire is a safe self – but a self unmistakeably, lyricised and mythicised. Millett's deliberately echoing the poets, in particular Donne's kind of 'dialogue of one' ('The world is here.' 'Our bodies are spread out between us.') in which 'I' and 'you', insides and outsides are exchanged with the solemnity of a mock-marriage. Its literariness, though, is appropriate, since despite echoes of 'woman itself' ('One never has this with a man, his experience hidden as mine is. But two women have the same nerves', p. 483) these two have no automatic access to intimacy. Hence the need (the same applies to the marriage service when you think about it) for this magic litany to make them 'one'. They are making themselves up (Millett is making them up). The world had no place for them, and to use words like 'home' and 'married' is to make a place on the page.

This happy ending – fragile and provisional though it is – gives *Flying* the structure of fiction. Like many novelistic marriages, it has to stand for a whole network of relationships, in this case with the women in the movement, whose splits and enmities have been chronicled blow by blow throughout the book. Inevitably, there's an ironic gap between the unanimity of 'the two of us' and the divisions it heals (so that it can hardly be said to heal them). The sub-text says that the group-grammar is a fiction too, and probably an unwritable one. So although, in contrast with Joyce Johnson, Millett tips the scales in favour of invented time ('This is our time') she shares Johnson's uncertainty about living with fictions. The 'girl gang' is something she cherishes and comes to dread. It's founded in the notion that identities are re-inventable – a recipe for change, but also for breakdown and exhaustion.[3] She and her characters are creatures of this time, this moment, not the 'old ladies' who look after the continuation of the species, not united in some timeless essence. Loneliness and panic lurk not far beneath the surface. The final sentences of *Flying* invoke a natural metaphor for community and movement, as a tribute to some possible synchronicity that its human subjects can't quite see in themselves:

> Gulls so many of them I try to count them but they split and break I cannot place and order them in the sky. Flying in a haze of wings noises cries. Chaos and serenity together. (p. 546)

Like Johnson's 'endless family', this image gestures towards an imagined security. Millett sets up a lot of awkward questions: is the woman writer who addresses herself knowingly to other women freed or inhibited, supported or undermined by that awareness? 'I have spilt myself in this book,' she says at one point (p. 338). That is: I am all here (but in pieces). Spilt like milk (you'd better not cry over)? Sperm (a female Onan)? Blood? Ink? When women writers lay claim to the territory of nakedness, it's their textual strategies that are exposed. 'I' is the most glaring, and the most problematic. The re-birth of feminism inspires and/or coincides with a proliferation of first-person fictions by women inventing themselves as writers. Or is it the other way round? I've chosen here to look at three novels that construct the first person in different ways: Erica Jong's *Fear of Flying* (1973), Diane Johnson's *The Shadow Knows* (1974), and Marilyn French's *The Women's Room* (1977), which stages a comeback for the third person as part of a salvage operation, stepping out of the looking-glass. Scandal, Horror and Self-Help, in that order.

ERICA JONG

> One by one, I peeled off the masks: the ironic mask, the wise-guy mask, the mask of pseudosophistication, the mask of indifference.
>
> (Erica Jong, *Fear of Flying*, 1973)

Fear of Flying is the work of a female impersonator. The book's 'honesty' is a fairly elaborate act, technically (and in more everyday senses too) a travesty. Reviewers registered this by describing it as 'uninhibited', 'bawdy', 'explicit', or (in the blurb to the British edition) as displaying 'the sort of absolute candour that for centuries was permitted only to men'. Far from peeling off masks, Jong – in the person of her heroine Isadora Wing – is trying them on; or rather, the peeling off is itself a form of dressing up. 'Candour' is a time-honoured confidence trick, with a good eighteeenth-century provenance.

This is Isadora mock-moralising:

> How hypocritical to go upstairs with a man you don't want to fuck, leave the one you *do* sitting there alone, and then, in a state of great excitement, fuck the one you *don't* want to fuck while pretending he's the one you do.[1]

And this is Fielding's *Shamela*, parodying Richardson's *Pamela*;

> O! What a devilish thing it is for a woman to be obliged to go to bed with a spindle-shanked young squire she doth not like, when there is a jolly parson in the same house she is fond of![2]

Eighteenth-century echoes have a particular point: they shake up time by reminding you of a pre-romantic, supposedly merrier world that hadn't yet convinced itself of the 'timeless' truths that women were naturally lustless, and that self was necessarily constructed on guilt. Jong's more contemporary subjects of pastiche – Roth, Nabokov – similarly stand for scandalous refusals (*Portnoy's Complaint, Lolita*) of 'maturity', and, more precisely, for irreverence towards the analysis of adulthood propounded by Freudian psychiatry. *Fear of Flying*, at least initially, operates in a culture of quotation marks. For example – 'Pia and I were "free women" (a phrase that means nothing without quotes)' (p. 97). In this case, quotes within quotes, since the phrase recalls Doris Lessing, while the parenthetical gesture is borrowed from Nabokov. 'Freud' here is the policeman of matrimony (and of divorce for that matter), the father of the Jewish family romance, the reductive diagnostician who naturalises discontent.

Jong's 'I' sets out to offend by being at once more and less than a character. More because Isadora is a writer who's deliberately, flirtatiously and maliciously 'confessional', a near relation of the author; and less because she's pieced together on the page, out of books. There's even the (seemingly inevitable) allusion to the Beats:

> Those longings to hit the open road from time to time, to discover whether you could still live alone inside your own head, to discover whether you could manage to survive in a cabin in the woods without going mad. (p. 18)

Isadora's central perversity is her refusal to '"ackzept being a vohman"' (p. 12), as one of her many analysts, Dr Schrift, puts it. She rejects the alternatives she finds on offer – celibate intellect or sex-and-motherhood – in favour of sex as self-invention: 'What I really wanted was to give birth to *myself*' (p. 52). She associates sex for pleasure (compare Nabokov's nymphets, Roth's masturbatory hero) with potency on the page. Instead of offering her fantasies up for dissection (and settling down to have real babies) she coddles them and wraps them in writing. The camped-up daydream she christens the Zipless Fuck is her prize example, 'more than a fuck . . . a platonic ideal. Zipless because when you came together zippers fell away like rose petals . . . . Tongues intertwined and grew liquid. Your whole soul flowed out through your tongue and into the mouth of your lover' (p. 19). Although, in contrast to all those depressing analytic sessions, 'there is no talk at *all*' (p. 22), it is an obsessively oral scenario, and it announces the novel's main idea about creativity, which is that mouths are sex-organs.

You too can talk dirty: having the words is tasting illicit pleasure. So, to casually drop 'motherfucker' in the book's third paragraph constitutes a claim to forbidden textual territory. It's a theme worked through with some thoroughness: Isadora's marriage to inscrutable Chinese analyst Bennett separates the sex off from the words, the mouth from the genitals ('hating Bennett for . . . being such a good lay but never kissing me . . . . And never going down on me, ever', p. 30); and conversely, her runaway affair with Laingian Adrian is focused on mouths and tongues ('the wettest kiss in history', p. 77) and loose talk – all of which promises to make him a most satisfactory Muse. Verbal excitement takes other forms too. Their adulterous joyride 'through the labyrinth of Old Europe' is done in a speedy parody of the trip Nabokov's Humbert Humbert takes with Lolita through the States, on a magic carpet of words. They are the secret agents of freedom, tenderly contemptuous of settled, ordinary life:

> We came to know the meager Austrian pension with its white lace curtains in the parlor, its windowsill full of cactuses, its red-cheeked proprietress (who always asked how many children we had – as if she had forgotten what we told her double some kilometers back) . . . . We came to know the German *Autobahn* automats with their plates of sauerkraut and knockwurst, their blotting-paper coasters advertising beer, their foul-smelling pay toilets, their vending machines for soap and towels and condoms. . . . (pp. 164–5)

Being without place or roots, on the run, produces a dizzying sense of unreality – like living in a movie. It's an effect multiplied by the Nabokov echoes: when writing is seen to be made out of writing, the entailments of realism are attenuated, drawn out to near-invisible thinness. The text is taking a holiday from the narratives of stability and family romance.

But only, as it turns out, a holiday. Jong writes about writing as though it were a playground game where the girls could join the boys behind the bicycle sheds and tell their side of the story. What she reveals, however, is that the sides don't fit together. Isadora comes down with rather a special case of what Sandra Gilbert and Susan Gubar call the 'anxiety of authorship'.[3] It's this that makes *Fear of Flying* a necessary text – that in it the women as writer and the woman as (already) written fall apart. Isadora's poetical body language, with its strategic analogies (men write with sperm, women with menstrual blood) and its merging of sexual want into one large hunger – ' a kind of pounding in my gut . . . . as if my stomach thought of itself as a heart, and no matter how I filled it – with men, with books, with food, with gingerbread cookies shaped like men and poems shaped like men and men shaped like poems – it refused to be still' (p. 153) – makes the womb a mouth as if to match the pen-penis. Except, of course, that in the male versions of the metaphor both the writing and the sex depend on your own desire. So long as you don't spell out the physical details this vital fact is obscured, but Jong's novel uncovers it:

> We kissed for a long time, his tongue making dizzying circles in my mouth. No matter how long we went on kissing his penis stayed soft. He laughed his sunny laugh and I laughed too. I knew he'd always hold back on me. I knew I'd never really possess him, and that was part of what made him so beautiful.

I would write about him, talk about him, remember him, but
never have him. The unattainable man. (p. 238)

Adrian's exit from the text ought in theory to be a blessing in
disguise ('A lifetime of Freudian interpretations or a lifetime of
Laingian interpretations! What a choice!' p. 121); instead, it's the
moment from which one can trace Isadora's decay into a more-or-
less conventional character. Suddenly writing becomes unreal in a
negative sense, unserious. She can put her tongue in his mouth, give
him his lines (take her revenge by making him a chauvinist swinger,
a fraud) but nonetheless his male mystique stays oddly intact. He
has, it seems, the power to make her feel incomplete. His desertion
leaves her not just alone, but in a state of vertiginous panic. One
can sum it up by saying that her libidinal freedom is in a man's
gift. The very literalness with which she has followed through the
notion that one thinks with one's body is what brings her to this
point of (as Andrea Dworkin would grandly put it) 'metaphysically
compromised privacy'.[4]

Intercourse is an unequal relation: strip it of its association with
ownership and the fear of pregnancy and you still can't quite make
it into a metaphor for being your own woman ('What I really wanted
was to give birth to *myself*'). On her own Isadora loses her sense
of being a subject. The sex she does want (a male Muse, someone
who'll make love with the writer) is perhaps 'unattainable'. The
sex she doesn't want is ubiquitous. Travelling turns into an assault
course – her encounter with the train attendant on the journey from
Paris to London replays the Zipless Fuck as nightmare:

'You are *seule*?' he asked again, flattening his palm on my belly
and pushing me down toward the seat. Suddenly his hand
was between my legs and he was trying to hold me down
forcibly . . . . (pp. 271–2)

However, her escape is unfrightening and even comic ('"You pig!"
I spat out . . . . with a burst of energy I leaped up on the seat and
grabbed my suitcase, nearly bringing it down on my own head. I
stormed out of the compartment while he just stood there smiling
his crooked smile and shrugging', p. 272) – and it needs to be in
order to salvage the novel's ending, which returns her to husband
Bennett clutching her 'freedom' like a battered souvenir. Isadora the
writer started off in the company of male writers who'd imagined,

perversely, alternatives to 'straight' sex (what Nabokov's Humbert Humbert calls nastily 'the routine rhythm that shakes the world');[5] Isadora the woman, however, recoils from the logic of this kind of plot, which would suggest that you settle for the masturbatory pleasure of the text. Losing the man inside you would be to lose your definition. Andrea Dworkin again: 'We need [men's] approval to be able to survive inside our own skins'.[6] This is graphically displayed in the last paragraphs of *Fear of Flying*, as Isadora waits for Bennett:

> I ran more hot water and soaped my hair. I thought of Adrian and blew him bubble kisses. I thought of the nameless inventor of the bathtub. I was somehow sure it was a woman. And was the inventor of the bathtub plug a man?
>
> I hummed and rinsed my hair. As I was soaping it again, Bennett walked in. (p. 277)

So everything fits together after all: holes and plugs, women and men, naked Isadora and Bennett with all his clothes on.

It's a short step from here to the insatiable Isadora of Jong's sequel, *How to Save Your Own Life* (1977), who'll try anything once (a lesbian relationship, an orgy), but who is of course inalienably heterosexual (the lesbian lover is exhibited as a grotesque), and who finds an updated happy ending with a new style of younger man whose ego she massages shamelessly. This is Erica Jong the 'man's woman', hailed by John Updike in *The New Yorker* as 'A winner . . . . the Wife of Bath, were she young and gorgeous, urban and contemporary, might have written like this'. The Wife of Bath however wasn't a writer, but a character – and that's what Jong more or less became. Having started out to invent a writer-heroine, she colluded in her own assimilation to Isadora, who does indeed end up as a mere mouthpiece. Not, this time, for the generic wife-and-mother, but for the 'bawdy' insatiable woman, equally nearly 'anon' and equally 'natural'. The contradictions of the earlier novel are disposed of with a theory about 'the language':

> 'There is the language, and we are its vessels. We speak for the mouths that can't speak, we speak *their* thoughts – not our own. . . . a river doesn't care if it stays in a given state . . . . It doesn't care if it's masculine in one state, feminine in anoth- er . . . . All the rest is foolishness, distraction, jockeying for

    position and reputation – politics, in short . . . . the river cor-
    responds to the rights of the readers.'[7]

This argument, put into the mouth of a woman poet shortly to be
sanctified by suicide, reduces the problem of representation to a
question of sales figures. The cultural conflicts over the boundaries
of self revert, via the river image, to a state of nature (a United States
of nature) and natural rightness. True, Isadora speaks for others, and
it's important to notice *which* others when she produces a line like
this one in *How to Save Your Own Life*: 'Man or woman, vibrator
or shower spray, I come in three minutes flat. If I don't, I am
angry . . . . My cunt growls, howls, bays at the moon' (p. 154). As
Toril Moi points out in a rather different context, in *Sexual/Textual
Politics*, 'To be "against" power is not to abolish it in a fine, post-1968
libertarian gesture, but to hand it over to somebody else'.[8] Not, here,
to the readers, but to the pornography establishment whose clichés
Isadora is mouthing.

    Jong illustrates with (I think) painful exactness the fact that you
don't 'live alone inside your own head' – that imaginary 'cabin in
the woods' is overcrowded, a fun-house full of mirrors, a textual
space. *Fear of Flying* has (at least) two novels lurking in it: in one
(the one that deals in pastiche and quotation marks) the woman
writer is looking for a version of sensuality diffused, a love-affair
with a male Muse that focuses on tongues and mouths; in the other,
she's seeing herself in the mirror of male desire, and reverting to
type. The result is a book that flatters the male reader with a vision
of woman as more or less insatiable, and the female reader (for
very different reasons) with the same vision. The Isadora who
wants wet kisses has, it seems to me, a good deal in common
with the women who've responded over the years to Shere Hite's
questionnaires, where the theme is, increasingly, the difficulty of
translation between women's and men's body languages. In *Women
and Love* (1987), for instance, talk and its intimacies are the subject
of many sad refrains: 'When we were first in love, I used to talk to
him about so many things, and he would listen – or I thought he
listened . . . . later I noticed when I spoke, he would walk out of
the room'.[9] Hite's respondents to this particular questionnaire put
in, she estimates, some 40,000 woman hours writing their answers.
The plots of their lives – 'Women are deserting marriage in droves,
either through divorce, or emotionally, leaving with a large part of
their hearts' (p. 526) – are not so different from Jong's first plot.

The writing of *Fear of Flying* did change Jong's life, of course; but it also turned her authorial persona into an updated version of the available woman and good sport. It's when Jong loses her grip on the quotation marks that that her 'I' becomes an easy lay for the *zeitgeist*. Isadora is nowhere near paranoid enough. 'I' may always be a fiction – a fake, an assemblage of voices – but there is a crucial distinction between the writing self that stays on top and the one that goes under. In Isadora's case, the 'subject position' and the sexual position coincide with embarrassing exactitude, in the end. The language of 'naked' greed and want ('poems shaped like men and men shaped like poems') loses its self-consciousness, until she's just a *consumer*, someone else's words in her mouth. Indeed, the imagery of mouths, obscenely, says it all – though not in the way the text once upon a time intended.

DIANE JOHNSON

> Outside I am a round-faced little woman with golden curls and round blue eyes, with round breasts and toes, surrounded by round babies; I look like a happy moon – now who would have thought I am riddled and shot through invisibly with desperate and sordid passions . . . ? Not even I would think that, looking at me. But I am, sometimes.
>
> (Diane Johnson, *The Shadow Knows*, 1974)

The 1970s novels of paranoia – Judith Rossner's *Looking for Mr Goodbar* (1975) was perhaps the most notorious – are often tacitly excluded from 'movement' literature. They shouldn't be, however, since they are intimately connected with those questions about the boundaries of self that follow from stepping into the looking-glass. In the plots about murder, rape and death-by-exposure the fears buried in *Fear of Flying* are exhumed. Diane Johnson's *The Shadow Knows* is among the most accomplished and cunning of these books. Her first person, Mrs Hexam to the world, is known to the reader as 'N.' – for nobody, perhaps, or for an indeterminate number. She is divorced, deserted by her lover, and lives in a 'unit' with her children and her black maid Ev in the vandalised outer suburbs of North Sacramento. N. is fancy-free in a very different way from I-for-Isadora, haunted by suspicion and dread. She lives in the suburbs of reality, you soon discover – on the very margins of that common ground which sustains people in their sense of what's actual, and who's who. She has lost her place, taken flight, cannot trust her perceptions – 'Entering into fear and liberty is exhilarating and elating as it must be to fly in an open plane, but also the thin air makes you giddy and liable to error'.[1] Sentences (like this one) are constructed stiffly, with exaggerated care, as though struggling for balance and precision.

N. writes (it's important that she's a writing narrator, among other things a reminder of her isolation) the body-language of vertigo. *Knowing* her world has become a compulsion, at once an imperative need and a seeming impossibility. The conventions of the crime novel (clues, suspects, the Famous Inspector) add an element of black farce, recalling as they do a world-picture in which the evidence makes sense in the end, and mysteries are resolvable. It's a genre in which order and stability of signification are generally guaranteed by the figure of the detective – the one who sorts out clues from red herrings, and makes causes and effects into chains of meaning. The Famous Inspector polices the frontier between us and them, substance and shadow. Joyce Carol Oates's *The Mysteries of Winterthurn* (1984), a lush pastiche of nineteenth-century detective yarns, has a narrator who's a fan of Famous Inspectors and who spells out the assumptions behind the role:

> . . . thus, in emulation of God, the detective aspires to invent that which already exists, in order to see what is *there* before his (and our) eyes. He is the very emblem of our souls, a sort of mortal saviour . . . . [2]

In *The Shadow Knows* N. decides she has to play this role herself in her scary new world, since – like her ex-husband Gavvy, and her ex-lover Andrew (both lawyers) – the Inspector proves comically, and horribly, unreliable.

So the novel's setting is outside the Law, a kind of no man's land – in the punning sense of those words. N.'s situation is banal enough: she has rejected her husband, and lost her lover (who has returned to his wife), and as a result has lost caste in everyone's eyes, including her own. In the process, however, she is coming to see herself as less-than-obvious, less the blonde and faithless mother of four (that 'round' character), more the sceptical, panicky analyst, inspired to dangerous invention, or divination, by fear. She sees she has joined the underclasses, economically and geographically speaking, but also in a more metaphysical sense. That is, having forfeited the security of (white, middle-class) marriage, she feels the reassuring habits of perception it nurtures withering away. People and things lose their safe definitions outside that charmed circle. Her story starts with a New Year and a vandalised front door ('hacked and slashed . . . smeared . . . with some disgusting substance like a mixture of blood and vomit and crankcase oil', p. 5), marking all sorts of thresholds, but most obviously the one between thinking of violence as outside, and taking it personally, letting it enter your imagination. In no man's land it's not as though there's no intimacy. There is, and it is an intimacy of strangers – whether unkown vandals, or people you thought you knew but didn't. Her secure past, as she recalls it now, is destabilised too. The things that turn out to have mattered are moments of fractured realism, flaws in the glass.

The style Johnson gives N. plays obsessively on 'I' and 'eye'. Sight is supposed to be the sense that provides us with evidence about the world without having to get too close, the one that enables us to 'read' experience, and supplies us with metaphors about insight and (moral) blindness. Here, it's reconnected with the body's messy limits – 'After Ivan was born I got contact lenses, and it seemed to me the world had grown brighter, not metaphorically but literally . . . Then I caught on that this was so because the spectacles I used to wear had always been covered with sticky fingerprints, from fat baby fingers . . . . ' (pp. 35–6). And in a way she does see with a new clarity: sees in the children's eyes 'intense and proper self-preoccupation'; sees she should go back to college; sees she doesn't love Gavvy, makes a bid for freedom . . . . But her new vision isn't single: she sees herself seeing, sees double.

N.'s perceptions have been *denatured*. She's simply not able to take them for granted: ' . . . I looked out into the leafy tree that screened the window of my dressing room and someone seemed to look back at me. I thought at first it was a person . . . . ' (p. 75). Her account of the vision that triggered her emotional divorce from Gavvy is splendidly equivocal – one of the most surreal of all the images of birds and flying that darken the air in the early 1970s. Out of her window she sees not a person, but an escaped parrot ('an immense bird of yellow and green') glaring in at her. The message of liberation is there all right (I have been a caged parrot, I too can escape, my wings weren't clipped after all) but it gets refracted in the telling. She beomes something else than 'a person', the parrot's reflection:

> . . . nor could I wrest my imprisoned stare from his staring eye. He knew me . . . . All that day and all the next my head was full of parroty phrases of wifely love and obedience and motherly concern but my voice developed an odd croak . . . . The day after that . . . . I glared with lidless eyes . . . . I felt myself to have grown bright green wings . . . . You never know what will set someone off. (p. 76)

The dry tone of this last shrugging sentence is the tone of the one who knows that 'You never know . . . . ' The window proves to be a mirror, not a cage-door left open. Even worse – her very self seems flattened into a mirroring surface. No wonder she sees a parrot.

Or rather, no wonder the 'I' sees this way. Paraphrasing Johnson's plot and transposing N. into the third person make her sound at once too solid and too mad. What it means to be a person is in question – in part because we're down among the women (and children), alien 'species' on the wrong side of the tracks. In this class system power makes some people more real than others. Osella, Gavvy's one-time nanny – who ran the house, cooked, looked after their children – now pursues N. with poisonous phone calls, and (more chillingly still) as a figure of guilt and fear lodged in her brain. This connects with 'I' and 'eye': Osella is bodily foreign, her colour and size ('an alien . . . so dark and fat . . . . like someone reflected in a fun-house mirror', p. 42) made it easy then to keep her on the periphery of consciousness. She arrived widowed and bereft, riven (N. now conjectures) with sexual need, and the 'hatred which is held by the powerless' (p. 33), passions whose bitter taste N. herself is beginning to savour; Osella 'went mad, living all by herself in a cold world of stony people who couldn't seem to see or hear her . . . . battering at us, us not feeling her at all' (p. 43); and Osella, N recalls, has 'the same birthday . . . also we are both left-handed' (p. 46). Osella's madness took the form of suspecting N. of witchcraft. N., contemplating her bloody front door, the strangled cat someone leaves for the children to find, the vomit splattered on the car windscreen ('I saw the world . . . through a film of someone's hate smearing everything over', p. 72), wants to suspect Osella. However, she's also beginning to recognise her: soul-vertigo done with (narrative) mirrors.

There are, besides, many other plausible suspects, not to mention the faceless, roaming and it's worth noting perfectly 'realistic' somebodies who may be venting their spleen or hatred randomly, in passing, and are part of no plot at all, except perhaps the one called poverty and dereliction. The novel's power derives from its radical transformation of a familiar pattern - the woman exposed, who's stalked and attacked (raped/murdered) by a well-disguised psychopathic killer. In *The Shadow Knows* the pattern is multiplied and dispersed (in a parody of the kind of crime novel where you find yourself suspecting each of the characters in turn) so that 'murderer' becomes a floating signifier, a name that could almost belong to anybody, even to N. She should have called the doctor when Ev was beaten up by a faceless assailant in the dark laundry room. Ev, Osella's successor, is not in the least invisible to N. – 'We were like two halves of a mirror. In her was a deep unspoken fear. In me was a deep unspoken fear' (p. 104), but still, N. lets her slip away. Ev has always lived on the margins and dies with dreadful ease in her sleep, perhaps partly from the blows, mainly from the effects of her pancreatitis, caused by drinking, caused by . . . ? We realise that 'victim', too, is a wandering signifier. To the Inspector, who finally puts in an appearance, Ev is at best an unfortunate statistic, at worst a minor criminal (arrests for drunkenness and brawling). So untidy and shapeless was her life, with so much waste and violence inside it – inside her – that her death seems to make no real difference. As he explains to N., '"A murder is a serious business . . . . Unsolved murders are very demoralising . . . . If it seems to people that the world is a place full of violence and crime, and that murder is not followed by discovery and retribution, then they are encouraged to indulge their desperation . . . ."' (pp. 202–204) Ev died from 'unknown causes', because it will not do to have a murder without a murderer. So 'peace and order' will be maintained by excluding this event from the realm of reality.

N., though, can't any longer draw a dividing line between the solid people and the others; or at least, can't be sure she's on the right side of it. 'Unknown causes' threaten her identity, and she continues the hunt for her murderer, in the underworld Osella vanished into – the world N. and her white friends used to regard with incredulity (an exotic sideshow, if it existed) where Osella had a sex-life and a singing career, the Zanzibar club. Here in 'the heart of darkness' (p. 271) the novel arrives at the naked truth. Famous Inspectors have a tendency to discover their alter-egos, cunning, anarchistic types playing God (or in the case of Conrad's classic *Heart of Darkness*, colonising reason and enlightenment discovers its own corrupt underside, Kurtz and 'the horror'). Here, in a parody of those revelations, N. sees Osella, stripped and oiled and exhibited for a cabaret act and the cameras: 'the naked Osella . . . . the light gleaming down on the folds of her body, on her tremendous breasts . . . . She seemed the embodiment of a principle, passive and patient, frightening to men, I guess, absorbing them into her immense proportions' (p. 267). It's the triumph of Osella's despised flesh, of her blackness, her sheer size (she's got her place in the world now). It's also a travesty and an obscenity, and the promoters are rubbing their hands in the wings. This image exposes more than Osella's flesh. It exposes the romance of Otherness, one of the female archetypes ('one of those frightening and horrifying fertility goddesses with swollen bodies and timeless eyes', p. 267) that make the weak seem strong, and keep the underworld under. Osella loses her black-magic aura for N. in this extraordinary scene. 'I' cannot see Osella as the 'other' (or rather, can see herself doing it and so break the spell). She has lost the habit of white, daylight civilisation, and the myths shared with the men.

The darkness has no 'heart'. N. drives home exhilarated and defeated, and in the last of the book's dark rooms, her garage, she is raped. In a sense the whole narrative is a device to postpone and set up this moment. Hence, I suspect, my urge to paraphrase the plot's progress, and replay the trick. N. has been looking for a murderer, and has at last found him – except that there's no murder, 'only' rape ('And that was all. There was no murder to follow', p. 276). Rape, though, solves the mystery of the source of her fear, of her sense that her personality is shadowed, her humanity insecure, her life threatened. Rape is the shadow-crime, a crime against the personality and the will, a fatal assault on the notion of the free-choosing moral individual. And it makes sense of what's gone before in rather the same way that a conventional happy ending does in a romantic novel: that is, it establishes a sexual relation, and suggests it's a symbol of the way things are; and answers the question, posed more than once in this book, 'What is the pattern of human life?' The rape has this kind of conclusiveness (reader, he raped me, you might say), substituting the unknown man ('he could have been anybody. He could have been black or white', p. 276) who makes you an object for the known man who makes you feel safe, and a subject. *The Shadow Knows* overlaps here with *Fear of Flying* :

either way you're not alone in your head. N., who is learning to see in this darkness, thinks perhaps the man's identity doesn't matter after all:

> The man could . . . have been Andrew . . . . or Gavvy . . . . Most likely it was some madman neighbour . . . . It could even have been the Famous Inspector. It did seem to me as he passed out the door that the moon illumined the imperturbable and knowing features of the Famous Inspector. (p. 276)

The law-men parade past in her mind's eye wearing their masks, but she has found them out.

So N. finally becomes the 'shadow' of the book's title – the one who knows. Who knows that 'I' am not one (not safe, not whole), and in that knowledge suffers a version of soul-death:

> You can change: a person can change. I feel myself different already and to have taken on the thinness and lightness of a shadow, like a ghost slipping out from his corporeal self and stealing invisibly across the lawn while the body he has left behind meantime smiles stolidly as usual and nobody notices anything different. You can join the spiritually sly, I mean. (p. 277)

A murder of a sort has been committed. N. is no longer convinced of having an essence, of being a 'real person'. She's a ghostly guerilla, a subverter of the Inspector's 'peace and order', someone who may well indulge her desperation. Her 'I' is criminal, or is it her 'eye'? She's outside the law in a positive and perverse sense. She is a heretic who has rejected her 'mortal saviour'. The metaphysical terminology is irresistible, since this is a power-struggle over who has the overview. N. has usurped the role of the Famous Inspector, whose penetrating vision fixes the nature of things. The book uncovers that order of representations (of which Poe's 'Mystery of Marie Roget' is a splendid example) in which a woman's body becomes the site of a contest between a great detective and a deviously ingenious criminal, and the 'solution' a triumph of mind over matter (in the form of the corpse, who anyway when she was alive lived in a careless, marginal fashion). Perhaps one of Diane Johnson's most impressive and spooky effects is to have N. speak for 'the body', the one witness not usually called.

Of course the narrating 'I' can't die in the book, though Johnson
has N. write up her story in daily instalments so that this piece
of sleight of hand is in a sense hidden, the better to make the sly
associations between murder and rape, sexual safety and life itself.
Early on N. imagines herself and the children appearing as a news
item:

> I am a divorced woman. I feel chagrin at the certain knowledge
> that the newspapers will put this in as if it explains why we were
> murdered . . . . (p. 6)

The black comedy (murder as an intrusion on privacy) turns serious.
Safe lives are those lived within the charmed circle of 'marriage',
extended with metaphoric knowingness to include that state of
identification with peace and order where you're allowed to share
in 'free' will – a fiction of security. *The Shadow Knows* is a fiction
of insecurity, not after all *outside* the Law exactly, but a rival
representation in shadow-play. Hence the Inspector's doubling as
a possible rapist. N.'s criminal eye 'frames' him.

Johnson provides the narrator and the reader with a glimpse of
the power in powerlessness (knowing the worst, surviving that
proverbial fate worse than death). The experience is bitter and
heady, N. seems to merge, *trompe l'oeil* fashion, with her author –
but writing is a slippery symbol for freedom. True, the writer can
slip out of character with 'the thinness and lightness of a shadow'.
This is what fuels, for example, Helene Cixous' memorably sly and
euphoric assault on 'The Character of "Character"'[3] – 'the single,
stable, socializable subject, represented by its types or characters'
– and her boast that '"I" am always on the run'. What Johnson's
novel does, with high irony, is underline that such freedom exists
anomalously, in the interstices of the public world:

> Trying to understand the personality: it is so mysterious; it is
> like being stood in a closet, baffled and fearful, with dark,
> strange-smelling coats stifling you, and then someone reaches
> a slim hand in, takes out his coat, and beyond you see a normal
> bright pacific world. People peer in at you; the world must seem a
> dark and stifling place indeed to you, they say, choosing to stand
> in that closet in that odd way. (p. 147)

The narrative of paranoia is just such a dark closet, its pleasures
arcane and wayward. 'I could imagine my room a cave now,'

N. writes, 'myself a cave dweller forever made to look at the shadows of the real' (p. 247), echoing Plato's *Republic*, where that ancestor of all Famous Inspectors argues that only a vision of the immortal Ideas outside this realm of shadows will enable us to understand its order, and dispense Justice in the dark. It's that claim to proprietorship of the real that *The Shadow Knows* so knowingly disputes.[4]

'There is a badness to things that satisfies your soul,' N. says, 'confirming that you were right about what you thought was what' (p. 276). She is both victim and criminal, a double role she shares with a remarkable number of heroines of her decade. There is Lise, for example, in Muriel Spark's *The Driver's Seat* (1970), who goes in search of the man who will kill her, dressing appropriately for the part (garish and memorable clothes that will hold stains well, and help the police with witnesses), and impatiently rejecting any offers of distraction (sex, say) that might obscure the real goal of the plot. In *The Driver's Seat* God-like omniscience obtains ('She will be found tomorrow morning dead from multiple stab wounds . . . . ')[5] and the ritual process of mystery and detection is rendered redundant. Spark's concerns are with literary theology, and the way contemporary life looks from the improbable perspective of Almighty irony, but she converges with Johnson because she unhesitatingly takes women to stand for the human condition, caught up in Someone Else's plot. In other words, she too outflanks the middle men – detective, murderer – who maintain peace and order and plausibility.

Spark was also, I imagine, mocking a forensic fashion of the time – victimology, the investigation of the active role of the victim. Joyce Carol Oates's 1973 novel *Do With Me What You Will* where, as in Johnson's, the heroine's husband and lover are both lawyers, fixes on victimology as a means by which the Law defends itself in the face of the diffusion of crime:

> . . . the guilt of the victim . . . . And rape was an excellent issue, because it involved not only some very subtle degrees of physical activity, but because – in a sense – it was a crime only if the victim resisted; it *became* a crime only through the strenuous activity of the victim.[6]

The defendant is black, the raped woman white. By successfully blaming the victim (she looked back over her shoulder, ran, screamed, struggled) Oates's lawyer makes both these messy persons and the crime vanish – rather as the Inspector disposes of Ev. Fear, it's implied, is an invitation, an acknowledgement of what's about to happen. This quaint scheme of causation, in more sensational form, also accounts for the structure of Judith Rossner's *Looking For Mr Goodbar*, where Theresa is murdered before the story starts, and the narrative conducts her back to death by showing how her personality is constructed around a bodily sense of original sin (a minor spinal deformity caused by polio), so that the only intimacy she can bear is the intimacy of strangers, men picked up and discarded to confirm her self-disgust. Her last words are 'Mommy Daddy Dear God, help me – do it do it do it and get it over w . . .'[7] Rossner's book (in which Theresa is very much a third person) lays down its own law, in the form of a dubious moral about the innocence of self-love, personal integrity regained through consciousness-raising. Theresa dies for her sexual character, not in the old-fashioned sense that she's loose (asking for it) but in the newer sense that she has a lousy self-image and lacks sisterly support.

Johnson is a great deal more subtle: N. has no 'character' (less and less as her narrative proceeds). Her 'I' disappears into the uncanny, 'spiritually sly' voice of the text, with all its knowingness, its lack of purchase in the real world, and so disappoints readers who want realism. *The Shadow Knows* is an 'alternative representation' that doesn't go in for the essentialism Stephen Heath worries about in *The Sexual Fix* – though it certainly doesn't go in for androgynous gestures either. It's about the separation out of a female point of view which has no secure boundaries, and no soul, but survives to say so.

MARILYN FRENCH

> I will write it all down, go back as far as I have to, and try to
> make some sense out of it. But I'm not a writer . . . .
>
> (Marilyn French, *The Women's Room*, 1977)

In *The Women's Room* Marilyn French collected up a lot of feminism's
fragments and fictions and returned them to the realist fold. It's a
novel that sets out to shelve the problems of the first person, and
though it disclaims 'art', its narrative strategies are crafty. In the
opening pages 'I' am exposed, isolated, possibly on the edge of
craziness, wandering on the seashore in Maine:

> I feel terribly alone. I have enough room, but it's empty . . . .   So
> I walk the beach . . . .   I know I am already pointed to, whis-
> pered about as a madwoman. . . . [1]

This writing 'I' on the margins, envious of the snails in their shells
and the mussels anchored to the rocks ('they don't have to create
their order, they don't have to create their lives', p. 14), is the kind
I've been describing as denatured. 'I' live in the present tense,
having to invent myself (having no ready-made place). Whereas
'she', in the past, in the third person, is a solid, describable person
with a life . . . .   *The Women's Room* fills up the emptiness of 'I' with
histories - lives that have at least the simple stability of pastness:

> My head is full of voices. They blend with the wind and the
> sea as I walk the beach, as if they were disembodied forces of
> nature . . . .   I feel as if I were a medium and a whole host of
> departed spirits has descended on me clamoring to be let out.
> (p. 17)

Though this sounds uncanny, it turns out to be a case of haunting in
reverse, a ghostly un-person being assaulted by realistic characters.
French accumulates third persons in order to crowd out the 'I's'
singularity.

Writing, of course, is a part of that singularity, and it's important
to the novel's effect that fiction should seem a matter of recording,
memorialising, transcribing – so that the 'I' can say 'I'm not a
writer . . . .   Writing is hard for me' (p. 17). The story is regularly

punctuated by references to writing as an act of reluctant piety, a
kind of chore almost:

> Truthfully, I hate these grimy details as much as you do. I
> love Dostoevsky, who doesn't harp on them, but suggests
> them . . . . But grimy details are not in the background of the
> lives of most women; they are the entire surface. (p. 62)

> Sometimes I get as sick of writing this as you may be at reading
> it. Of course, you have an alternative. I don't. I get sick because,
> you see, it's all true, it happened, and it was boring and painful
> and full of despair. (p. 189)

> Everything I write is lies. I am trying to tell the truth, but how
> can I tell the truth? . . . All I can do is talk, talk, talk. Well, I will
> do what I can. (p. 582)

In a way, these testimonies to the text's honesty are merely traditional – realists have always constructed themselves as scribes,
after all. There seems to be something more going on here, however.
What this book wants to do is revalue the act of representation as a
version of women's work – like 'scraping shit out of diapers with a
kitchen knife, finding places where string beans are two cents less
a pound' (p. 62). This way, you avoid the isolation (the author as
traitor) Millett explored in *Flying* – 'could I give my friends life on
paper? . . . So far I am trapped in self, trying to find me'.[2] You also
edge back towards a notion of women's 'nature': they reproduce life
in the double sense of having the children and caring for them, and
of being the patient historians who register the texture of living.

Again, this looks very like what realists have long claimed: I love
Dostoevsky, but . . . . (George Eliot, for instance, often implies how
much she loves Milton, but . . . .) French, though, is consciously out
to capture the realist middle ground for feminism. She's acting as a
mediator not between men and women, but between women whose
lives and interests circle back into home, and the private sphere,
and women who see themselves as 'outlaws' (p. 66). Her central
figure, Mira, whom we follow through from childhood to marriage
in the 1950s, divorce and college in the 1960s (and reabsorption
into the writing 'I' in the 1970s) spans that divide. She's a 'child'
of the times, with something of the powerlessness that suggests
– a consciousness that reflects the world around her, a reluctant
experimenter whose only way of expressing her inner dissent, over

the years of her marriage, is late-night lone pondering, smoking and drinking brandy in the dark. Mira (at considerable cost – she's prim, puritan, self-righteous) tries to be what she's told, and is only gal-vanised into taking her own life on (and indeed, nearly takes it in a botched suicide attempt instead) by her husband Norm's defection. You could say that the main, overarching plot is the one in which she converges with Val in Harvard in 1968, since Val represents the outlaw, the veteran radical and sexually-liberated woman who is Mira's 'other'. But that would be to ignore the novel's most striking feature, which is quite simply its compendious size, its attempt to abolish the class-distinction between major and minor characters (where women are concerned) and to rediscover in late twentieth century America a society a bit like those 'primitive' ones where women are the solid nexus of continuity, men the vagrants. Women are, as it were by definition, *plural* in this text (hence the need to exorcise the 'I'). They 'talk, talk, talk' with each other (whereas the men tend to be monologuists), and this routinely devalued activity turns out to be the clue that links private to public. Val, in the end, opts for non-communication and violence – but by then her positive outlaw qualities have been absorbed by the group in general and Mira in particular.

The very word 'group' recalls McCarthy, and *The Women's Room* is in many ways a revision of *The Group*'s dry, satiric portrait of women as bit-part players in a masculinised world. There are three phases in this revisionary strategy. First, we're given Mira's sense (intermittent and uneasy though it is) of women's traditional culture: glimpsed in the conversation of the women in the maternity ward after the birth of her first child ('never linear, it did not have a beginning and an end, a point to be made', p. 73); in the suburban ghetto of her later married years ('There were two cultures – the world, which had men in it, and their own, which had only women and children' p. 103); and in the home-made philosophy she patches together out of stoicism and disappoint-ment ('It was women who kept the world going, who observed the changing seasons and kept the beauty high, women who cleaned the world's house' pp. 247–8). These passages are intercut with later sceptical and jeering comments from Val ('"You might as well say women's place is in the home . . . . you're admitting an identity among all women, which implies lack of individuality"' pp. 78–9). However (this is the third move) consciousness-raising doesn't so much undermine the common ground as translate it into articulate communion. French's characters naturalise their discontent as a new version of the shared female culture. Gradually you realise that thinking and talking compulsively about their lives (Harvard conversations included) is indeed the women's 'thing' – a culture that 'specialises' in rehashing experience. The arguments about marriage or the family or rape – or the 'nature' of women – become part of their sort of literacy, which the men don't share.

Husband Norm, a 'stick figure' the narrator can't find much depth in (a double-take here – Norm is, we're told, *'life's* stereotype, not the author's, p. 260) sets the pattern. He is humanly illiterate, no good at 'talking people' (p. 518), and affects a superior distaste for hearing about the love-affairs, jealousies and hidden currents that surround them in suburbia. Harvard graduate school, on an altogether grander scale, also 'transcends' the grimy details with its 'pure thought, pure mind, pure marble busts of pure marble men' (p. 387). Val jokes about the 'sanitary' problem women present in the temples of learning ('Splat, splat, a big clot of menstrual blood right on the threshold', p. 387), and Kyla has a nightmare about an incriminating pile of sanitary napkins in the corner of the exam room on the eve of her literature orals. Mira reflects:

> . . . here, underneath all the intellect, the abstraction, the disconnection, were the same old salt tears and sperm, the same sweet blood and sweat she'd wiped up for years. More shit and string beans. (p. 387)

This language of spilt self, '"Women's troubles" . . . . oozings and drippings' (p. 268) generates the novel's most violent (offstage) action, Val's death as a terrorist at the hands of the police, her body a mass of 'exploded flesh' (p. 628). But its main use is as a metaphor for the 'stuff' of life, the texture of the text:

> . . . not the stuff of fiction. It has no shape, it hasn't the balances so important in art. You know, one line goes this way, another must go that way. All these lines are the same. These lives are like threads that get woven into a carpet and when it's done the weaver is surprised that the colours all blend: shades of blood, shades of tears, smell of sweat. Even the lives that don't fit, fit. (p. 269)

Does French really mean to be echoing Winston Churchill's wartime rhetoric ('blood, toil, tears and sweat')? Very possibly, I suppose, since she's thinking of an alternative heroism, not (despite Val) Amazon warrior virtues, but the toil of multiplying lives.

At Harvard Mira discovers the vocation that will turn her into the 'I' who writes it all down: literary scholarship. The novel prepares for this in a rather clumsy way by having her start a card-index long before, when she's the model housewife engaged in 'an orgy of planning' (p. 209) which involves a serial spring-clean. Mira finds herself in her work ('*I am, I am, I am . . . I want, I want, I want . . . .* two statements she had never felt per-mitted to utter' p. 620). She finds herself in order to submerge herself anew, however, since writing here is remarkably similar to housework, a matter of scholarship applied to the shit and string beans. The card-index model of composition, in fact, fits the novel all too closely for comfort – 'Even the lives that don't fit, fit' because they're part of the inventory, and because *quan-tity itself* (representing piled-up labour) is being presented as a value.

The Women's Room takes up a lot of space. Its length has a pathos of its own: like the roll of honour in a military cemetery, it testifies to the cost of women's struggles. It's also a measure of what one can only call the failure of any individual life to symbolise woman's lot, so that it has the message, as I've already suggested, that women's nature lies in the group:

> . . . and in time, everybody would know everything about every-body else, and everybody would talk about everything they knew about everybody else, and everybody accepted everything about everybody else. (p. 310)

This is French's version of the paradox of feminist self-consciousness – the realisation that you're not alone in your head, and that there is nothing timeless or inviolable about the 'I'. However, in her revisionary perspective, female character acquires a col-lective integrity. This is why I think Nicci Gerrard is wrong, when she suggests that the book belongs imaginatively to 'first-wave feminism'.[3] It belongs rather with, for example, the later Germaine Greer who stresses the importance and dignity of 'femi-nine' values her earlier self despised – nurturing, fostering, com-munity feeling, continuity . . . . One reason why *The Women's*

Room claims so often not to be 'art' or 'fiction' is because it's retreating from the 'first-wave' notion that *women* are fictitious constructs. Indeed, its construction of the narratorial 'I' as a scholar-housewife is designed to undercut any association of writing with invention.

Still, *The Women's Room* is an invented space, and does, despite disclaimers, have a shape. Even a list has a shape, of course, but there's more to it than that, witness Nicci Gerrard's description of the novel as 'fat, satisfying' (p. 137). French herself, in a later, even fatter novel, *Her Mother's Daughter* (1987), has her heroine reflect that 'art is what nourishes, what feeds: art is food. The oversweetened or over-spiced food that is most of popular culture makes a society sick, thin-blooded and vacant; but the wan, delicate work of the self-engrossed nourishes not at all, is papery dry as communion wafers offered as body and blood.'[4] The image lurking here is that of the pelican mother, who feeds her offspring on 'body and blood', and mothering is indeed the 'authoring' activity French's books enshrine. Not only do the women she portrays mother each other in myriad metaphoric ways (like the childless lesbian Iso in *The Women's Room*, who is always 'there' for her friends), but the narrative preaches an unjudgmental maternal celebration of women's lives, their mere existence a triumph ('everybody accepted everything about everybody else').

So French reclaims the novel as a home for women – but at the cost of denying its 'papery dry' fictionality, its inventiveness, its ambivalences, the loneliness and vertigo her 'I' suffers at the start. *The Women's Room* is a refuge, and as a result feels claustrophobic despite its size: the 'man's world' outside its covers remains uncharted, and indeed the book's version of separate spheres has the ironic effect of confirming women's identification with 'nature', species, survival. In her mammoth moral history *Beyond Power* (1986) French explores 'male' civilization as a suicidal conspiracy, and concludes that 'The end of life is the continuation of life'[5] – and you can see the roots of that position in the novel, in the insistence that women don't 'create' things ('I'm not a writer'). To play the author in that sense would be, you feel, a betrayal for French, an entry into the men's power-games. *This* writing re-produces, and therein lies its virtue.

*   *   *   *

Marilyn French's style of fiction has analogies with the feminist scholarship that has recovered women's writings, and reconstructed female traditions. Her own idiom claims a foremother in Doris Lessing – though it's both interesting and revealing that *The Women's Room* recalls the 'frame' narrative of *The Golden Notebook* ('Free Women') with its stress on 'boulder-pushing' labours, rather than the disintegrating first-person fictions of the notebooks. French's novel is very much a *Golden Notebook* without the formal and imaginative risks. Indeed, whereas Lessing plays the multitude of 'I's' off against the realist frame, French aligns her characters with the narrator. Her re-writing – and simplification – of Lessing is part of the process of establishing a women's culture. Even the writers that don't fit, fit: 'All these lines are the same'. And yet, of course, the very insistence on artlessness is coercive. In terms of the literary politics of feminism, it signals a revaluation of the women writer's role as scribe, go-between, moralist (corresponding to nurturing, maternal tasks in the social sphere); and a devaluation of 'self-centred' stories and deconstructive slyness.

This is tied up with nostalgia. French, in fact, is looking back beyond Lessing, and has a good deal in common with British writers like Murdoch and Drabble, who look to nineteenth-century traditions. In the coda to the last chapter I quoted Adrienne Rich on similar lines – 'pulling the tenets of a life together/ with no mere will to mastery,/ only care for the many-lived, unending/ forms in which she finds herself' – and such pictures of women's material wisdom, thinking small and growing by accretion (the image comes from patchwork), struck many feminists during the 1970s (some, like Greer, having second thoughts) as a clue to 'real' female culture. Women naturally, on this view, turn away from high art to craft; their work deals in solid things, and changes very slowly; and it's rooted in crypto-biological imperatives (compare Drabble on 'the pulls of sex and blood and society').

One can see why the return to realism appeals: it's a reaction against the consumerist, competitive takeover McCarthy writes about, which has disinherited women by professionalising and packaging sexuality, childbirth and child-rearing, housework and so on and on. So far as writing is concerned, it's a return to a kind of novel in which women have been 'at home' – one with an extended-family plot, in which individualism is punished, the 'will to mastery' discounted, and identity stabilised as part of the book's wider community. From this angle one can see that French's plot, while obviously marginalising men, is also more covertly castigating women who live in the present. The female present is the site of confusion, fantasy (compare Millett's Rhoda – 'This is our time . . . . we have magic now'), wandering signifiers, mobility in meanings, women as I-for-Isadora or N-for-nobody.

Or indeed, M-for-mother. Going back is never the same as being there in the first place. Differences among women dictate French's narrative strategies, even as the book seeks to submerge difference in its huge body, its 'shades of blood, shades of tears, smell of sweat'. It remains the case that *The Women's Room* looks very like Stephen Heath's depressing kind of 'alternative representation' which actually confirms 'the old identities, "male" and "female"'.[6] Its 'separate' sphere is a space assigned long before in patriarchal patterns of thinking (very close, for instance, to the new-old opposition Joyce Johnson saw in Kerouac's identification of the 'old ladies' with babies and staying put, the Beats with mobility and change). However, even a woman writing it out does make a difference: after all, the point about the old ladies is that they're outside literature. Getting in on the act, women writers, endlessly reimagining women, at the very least take up space – in bookshops, in readers' minds, in people's picture of the cultural scene. In *Nostalgia and Sexual Difference* (1987) Janice Doane and Devon Hodges, exploring reactionary reactions to feminist writing, suggest that 'its very volume becomes a force that challenges male authority'[7] – a glum but humorous (and convincing) notion.

Getting the person onto the page multiplies the rival fictions. What it doesn't do is provide an authentic body-language that speaks for Woman. 'There are books,' as Joyce Johnson observes, 'that serve as mirrors in which one catches reflections of oneself.' But such recognitions – always partly misrecognitions – also serve to disseminate doubt. Fiction seems to have entered into our condition, rather than the other way round. One final quotation, from Angela Carter's *The Infernal Desire Machines of Doctor Hoffman* (1972), succinctly retitled *The War of Dreams* in the United States:

> The Minister sent the Determination Police round to break all the mirrors because of the lawless images they were disseminating. Since mirrors offer alternatives, the mirrors had all turned into fissures or crannies in the hitherto hard-edged world of here

and now and through these fissures came slithering sideways all manner of amorphous spooks.[8]

Carter doesn't 'come after' the women's movement, nor do the other writers in my final chapter. They are contemporaneous with it, and part of it – but only if you see the movement as dispersed, divided and far-flung, a kind of diaspora.

5

Divided amongst Ourselves

FAY WELDON

> If thine eye offend me take a good look at yourself. If thine I
> offend thee, change it.
>
> (Fay Weldon, *The Cloning of Joanna May*, 1989)

Fay Weldon's reputation as a 'woman of letters' is itself a measure
of how our picture of such a personage has been changing, and how
far niceness has fallen out of fashion. She writes in a survivalist spirit
(anger, hate, bitterness, laughter taken as signs of life), and if her
characters frequently moralise about 'us', the tone is bleak:

> We shelter children for a time; we live side by side with men; and
> that is all. We owe them nothing, and are owed nothing. I think
> we owe our friends more, especially our female friends.[1]

The reference to 'female friends' in this quotation from *Praxis* (1978)
has a double edge. Three years earlier in a novel titled *Female Friends*
Weldon had given her narrator Chloe some lines that compose a
memorably bitter lttle song of sisterhood:

> Marjorie, Grace and me.
> Fine citizens we make, fine sisters!
> Our loyalties are to men, not to each other.
> We marry murderers and think well of them. Marry thieves,
> and visit them in prison. We comfort generals, sleep with
> torturers, and not content with such passivity, torment the
> wives of married men, quite knowingly.
>   Well, morality is for the rich, and always was. We women,
> we beggars,we scrubbers and dusters, we do the best we can
> for us and ours. We are divided amongst ourselves. We have
> to be, for survival's sake.[2]

153

It's a savage, stylised refrain, a bit like Brecht's favoured lyrics in its alienation effect – being honest about dishonesty.

The language of sisterhood is an underworld argot in her novels. To speak it (to be spoken by it) you have to collude in treachery. Explicitly, treachery to 'morality', citizenship, and other elevated ideals ('We live at floor level, washing and wiping. If we look upward, it's not towards the stars of the ineffable, it's to dust the tops of windows');[3] treachery, too, towards the notion of fiction as a metalanguage that should strive to be accomodating, celebratory, patient, inclusive . . . . This makes Weldon herself a traitor to certain kinds of literary sisterhood, especially women realists in the nurturing, matriarchal mould. On the one hand her plots are invariably partisan and have female characters centre-stage (this is what distinguishes her kind of 'world' from those of Murdoch, say, or Drabble); and on the other she refuses to see women as experts in continuity or communion, and here she parts company with Marilyn French, who makes of women a moral minority.

Weldon's very briskness, her impatient and mocking manner-isms, her shameless appropriations and her slapstick plots all call into question the *solidity* of fiction. She insults work – work, that is, in the sense of piling up detail and transcribing the processes of living. This seems to be because she sees description as invention in disguise. We flatter ourselves when we pretend that the 'crazy culture' (*Praxis*, p. 253) deserves to be dignified as a vale of soul-making. Not all the washing, wiping, scrubbing and dusting in the world will make you whole. Her women (like her men) live out roles they've sold themselves, including 'the fulfilling of other people's needs . . . the sense of self-righteousness' (*Praxis*, p. 256) that have made the realist novel so congenial. Her heroine Praxis is a special case only because she enacts the contradictions in exaggerated, emblematic fashion, performing a set of confidence tricks on herself. In one of her several lives, for instance, she flourishes in a high-powered job in advertising, selling domestic appliances and (naturally) domesticity – '"God made her a woman," she wrote blissfully, "love made her a mother – with a little help from electricity!"' (p. 218). At the same time, she exhausts herself at home in order to sustain the illusion that (being a good women) she doesn't go out to work. Weldon's own career in advertising obviously sharpened her sense of how thoroughly people are sold 'nature' (she worked on 'rather cosmic things like eggs and milk'). Indeed, her characters sometimes sound as though they are shaking off the effects of a particularly successful campaign on behalf of Biology:

> It's nature that makes us love our children, clean our houses, gives us a thrill of pleasure when we please the home-coming male.
> Who is this Nature?
> God?
> Or our disposition, as laid down by evolutionary forces, in order to best procreate the species . . . ?
> Nature does not know best, or if it does, it is on the man's side . . . .
>
> It seems to me that we must fight nature tooth and claw. (pp. 146–7)

The very look of her writing on the page, with its exaggerated paragraphing and suggestive use of blank space, announces a didactic design – parody-ad, parody-catechism.

Writing copy against Nature, Weldon privileges first persons and the present tense. The logic behind this should by now be fairly clear: the past tense has a tendency to conspire with Nature, rooting 'now' in 'then'; and third persons fit in with the same rhetoric, since they give individuals a continuous identity *from outside*. So we dignify unfreedom. One's context is a material condition, but with metaphysical overtones – it's 'there', ineluctably, and from it one borrows a 'nature' (compare Marilyn French: 'not the stuff of fiction'). Weldon's novels do of course describe blood ties and the pressures of the past, but their meaning is unsettled, they have no ontological priority. Witness Praxis unravelling her account of her mother:

> We are the sum of our pasts, it is true . . . but a memory is a chancy thing, experience experienced, filtered coarse or fine according to the mood of the day, the pattern of the times . . . .
>
> Was my mother in a strait-jacket, a real tangible, canvas strait-jacket, or is this merely how I envisage her? Do I pinion her in fact as she was pinioned in her mind . . . ? (p. 81)

This kind of mirror-effect ('experience experienced') reveals the past as structured by the present, as well as the other way around.

Similarly, Weldon's intercutting of narrative with polemic breaks up the sense of continuity, and deprives 'backgrounds' of their moral authority.

Not that her novels always deploy the same formula – but whether there are multiple first persons (*Remember Me*, 1976) or one looking back (*Praxis*), the effect is to isolate what I've called 'matriarchal' realism as an episode, or one kind of destiny, rather than a governing paradigm. Thus Chloe in *Female Friends* starts off despising women who aren't part of her own rich, reproductive text – 'Poor little Marjorie . . . . Childless, deprived of those pilferings into past and future with which the rest of us, more fertile, more in the steady stream of generation, enrich our lives'[4] – but arrives at the sardonic, self-knowing accents of the underworld. As Praxis points out, most women are left alone with themselves, or other women, in the end (if not a lot sooner). Her history is made up of a series of roles – domestic drudge, part-time prostitute, suburban hostess, metropolitan superwoman, feminist convert and mercy-killer; indeed the part she plays for most of the novel, an old woman dying, is itself discarded at the end: 'My skin is already better, my eyes are brighter, my hair is almost thick. I am not nearly so old as I had assumed' (p. 282). Such discontinuities are compounded by Weldon's use of flashbacks; and by the prominence of dialogue, which is sometimes set out as in a script for performance:

> OLIVER: Tell me about yourself.
> CHLOE: There's nothing to tell.
> He believes her.[5]

Other texts are punctuated by voices saying 'Listen' or, simply, 'Now'.

All of these devices work to translate life-histories into a form of picaresque. That is, the characters' lives are seen as episodic, opportunist, short-sighted; they live on their wits, and often at each others' expense, even when they seem to themselves (like Chloe) to be borne along by 'the steady stream of generation'. In fact motherly women are accused remarkably often of taking over other women's children (and sometimes husbands) in this beggarly economy. Sisterhood is founded in the recognition of mutual wrong; and by a logical if shocking progression, bad, superficial women who openly barter their assets and travel light (Helen and Grace in *Female Friends*, Irma in *Praxis*) become anti-heroines, because they at least don't mystify the means of survival. If there is an underlying, all-purpose Weldon plot, it consists in uncovering the adventuress in the most outwardly stable, even matronly character, and so revealing her and her seeming 'others' as sisters under (or perhaps merely 'in') the skin. It's a plot about living in the present, and possibly its oddest embodiment is the haunting in *Remember Me*, where Madeleine, dismembered in a road accident, invades the text from the mortuary.

The Gothic trappings give the underworld of women a fantasy dimension, and offer a further insult to the notion that living the way we do is natural. Weldon slides over into the idiom of haunted houses, possession, doubles and devilish inversions with mischievous ease: perhaps women have shadowed characters in any case? Madeleine, even when alive, is redundant, an ex-wife and manless (she dies driving back from a desperate assignation arranged through a dating agency), a thin, fierce, ragged female who subsists on hate, resentment and inadequate alimony in a gloomy basement:

> . . . . what is there left of Madeleine without her titles? . . .
>
> Oh, I am Madeleine, I am the first wife. . . . My house, my home, my life gone with my marriage. Myself left walking about the world, stripped of my identity.[6]

Her unwanted presence ('the ogre, the vampire', p. 46) lurks on the margins of nice people's world-pictures, in particular Lily's, since Lily the second wife has supplanted her, and is bent on being the model mother, sex-object and housekeeper Madeleine never was. Refusing to die is (though more extreme) like refusing to be silent or hide oneself away. Madeleine won't accept her social death: she rants on.

The 'medium' for her posthumous career is Margot, complete with all the titles ('daughter, wife, mother', p. 34), the book's self-effacing matron, who once shared a moment's dangerous complicity with Madeleine – 'A manic malice, momentary but there: felt like a contraction in her private parts' (p. 47) – and finds herself speaking with tongues, possessed by a spiteful, alien spirit, 'the very devil floating, as you might say, on the beam of interpersonal communication' (p. 50). There's authorial malice at work here too, signalled in the coy aside, 'as you might say', which reveals Weldon in the process of cross-breeding the jargon of social therapy ('interpersonal communication') with Hammer-movie horrors. Giving the Margot character the role of spokeswoman for her opposite is a way of serving her right for being so useful and suppressing her own devils; also for having, as it turns out, slept with Madeleine's husband herself once upon a time. One way or another, people invade each other's private parts. The plot's elaborate machinery lays Madeleine to rest by making space for her 'spirit' in the lives of those who betrayed her, including Lily's. The Gothic conventions provide a handy framework for accomodating characters who are dismembered, obsessed, imaginatively homeless. Weldon in fact reworked the plot of *Remember Me*, first for television, then as a short story, 'Watching Me, Watching You', for *Women's Own* in 1981. Here the usurping second wife, supplanted by a third, realises that the ghost that's been troubling her for years was her present sadder and wiser self – '"What I sensed was myself now, looking back; me now watching me then"'.[7] And she joins the first wife in her basement flat.

Is there more to Weldon's Gothic than a set of convenient metaphors? In a sense not: the point about such devices is that, unlike realist schemes, they announce their own flamboyant and ramshackle fictionality. Rewriting the domestic scene as a haunted house is thus two gestures at once – a black-comic joke about 'redundant', underworld women; and a reflexive comment on the novel form. Her texts, that is, demolish while they build. They are improvised structures – and this links them with much more obviously metamorphic fictions by other writers in this chapter, Angela Carter, or Joyce Carol Oates. Weldon's 1983 novel *The Life and Loves of a She-Devil* is perhaps most suggestive in this connection, since it stages a confrontation between genres – Gothic versus romantic fiction, hate story versus love story – and thus makes novelistic conventions themselves the protagonists.

Or to put it another way, the characters here are authors: not only blonde, petite, pretty Mary Fisher, who's a best-selling romantic novelist, herself a heroine of her own imagining; but also Ruth Patchett, whose husband Mary steals, and whose transformation from huge, clumsy, apologetic housewife to vengeful demon releases a flood of inspiration. Ruth becomes horribly inventive. Her journey in disguise through the underworld of drudgery and the 'caring professions' to sabotage the story of love triumphant is a viciously funny advertisement for the criminal application of domestic skills. (Doris Lessing's *The Good Terrorist*, 1985, exploits the same subversive thought.) Her final invention, the creation of herself, via cosmetic surgery, as Mary Fisher's double, completes the book's mirror-imagery. Mary Fisher is dead by now and so in a sense is Ruth, having successfully called her world's bluff –

> . . . I have no place, so I must make my own, and since I cannot change the world, I will change myself.[8]

This is the most mutilating kind of satire: Ruth is caged in the patterns of reversion, her anger bottled up to render it the more explosive.

The bars of the cage are cash and power. Weldon's worldliness in this regard is a further side-effect of demolishing the novel as home, as 'women's room'. In *The Life and Loves of a She-Devil*, women are, as it were, the suburbanites of the human race. The opening setting, 'Eden Grove', with its brand-new houses, half-grown trees, domestic seclusion and large-scale consumption of tranquillisers and Mary Fisher novels, is a luxury ghetto where wives are insulated (for the moment) from material pressures and opportunities. It could be anywhere in the developed world – a small hoard of investments and consumer durables that can be converted back into money at any time, a haven of insecurity. When Ruth burns the house down, rather than waiting for her runaway accountant-husband to sell it, she's free to wander in the world's market place. As if to underline the moral, Weldon includes amongst her picaresque adventures a spell in a separatist, feminist commune (where they've broken all the mirrors), but has Ruth reject the refuge it offers: 'She wished to live in the giddy mainstream of the world, not tucked away in this muddy corner of integrity' (p. 200). That this episode was cut in the American edition of the novel provides an indication of Weldon's power to offend. (That she allowed it to be cut is perhaps itself a sign of her relative indifference to 'integrity'.)

She remains a didactic deconstructor. The novels push things to extremes in order to demonstrate the nature of the ordinary – that is, that it is only nature in the sense of the current state of play, not God-ordained. *The Cloning of Joanna May* (1989) fastens on nightmares about genetic experiment to rehearse her 'mainstream' moral. Joanna, discovering that she has been secretly cloned by her Frankensteinish ex-husband Carl, turns her crisis of identity into a bitter triumph. Like Mary Shelley's Frankenstein, he has got more than he bargained for, women (in this case) unhampered by superstitions about having an 'essential self'. He has invented co-conspirators and rival inventors:

> He stole my soul . . . . when they took that part of me, the singular me, away, and interfered, they stopped me in my tracks . . . . I felt the pleasure of it. I felt what it was to be Carl, and want to change the world . . . . I wanted to see what I would be . . . the ageing Empress: not devastating, frightening, shocking any more – just how very *interesting* to see how it all turned out. What fun it would be – that rare commodity.[9]

The cloning idea, too, gives a new twist to sisterhood ('We are divided amongst ourselves'), as well as a satiric image of ordinariness (we're cloned in any case by the pressures to conform and consume).

Frankenstein is an especially suggestive text because it deals in re-invention, and hence (no accident) has proved endlessly rewritable. Weldon's preoccupation with its central notion of radical surgery on the soul is part of the pattern of picking and choosing your literary ancestors, and cultivating unnatural hypotheses. She too is a re-inventor, and one of the things she has changed is the image of the women writer. Her work is bold, schematic, often sketchy, frequently 'nasty', and singularly free from the need to be liked or approved of. The voices that get onto her pages – 'See how easily it comes to me to turn from "I" to "she" – joining my lot with other women, universalising an experience, as if to justify myself'[10] – all have a hint of the author about them; but this works in the opposite direction too, to make the author into a series of characters, a picaresque figure who lives hand to mouth, by her wits.

MARGARET ATWOOD

To live in prison is to live without mirrors. To live without
mirrors is to live without the self. She is living selflessly, she
finds a hole in the stone wall and on the other side of the wall,
a voice. The voice comes through darkness and has no face.
This voice becomes her mirror.

(Margaret Atwood, *Marrying the Hangman*
from *Two-Headed Poems*, 1978)

In 1972, with *Surfacing*, Margaret Atwood seemed suddenly to
stand for women, Canadianness, and a mystical return to wild
nature. As things turned out, none of this was exactly the case –
in fact, her *timeliness* was the sub-text, her capacity to impersonate
the moment's heroine, rather as Doris Lessing had in *The Golden
Notebook*. And like Lessing, Atwood registered some dismay at the
novel's reception. Her next book (*Lady Oracle* in 1976) was a comic
narrative about a writer of costume Gothics who becomes a guru
on the side and by accident. It's designed to turn 'the author' into a
multiple personality. Joan Foster alias Louisa K. Delacourt has faked
suicide in order to get out from under her 'visionary' identity, and
contemplates with distaste her posthumous success:

Sales of *Lady Oracle* were booming, every necrophiliac in the
country was rushing to buy a copy.
   I'd been shoved into the ranks of those other unhappy ladies,
scores of them apparently, who'd been killed by a surfeit of
words. There I was, on the bottom of the death barge where
I'd once longed to be, my name on the prow, winding my way
down the river. . . . I began to feel that even though I hadn't
committed suicide, perhaps I should have. They made it sound
so plausible.[1]

She has become a 'culture heroine' (p. 286): can she survive?
Joan/Louisa's fear is that her *book* has killed her – frozen her
in an impossible posture of truth-telling. *Lady Oracle* is a way
of staging the resurrection of a mutated author, someone who is
not *the* author at all, someone who wants 'to have more than one
life' (p. 141). Atwood was anticipating certain large-scale shifts in
feminist theory. In 1977, in her Introduction to the Virago paperback
edition of *Surfacing*, Francine du Plessis Grey was still celebrating

Atwood as 'a prophet in her own country', a female mystic turning
to nature as to a nunnery, 'a refuge from the patriarchal order'.[2]
Over the following years, though, positions have changed roughly
in line with *Lady Oracle's*, so that Coral Ann Howells, in her 1987
study of Canadian women novelists, *Private and Fictional Words*,
finds that what female and Canadian identities have in common
is 'an awareness of instability' – '[Atwood] has moved through and
beyond the primitivist myth of wilderness'.[3]

Retreating ahead of her critics, Atwood establishes a characteristic
pattern of self-division. For instance, her plots often supply the nar-
rator/heroine with a best friend who's wild, irreverent, swaggering
and – usually – a comedian (Ainsley in *The Edible Woman*, Jocasta in
Bodily Harm, Moira in *The Handmaid's Tale*). These characters are, I'd
argue, narrative traces of the novelist's split. They raise questions
about the relation between inside and outside views, 'I' and 'she',
author and character (and reader). In her most recent novel, *Cat's
Eye* (1989), this relationship is for once in the foreground, and loses
its comic-sub-plot lightness:

> I could give her something you can never have, except from
> another person: what you look like from outside. A reflection.
> This is the part of herself I could give back to her.
>
> We are like twins in old fables, each of whom has been given
> half a key.[4]

Atwood's preoccupied here with women as the mirror to each other,
each other's measure of reality. In the background, more or less
taken for granted by now, is the assumption that you can't define
yourself any longer in simple opposition to patriarchal attitudes, the
Gothic victim. *Cat's Eye* is the story of a woman painter's family
tree – the family tree that the *painter* descends from – and in it the
role of Cordelia, her childhood best friend (and worst enemy) is the
central one. Cordelia teaches her, by nearly killing her, the skills of
survival. She's 'the other woman' in an entirely new guise, the one
who comes between you and the old scenario of imprisonment in a
man's world.

This man's world for Atwood had in any case an odd remoteness
about it. Like Christina Stead, she was brought up by a father who
was a naturalist. He appears in the fiction (a daemon in *Surfacing*,
an eccentric in *Cat's Eye*) as obsessed with extinction. Here he is in
her short story 'In Search of the Rattlesnake Plantain':

My father has a list in his head of things that are disappearing: leopard frogs, certain species of wild orchid, loons, possibly. These are just the things around here. The list for the rest of the world is longer . . . . I have lived with this list all my life, and it makes me uncertain about the solidity of the universe.[5]

His legacy is just this loss of 'solidity', plus the ubiquitous Atwood survivalist vocabulary. It's as though he absents himself long before his death, leaving behind a world without secure landmarks, only fugitive memories of an early childhood spent on wilderness trails. Family life in the novels is always in the past, and even then a nomadic affair; the love-and-marriage plot seems never to have had any plausibility for her heroines, even when, as in her first novel *The Edible Woman* (1969), they can't imagine anything else to do. It's not that patriarchy has gone away, rather that its structures are altogether more distant and bleak, not domesticated in the form of realist plots nor, *Surfacing* apart, Gothic ones. To put it simply, the young men in her novels are generally inept, fake or childish, and the love-and-marriage plot is replaced by the stark Darwinian choice of extinction (suicide) or babies.

The nameless heroine of *Surfacing*, of course, all but conflates the two, disintegrating herself into stone, fur, gristle and godhead in the wilderness. Culture belongs to the enemy – 'Everything from history must be eliminated, the circles and the arrogant square pages'[6] – and is corrupt all through, a process of sorting, labelling, representing and denaturing the things and creatures of the world. One of the book's most thrilling and dizzying sensations is the sense that it's stripping away its own props, that any moment there'll be no words left:

In one of the languages there are no nouns, only verbs held for a longer moment.
The animals have no need for speech, why talk when you are a word I lean against a tree, I am a tree leaning . . . I am not an animal or a tree, I am the thing in which the trees and animals move and grow, I am a place. (p. 181)

But there are the words, waiting in readiness. This language of Nature – the language of a space, a ground or womb – is disturbing in two ways at once: first because it clashes the Godhead ('I am') against matter ('the thing'); and secondly because it's proclaiming with triumph the rediscovery of a banal truth, woman as a word in someone else's language (Nature, or Earth, or Silence).

Atwood's own revisionary reading of such passages in *The Handmaid's Tale* fifteen years on provides an ironic commentary. In the dystopia of Gilead women are 'two-legged wombs', all biological function with no outside life:

> I sink down into my body as into a swamp, fenland, where only I know the footing. Treacherous ground, my own territory. I become the earth I set my ear against, for rumours of the future . . . . I'm a cloud congealed around a central object . . . . inside it is a space, huge as the sky at night and dark and curved . . . . [7]

You realise that the words by themselves don't signal the horrors of Gilead. Out of context this could be the timeless language of gravid Nature (as her Commander says, 'All we've done is return things to Nature's norm', p. 232). What Atwood has done is situate this female space in a containing culture that legislates it. In *Surfacing* those surroundings are obscured.

Other revisionary gestures extend the argument with herself. The mirrors are all broken in *Surfacing*, because they multiply images, imitations, outsides. The heroine sees her friend Anna as a monster of unreality, a sixties odalisque brainwashed by reflections:

> Rump on a packsack, harem cushion . . . . a seamed and folded imitation of a magazine picture that is itself an imitation of a woman who is also an imitation, the original nowhere . . . . She copulates under strobe lights with the man's torso while his brain watches from its glassed-in control cubicle . . . . (p. 165)

In fundamentalist Gilead the essentialism that underlies this arrogant picture of Anna (it comes out of Plato's *Republic* and his *Laws)* is acted out and on display, in the terrorist state that identifies women with their inner space, their natural function.[8] It's the collaborator-Aunts, in *The Handmaid's Tale* who warn that 'To be seen – to be *seen* – is to be . . . penetrated' (p. 39), and it's Moira in the brothel, dressed in a Playboy Bunny's discarded skin, who offers solace and support and a saving reflection – the other woman. There's even a mischievous, nostalgic praise of women's magazines (long banned and burned): 'they suggested an endless series of possibilities, extending like the reflections in two mirrors . . . replica after replica . . . . ' (p. 165). The point here is not mainly, or only, that Atwood has shifted her ground (though she has), but that such shifts are symptomatic of the 'homeless' woman writer. Each novel faces over again the task of finding a perspective. 'What I need is perspective,' says Offred bitterly in *The Handmaid's Tale*, 'The illusion of depth . . . . otherwise you live in the moment. . . . Live in the moment, make the most of it ' (p. 153). The trick is to live in the moment unreconciled.

Life Before Man (1979) applies her special kind of perspective to materials that might have been the stuff of a solidly realist novel. An adulterous triangle in middle-class Toronto is set against a background of pre-history (the two women work in the Museum) and cunningly transposed into the idiom of fossils and taxidermy. The characters are confronted with the spectre of the death of the 'species' to which they belong – that is, the class who (in a realist environment) are allowed to concentrate on their personal relationships, and inhabit their patch of time well-insulated from the chill winds that blow across the millennia. Here it's their monstrous, pathetic and ill-adapted traits that are on display: Nate's overgrown boyishness ('An evolutionary mistake, the doctor said, meaning his height')[9] and his doomed attempt to recapture his innocence by giving up the law to become a toymaker; Lesje's day-dreams of a world before people ('tranquil seas, gentle winds, the immense fur-covered pteranodons soaring like wisps of white cotton', p. 238); Elizabeth's cold WASP-ish lust for real life, in the shape of her lover Chris, who seems 'archaic, indigenous, authentic' (p. 160) but isn't, and who commits suicide before the book begins. Nearly everyone contemplates suicide, but in a sense it would be a redundant gesture, they're coming apart in any case, and can hardly summon enough conviction to make the most ordinary of plots work: 'marriage is an event . . . . So is divorce. They create a framework, a beginning, an ending. Without them everything is amorphous, an endless middle ground stretching like a prairie on either side of each day' (p. 192).

Not that it's a structureless book, much the reverse. It's simply that the structure is a web of metaphors invented for the occasion, in order to focus on Life After Man rather than Before. Man, that is, in the sense of the synthesis that's called human. Lesje wonders whether the child she's conceived (rather than killing herself) might turn out to be 'a throwback, a reptile, a mutant of some kind with scales and a little horn on the snout' (p. 293), and sounds rather pleased with the idea. Some evolutionary quirk or miracle may (compare Angela Carter's rebirth sequence in *The Passion of New Eve*) unravel the cells and come to a better arrangement, given that the notion we're all members of the same species seems to be wearing so thin. When the characters in *Life Before Man* look back a generation or two they find their forebears shooting off in all directions (Finnish, Latvian, Jewish, Mennonite): they're supposed, on a synthesising view, to see themselves as somehow having ingested and unified all this into Canadianness, but the effect is the opposite, a sense of exploding personal universes. In *Cat's Eye* the painter-narrator does a portrait of her three Muses: a Scottish teacher, a Jewish neighbour, an Indian research student. The effect of Atwood's long-sighted perspective is to create the illusion not that she's writing *out* of a place or an identity, but that she's looking into one.

She has been making her own places on the page, inventing or borrowing alien perspectives – the political thriller's conventions in *Bodily Harm* (1982) (where Rennie 'feels as if she's returning after a space trip, a trip into the future');[10] the futurist dystopia in *The Handmaid's Tale* – in order to reflect on the present. Which is the present of the reader – 'I tell, therefore you are,' says Offred, parodying the grand Cartesian cogito, I think, therefore I am. Her narrative is a way of persuading herself that there's life outside Gilead, that an unknown reader or listener is her 'mirror': 'You don't tell a story only to yourself. . . . A story is like a letter' (p. 49); 'Because I am telling you this story I will your existence' (p. 279). She doesn't much resemble author-gods, nor indeed lady oracles. Gilead's creators, the patriarchal Commanders, have Plato and the Bible on their side, her own style is of necessity different, the style of a prisoner without reflections ('to live without reflections is to live without the self'). Moira supplies that part inside the text, the reader outside. But which reader? The 'Historical Notes' at the end show Offred's transcribed tape being received as an unsatisfactory document by a jovial scholar who cracks Chaucerian jokes (tale/tail) and laments with some eloquence the fact that 'voices may reach us . . . but what they say to us is imbued with the obscurity of the matrix out of which they come' (p. 324). Another reader might wonder whether it's not also the 'obscurity' of the world into which they go that's the problem.

There's an episode in the *Tale* that has some bearing on this, where Offred is smuggled into her Commander's study for an illicit game of Scrabble. Sex-for-procreation is obligatory, word-games are forbidden, and so Scrabble acquires a predictable but nonetheless enthralling erotic charge:

> The feeling is voluptuous. This is freedom, an eyeblink of it. *Limp*, I spell. *Gorge*. What a luxury. The counters are like candies . . . . The letter C. Crisp, slightly acid on the tongue, delicious. (p. 149)

Words and money are the crucial deprivations for women in Gilead. They are the means of exchange that give you a convertible identity, and their loss produces an almost unbearable nostalgia for the past, our messy present ('I want everything back the way it was', p. 132). It's a nostalgia for the kind of shared space that's represented by a game, or a marital row, the space of negotiable difference. Offred tells her story into this non-place, now, where 'the reader' is plural, heteroglot and partial (all that the rulers of Gilead deny). Atwood in her own person also has something to say on this topic:

> . . . it matters how old you are . . . and whether you're male or female, or from Canada or India. There is no such thing as a truly universal literature, partly because there are no truly universal readers. It is my contention that the process of reading is part of the process of writing, the necessary completion without which writing can hardly be said to exist.[11]

There's an obvious paradox here – that the matching-up of partial reader and partial writer can produce a fake universal, a culture of sameness. For her idea of 'completion' to work, Atwood needs the reader to be some kind of outsider with whom she can trade meanings.

Hence, I think, the role of 'the other woman', and indeed Atwood's ongoing argument with herself as author. Cordelia in *Cat's Eye* is a figure who's 'mimicking something, something in her head, some role or image that only she can see'.[12] She is, it turns out, mediating the patterns of authority in her family, passing on her fear of her father in the form of cruelty and emotional torture. But she's also the one the 'I' struggles *with*, changes places *with* – 'Cordelia is afraid of me, in this picture . . . . I'm afraid of being Cordelia. Because in some way we changed places . . . . ' (p. 227). Cordelia drags her out of subjective space, makes her fit to survive. You can translate this into the anti-essentialism argument: the important thing is to trade with the world outside, the culture of mimicry is where you find models of difference. It is, perhaps, because Atwood's clearly so attracted to the nunnery – to the refuge of inner space – that she is so cunning in her schemes for escaping from it. She's her own most intimate enemy. Her critics have mostly concentrated either on her oracular moments, or on her rewriting of traditional genres, but it's her re-writing of herself that's most interesting. One shouldn't take her abdications too literally – they are part of a pattern of deaths and resurrections, a way of surviving as an author through the artificial miracle of mutation.

ANGELA CARTER

> A universal cast of two-headed dogs, dwarfs, alligator men, bearded ladies and giants in leopard-skin loin cloths reveal their singularities in the sideshows and, wherever they come from, they share the sullen glamour of deformity, an inter-nationality which acknowledges no geographic boundaries. Here, the grotesque is the order of the day.
>
> (Angela Carter, 'The Loves of Lady Purple', *Fireworks*, 1974)

Angela Carter's fiction makes a new map of the realm of alterneity. She began her writing career as a connoisseur of 1960s cults of 'otherness', and was never inclined to think of fantasy (the grotesque, the fabulous) as simply oppositional – a return of the repressed, a kind of annexe to the solid novel. The world of outsiders is not, for her, either so securely marginal, or so confined as that. Her writing, in short, unravels the romance of exclusion. And this means it's in an oblique and sometimes mocking relation to the kind of model of female fantasy deployed by Gilbert and Gubar in *The Madwoman in the Attic* – where fantasy is a matter of writing against the patriarchal grain. You realise, in fact, that feminist literary history habitually attributes to 'madness' and marginality a rather suspect status. Not only are the 'Gothic' women cunning subversives, they're also *virtuous* because they didn't construct their prison. Carter's novels and stories start with more sophisticated assumptions, in a setting where the structures of power (literary and otherwise) are a lot less obvious.

Her early novels are fables about fake freedom. Wittily – cruelly – she held the mirror up to 1960s narcissism, framing a culture that was in any case already obsessed with appearances. The effect is at once spell-binding and mocking. A bleak eroticism pervades the whole scene, people have a patina like objects, and indeed objects take on a covetable, collectable air. We are in the world of the second-hand trade, where the inherited stuff of the past - clothes, furniture, imagery, ideas – is reassembled in travesty. The thread of a *necessary* history seems to have run out. The present is all, and all performance; any utterance or gesture shades over into pastiche. The titles of the first three books, *Shadow Dance* (1965), *The Magic Toyshop* (1967) and *Several Perceptions* (1968), announce these themes succinctly. Their plots move from one tableau to another, 'still' after 'still', quickened into movement by a kind of optical illusion – as in a flicker book, or of course a film. And the result is a powerful focus on the sexual fix. Sex is everywhere, and yet nowhere.

Partly this is to do with a breach of that time-honoured specular convention by which female figures alone are fully objectified. John Berger in *Ways of Seeing*, on nudes in paintings, spelt out this relationship with laudable plainness:

> . . . *men act* and *women appear*. Men look at women. Women watch themselves being looked at.[1]

In Carter's novels, the young men are described as erotic objects; not in the romance fashion (dark, active, strong – all signs of 'soul', since women in romances are 'looking' for love), but as self-regarding arrangements of flesh, pigments, clothes, smells and sidelong glances. This is Finn in *The Magic Toyshop*:

> . . . longish, bright red hair hanging over the collar of a dark blue, rather military looking jacket . . . . His clothes had the look of strays from a parish poor-box. His face was that of Simple Ivan in a folk-tale, high cheek-bones, slanting eyes. There was a slight cast in the right eye, so that his glance was disturbing and oblique. He breathed through his slack-lipped mouth, which was a flower for rosiness . . . . [2]

Finn joins adolescent heroine Melanie in the realm of narcissism. The plot makes both of them puppets of the nightmare toy-maker and

patriarch Uncle Philip, and so gives them a shared if shaky reality –
toys who rebel, objects who insist on being subjects. Possibly Finn's
obliquity (that squint, which means you can never meet his eye)
preserves for him a dying glimmer of male mystique; however, his
'regard' does nothing for Melanie's sense of who she is. Once the
tyrannous patriarch is foiled, the two of them are subject to a horrid
vertigo. Uncle Philip gave a meaning to sex roles by his grotesque,
pantomimic maleness. Without him Melanie and Finn are possibly
not *different* enough to make the happy ending convincing:

> They looked at each other . . . . she saw herself in the black pupils
> of his squint. 'My face in thine eye, thine in mine appears,
> And true plaine hearts doe in the faces rest.' John Donne,
> 1572–1632 . . . . In the school poetry book . . . . How all the
> young girls loved John Donne. And John Donne thought souls
> mingled as the eyestrings twist together, tangling like the puppet
> strings . . . . She sat in Finn's face; there she was, mirrored twice.
> (p. 193)

Once upon a time male subjectivity lent a shadow of itself to the
chosen female; Finn, though, is only another denizen of the mirror.
The book's ending is full of quotations that act as ironic reminders
of a time when there were 'souls': these two confront each other in
'wild surmise' (a phrase from Keats's sonnet on Chapman's Homer)
in a dark garden with shades of paradise lost.

There's a recurrent Carter plot from these years which, if you
translated it into more or less realistic terms, would go like this:
a middle-class virgin bewitched and appalled by the fictions of
femininity falls in love with a working-class boy, a dandified,
dressed-up tramp who's meant to make sense of her desires, but
doesn't. Marianne in *Heroes and Villains* – the heroines often have
names that are double, to fit their brittle, mirrored personalities –
makes a speech which bitterly arraigns the charm of the new-style
homme fatal:

> ' . . . you with your jewels, paints, furs, knives and guns, like a
> phallic and diabolic version of female beauties of former periods.
> What I'd like best would be to keep you in preserving fluid in a
> huge jar on the mantelpiece of my peaceful room, where I could
> look at you and imagine you . . . . You, you're nothing but the
> furious invention of my virgin nights.'[3]

This novel's patriarch, the shambling guru Donnally who cynically supplies Marianne with a wedding dress and a ritual role, isn't of course the real threat. That comes with the demystification of the hero. In *Love* (written in 1969, published in 1971, revised and reissued in 1987), the theme of sexual fixation plays itself out with cold brilliance, like the last act in a firework display.

The backdrop is a municipal park, once the landscaped garden of a great house, only its follies still standing to mark out Classical south and Gothic north, though its gates are still in place:

> . . . a massive pair of wrought-iron gates decorated with cherubs, masks of beasts, stylised reptiles and spearheads from which the gilding flaked, but these gates were never either open or closed. They hung always a little ajar and drooped from their hinges with age; they served a function no longer for all the railings round the park were gone long ago and access everywhere was free and easy.[4]

This studied and beautifully ominous opening description marks the threshold of a place of ambivalence. The lord of this manor is long-departed, and our trespasses will neither be forbidden nor forgiven. Inside and outside, self and other, lose their definition. The central love-triangle composed of Annabel, her husband Lee and his dark, deranged half-brother Buzz, is a fight to the death over this amorphous space. They construct their selves, cannibalistically, out of each other, and inscribe their meanings on each other's flesh. Lee seems the most innocent of the three, though that is because he is the most thoroughly narcissistic:

> Lee looked like Billy Budd, or a worker hero of the Soviets, or a boy in a book by Jack London . . . . he had become self-conscious very young in life and so profoundly aware of the effect of his remarkable appearance on other people that, by the age of twenty, he gave the impression of perfect naturalness, utter spontaneity and entire warmth of heart. (p. 12)

Moreover his point of view is privileged by the authorial voice, whereas Annabel ('When she told him her name . . . [Lee] knew at once she was middle-class' p. 15) and Buzz are described in terms of the alien ways they perceive the world. Buzz sees through a camera lens, 'everything at second hand, without depths . . . . he was surrounded by frozen memories of the moment of sight' (p. 25). For Annabel, who carries her imagery home from art school and plasters it on the walls, Lee is 'at first . . . a herbivorous lion, later . . . a unicorn devouring raw meat' (p. 34):

> . . . it hardly occurred to her the young man was more than a collection of coloured surfaces and she had never learned to think of herself as a living actor anyway. (p. 30)

Their intimacy is a mutual violation, like intercourse between creatures from different species: 'she gazed at him with wonder, as if he might be magic, and he looked at her nervously, as if she might not be fully human' (p. 34). Ironically, this distance derives from the very thing that brings them together, their lack of purchase in the world, in which they are alike ('as though both could say of the world: "We are strangers here"', p. 17). Sexual love, though, depends on a certain complementarity (a *domesticated* difference, you might say), which these two can't contrive. They are at once too different and too similar ('strangers'), and their love-making estranges them further. Buzz compounds the obscenity ('they often woke in the morning to find him perched on the end of the bed, clicking away', p. 25).

The marriage comes to a bitter end with a 'mutual rape' (p. 97) which demolishes Lee's good opinion of himself and perfects Annabel's despair. Her final gesture (compare Fay Weldon's she-devil – 'since I cannot change the world, I will change myself') is to make herself over into a parody-woman (a blonde, painted doll) and then, by a logical extension, a dead one:

> . . . she could not draw anything any more and so was forced to make these imaginative experiments with her own body which were now about to culminate, finally, in erasure. (p. 103)

It's a nastily plausible conclusion, rendered all the more disturbing by the narrative's refusal to blame Lee (or even the horrible Buzz). Carter's 1987 revisions to the text are interesting in this connection. She remarks wryly in her Afterword on 'its almost sinister feat of male impersonation' (p. 113); she has also deleted several passages which in the original made Lee Annabel's victim. For example:

'since he loved her, he did not wish to believe his occasional intuitions that she was obscurely calculating and malign';[5] and 'She filled him with revulsion; her curiously pointed teeth might be those of a vampire' (p. 107). In 1971, Annabel 'slavered' kisses on him in her final doomed attempt to force sex to have a meaning, whereas in 1987 she 'lavished' them, and so on. The effect of these changes is to diminish the amount of subjective sympathy Lee is allowed, and so reinforce what was anyway the original implication: that 'the hero' has no power to redeem. Lacking that power he loses his moral meaning, and can't uphold the opposition between light and dark, good magic and bad – 'He thought a door must either be open or closed . . . . '[6]

Carter has fun in her 1987 Afterword, sketching futures for the surviving characters of *Love*. However, she'd already put the cast to work in the books between, where she explores a wealth of other ways of writing these themes – in (for example) the 'sleeping beauty' motif of *The Infernal Desire Machines of Dr Hoffman* (1972), where the prince is a bringer of death; in the authorial transvestism of *The Passion of New Eve* (1977), where male narrator Evelyn is remodelled *Frankenstein*-style as 'the *Playboy* center fold';[7] in the story of the vampire 'Lady of the House of Love' and the male virgin in *The Bloody Chamber* (1979). During these years she got more explicitly and systematically interested in narrative models that pre-date the novel: fairy tales, folk tales, and other forms that develop by accretion and retelling, like medieval allegories of love. The flicker-book technique develops into a journey from one imaginary locale to another, her world becomes more spacious and multifarious without in the least surrendering its surreal quality. The effect of this carnival of re-writing is to shift the narrative focus onto transformations, metamorphoses and exchanges of identity. She moves away – actually, she always had, so that one should say further away – from the notion of fantasy and the language of desire as *either* repressed *or* produced by some central patriarchal authority. The best description of the significance of such a move is probably that given by Michel Foucault in *The History of Sexuality*:

> The omnipresence of power: not because it has the privilege of consolidating everything under its invincible unity, but because it is produced from one moment to the next . . . . Power is everywhere; not because it embraces everything, but because it comes from everywhere.[8]

For Foucault there is no big binary opposition between (for example) 'law' and 'revolt'; but rather 'a plurality of resistances . . . resistances that are possible, necessary, improbable; others that are spontaneous, savage, solitary, concerted, rampant or violent; still others that are quick to compromise, interested, or sacrificial . . . . ' (p. 96). This conceptual 'plot', it seems to me, bears a striking resemblance to the narrative shapes Carter produces. Like Foucault, she is interested in locating 'matrices of transformations' (p. 99), telling stories that branch and subdivide to reveal continuously shifting definitions of character, gender and genre.

Her own contribution to cultural studies, *The Sadeian Woman* (1979) makes the same point in slightly different language – 'flesh comes to us out of history'; it is not changelessly natural.[9] It's an observation that, if taken seriously, ought to modify the way we think of history, as well as the way we think of sex. History, in other words, would take account of the changing strategies for fashioning selves. That is more Foucault's territory than Carter's of course, but her stories are richer because they acknowledge their own historicity, rather than appealing to 'timeless' fantasy. It remains true that, for her characters, there's no one *necessary* history, no solid, determining context. Instead, there are provisional, ambivalent structures – 'I'm in the demythologising business . . . . putting new wine in old bottles and, in some cases, old wine in new bottles'.[10] So, having started out anatomising fake freedom, she discovers a practical, creative freedom. As should be clear by now, it's a freedom to manoeuvre: opportunist, episodic and tactical, utopian perhaps, but not atopian. Her plots are altogether more self-consciously literary than Weldon's, but share the same picaresque feel. What it comes down to, perhaps, is imaginative mobility, the literary equivalent of being street-wise.

The Passion of New Eve is about melting the mirrors and setting symbols in motion. This assault on a vitrified culture has as its own central symbol a glass mansion where Hollywood goddess Tristessa St Ange has retired to brood on her immortality, a vulgar palace which revolves on its own axis like a roundabout; and which doubles as a mausoleum housing waxwork corpses (Jean Harlow, James Dean, Marilyn Monroe), with suggestions too of Sleeping Beauty's castle. The hybrid imagery – taken from fairy tales, fanzines, carnival and Gothic movies – is a fitting setting for the revelation that Tristessa's screen image was a monstrous masquerade. She is the world's most brilliant transvestite, a man who re-invented himself as the man's woman, and so contrived to be more tragically, narcissistically, essentially feminine than any woman born. Breaking his/her spell is the book's transparent design. However, this isn't a straightforward piece of iconoclasm. Carter insists that the only way to write oneself out of the labyrinth ('that hall of mirrors . . . the glass mausoleum that had been the world'),[11] is to take the mirror-images seriously. Here, that means reading doubleness 'back' into gender: 'new Eve' is surgically emasculated Evelyn, his/her marriage to Tristessa a complex and ecstatic travesty in which both play both parts. It's a scenario that's oddly reminiscent of the way the old Neo-Platonists read the myth of Narcissus. He drowned trying to embrace his own reflection in the water, they said, because he didn't love himself *enough*. That is, he didn't realise the source of the reflection. If he had, he'd have turned his mind round and freed himself.

New Eve takes a journey across a just-future United States that is disintegrating into ' a series of enormous solipsisms' (p. 167). Here, as often, Carter is describing a journey which is neither a flight nor a quest, but hints at both. The reason for this narrative ambivalence is that there's no going back to Nature. One of the book's 'solipsisms' is Beulah, the space-age Matriarchy where Evelyn becomes an 'artificial changeling' (p. 71) at the hands of self-appointed Goddess and plastic surgeon, Mother. She is a witty parody both of father-gods and earth-mothers, black and many-breasted and all her own work. Her followers have 'the look in their eyes of the satisfied Calvinist who knows he has achieved grace' (p. 79); and in this they resemble the book's other last-days sects, from the girls in the harem of the Manson-style guru Zero to the boy-scouts of the children's crusade. New Eve is endlessly on the run from these true believers, in search of an identity that can stay fluid and changeable. She finds 'herself' for a moment with the resurrected Tristessa; in the last scenes on the seashore she revisits Mother (by now 'a figure of speech', p. 184), and is treated to an extraordinary vision of beginnings, time unwinding, amber melting, birds and lizards converging in 'intermediate beings', an evolutionary movie run backwards. It's a suitably ambiguous last episode: new Eve is pregnant, yet still busy giving birth to herself; she is searching back in nature's womb for the kinds of 'monsters' (archaeopterix, and those other feathered-and-scaled, angelic-and-satanic intermediate beings) which have always been seen as unnatural, and are moreover extinct. She is looking for the future in the paths the past didn't take, and so becomes at the last an allegory for her author, who is also – increasingly – interested in freaks.[12]

The offspring of *New Eve* include the werewolves and wolf-girls of *The Bloody Chamber*, and Fevvers in *Nights at the Circus* (1984), a heavyweight Cockney trapeze artiste with wings, an 'intermediate being' with avengeance. Fevvers looks like a symbol for the undomesticated female imagination. She's hatched without parents towards the turn of the last century, brought up in a brothel, and thereafter evades the traps the world sets, escaping the cages of the 'real' (incarceration in a freak-show) by pretending to be an artificial bird-woman, a music-hall turn. Thus she levitates out of the clutches of classification, and the text escapes the gravitational pull of realism's settings, for this is a book with hardly any houses at all. The sheltering brothel is soon burned down (fictional arson seems to be becoming more widespread), and once we join the circus – a community where everyone is an outsider – the plot goes well and truly on the road, and divides into multiple sub-plots. Fevvers, however, proves to be both more and less than the symbol of potentiality the kindly Madam once saw in her – 'the pure child of the century that just now is waiting in the wings, the New Age in which no woman will be bound down to the ground'.[13] For one thing, the narrative insists on her physicality (indeed, she's not only material, but a materialist who knows about money); for another, she's garrulous on the topic of the significances people have tacked onto her – something no symbol can decently be.

Nights at the Circus is perhaps most radically picaresque in the way it refuses to settle down with labels – even the label 'freedom'. Early on in her adventures Fevvers is sold to a philosopher in search of eternal life, who sees in her a most satisfactory symbol of just about everything –

> 'Queen of ambiguities, goddess of in-between states. . . . virgin and whore, reconciler of fundament and firmament, reconciler of opposing states through the mediation of your ambivalent body . . . . ' (p. 77)

It's just as well that Fevvers has identified his school of thought ('H'm. This is some kind of heretical, possibly Manichean version of neo-Platonic Rosicrucianism, thinks I to myself', p. 77), since what he has in mind is sacrificing her on the altar of his beliefs. This episode strikes me as a kind of allegory against allegory – a warning that even adopting the most ambiguous of symbols still spells a rejection of living ambiguity. Women's images, of course, have traditionally been appropriated as signs for something else, witness the female figures (described, for instance, in Marina Warner's *Monuments and Maidens*, 1985) carved in stone to represent Truth or Justice or what have you, when actual women weren't supposed able to create or use such concepts for themselves.[14] Fevvers comes to recognise 'that shivering sensation which always visited her when mages, wizards, impresarios came to take away her singularity, as though they believed she depended on their imaginations in order to be herself. She felt herself turning, willy-nilly, from a woman into an idea' (p. 289).

On the other hand, she has to resist 'turning from a freak into a woman' (p. 283) too. Carter hovers between genres, savouring the feelings of vertigo produced by writing her way across the gap that has conventionally divided fantasy and realism. The book's tricks with time add to this fertile confusion:

'What we have to contend with here . . . is the long shadow of the *past historic* . . . that forged the institutions which create the human nature of the present in the first place.' (p. 240)

In other words, what we define as timeless ('human nature') hasn't that fixity or finality. Amongst Carter's pantheon of missing patriarchs, Father Time deserves an honourable mention, and indeed gets it here – '"Father Time has many children"' (p. 273), and not all of them are legitimate nor do they take after him.[15] Doubleness, self-division (not self-other division) and self-consciousness are the qualities that for her spell contemporaneity. You find space by teasing out the loose ends in the old stories, and then the loose ends in your own. . . . Her writing takes for granted not only the past constructedness of gender, but also its logical corollary – that it is continuously being constructed, not least in fiction. In this sense, we glamourise fantasy if we take it to be always 'in opposition'. Her most impressive achievement is to write fantasy which refuses to obey this time-honoured and insidious rule.

TONY MORRISON

> She was scared of being still, of not being busy, scared to
> have to be quiet, scared to have children alone . . . . She kept
> barking at him about equality, sexual equality, as though
> he thought women were inferior. He couldn't understand
> that . . . . His mother's memory was kept alive by those
> who remembered how she roped horses when she was a
> girl . . . . Anyone who thought women were inferior didn't
> come out of north Florida.
>
> (Toni Morrison, *Tar Baby*, 1981)

Matriarchal attitudes have a special place in black American mythology, rooted (that loaded word) in black history since slavery. In
Toni Morrison's *Beloved* (1987), which is set in the 1870s, murdered
Sixo is given a line about his lover that sums up with moving
brevity a good many of the meanings that cluster around the
black woman: '"The pieces I am, she gather them and give them
back to me in all the right order"'.[1] Sixo dies laughing, calling out
'Seven-Oh!', in the knowledge that he has cheated his owners and
killers because his woman is pregnant and has escaped with his
child. There's another message too, encoded in the person of the
speaker, even such an exemplary speaker as Sixo. Woman as the
bearer of continuity, the piecer-together, is a figure first of all in the
men's stories. Morrison's fiction gives male characters – whether
they're hunted, needy, footloose, wild, fearful or defiant – one point
of reference in common: the woman as their place, as home. This
figure they love or loathe according to their lights, but she's always
there.

So in *Tar Baby* (1981, and set in the present) Son, who's
'without human rites: unbaptized, uncircumcised, minus puberty
rites. . . . Unmarried, undivorced'[2] dreams of 'home . . . . That
separate place that was presided over by wide black women in
snowy dresses, and was ever dry, green and quiet' (p. 168).
Underground man and terrorist Gitar in *Song of Solomon* (1977)
despises and fears women on more or less the same grounds. They
are a place, a tie, a trap:

> "Everybody wants the life of a black man. Everybody. White
> men want us dead or quiet – which is the same thing as dead.
> White women, same thing. They want us, you know, 'universal,'

human, no 'race consciousness.' Tame, except in bed . . . .   And black women, they want your whole self. Love, they call it, and understanding . . . . but what they mean is, Don't go anywhere where I ain't. You try to climb Mount Everest, they'll tie up your ropes."[3]

Morrison's fiction includes many separate voices, and one product of that multiplicity is a strange unanimity on this point. Women, in men's stories, have continuity, and *are* continuity. They are what you define yourself in relation to (compare blacks and women in Kerouac's mythology, in the section on Joyce Johnson in Chapter 4) and their supposed immobility is thus a very relative matter. One last example, defeated Jude in *Sula* (1974): 'So it was rage, rage and a determination to take on a man's role anyhow that made him press Nel about settling down. He needed some of his appetites filled, some posture of adulthood recognised, but mostly he wanted someone to care about his hurt . . . .   The two of them together would make one Jude'.[4] These narratives inside the narrative reflect back on the woman-as-author. You might expect her – if she were acting like a matriarch on paper, writing novels that provided a home – to play the part of chronicler, piecing things together, but no. Morrison's narratives are spectacularly discontinuous, with time chopped up and voices in conflict – deliberate refusals to reproduce the world.

In other words, what I've been calling matriarchal realism (in the Anglo-American tradition, in any case more Anglo than American) turns into a peculiar provocation for the black American woman writer, since it's an aching truism. Morrison's poetical language has a worldly and sometimes satiric purpose. It acts against the myths that dignify black women by taking away their inventive powers. Her female characters aren't seen as bearing a natural burden of continuity, but as uncanny, slippery creatures who fit with the myths by default (they're so ambivalent they'd fit almost any paradigm). Their stories hang together by association, and are guilty of invention. Perhaps her most vivid and explicit version of a woman's uncanonical life (a portrait of the artist manqué) is *Sula*. The novel's eponymous anti-heroine is a pariah among pariahs, a black woman who won't play her part in the supportive conspiracy. Sula and her friend Nel share, as children, the hideous secret of the death of Chicken Little, who's swung around in a game by Sula on the river bank, lets go (is let go?) and drowns. Nel grows up and forgets, Sula (perhaps) remembers and becomes a 'loose' woman, an experimenter with life who's unconvinced of her vocation as mother-wife-lover:

> ' . . . When you gone to get married? You need to have some babies. It'll settle you.'
> 'I don't want to make somebody else. I want to make myself.'
> 'Selfish. Ain't no woman got no business floatin' around without no man.'
> 'You did.'
> 'Not by choice.'
> 'Mamma did.'
> 'Not by choice, I said. It ain't right . . . . '
>
> (pp. 85–6)

This exchange between Sula and her grandmother is an existentialist drama in miniature. Sula chooses herself, and so breaks down the fragile fiction by which (free) men are distinguished from the (stable) women they leave at home, whose loneliness is unchosen. '"I'm a woman and coloured. Ain't that the same as being a man?"' she asks nastily (p. 128). Though she's a good deal less sinister than her grandmother, who may have deliberately sacrificed a leg for the insurance money, and who certainly burns her junkie son to death ('There wasn't space for him in my womb. And he was crawlin' back . . . . so I just thought of a way he could die like a man', pp. 68–9), Sula becomes the black community's ritual outsider. People make sense of her, and preserve the decencies, by casting her as a witch, since a floating woman threatens everybody's sense of who they are. (Grandmother, by contrast, is a pillar of the place, self-mutilated, prepared to murder her son to uphold his manliness.)

Sula makes life up as she goes along, 'And like any artist with no art form, she became dangerous' (p. 110). In fact, the novel makes her an artist of sorts, a bitter, hilarious talker who says the unsayable: that black men, on their own account, are the envy of the world, their sex the object of white men's paranoia, white women's fascinated fear and coloured women's clinging need, 'And if that ain't enough, you love yourselves' (p. 95). She squanders her next-to-last breath on a carnival obscenity, a pariah vision of universal peace and satisfaction:

' . . . after all the black men fuck all the white ones; when all the white women kiss all the black ones; when the guards have raped all the jailbirds and after all the whores make love to their grannies; after all the faggots get their mothers' trim, when Lindbergh sleeps with Bessie Smith and Norma Shearer makes it with Stepin Fetchit; after all the dogs have fucked all the cats and every weathervane on every barn flies off to mount the hogs . . . then there'll be a little love left over for me. And I know just what it will feel like.' (p. 130)

The novel's final joke is to make pious Nel, years later, realise that she doesn't miss the husband Sula stole from her and discarded, but Sula herself, with whom she shares the secret of that long ago gratuitous act that let them know how accidental and contingent and absurd the world was.

There is a second plot in *Sula*, about crazed Shadrack, back from the First World War, who celebrates an annual Suicide Day to contain the murderous mayhem that's indelibly printed in his memory. Morrison multiplies and interweaves narratives that stay stubbornly separate: in *Song of Solomon*, the foreground story about roots, ancestry, tracing back names ('a name . . . given at birth with love and seriousness. A name that was not a joke, nor a disguise'),[5] belongs to the men, the sub-plot to the women. The magical patriarch in the legend flew back to Africa; his sons are still on the wing; and the women are still alone, whether they choose it like Sula or not. Every Morrison novel contains a love-affair (or hate-affair), a dialogue to the death, but only in *Tar Baby* is it a dialogue between the sexes. Elsewhere it's on the pattern set in her first book, *The Bluest Eye* (1970), where Pecola, a child herself, is impregnated by her father and disintegrates into merciful madness, talking to herself, imagining she's at last transformed into one of the blue-eyed dolls all blacks are supposed to covet. Dialogue is about the enemy within. To say it's white racism internalised is only partly true, because the most disturbing suggestion is that the inextricable, incestuous tangle of love and hate (however it came about) is as 'authentic' as you can get. Pecola, on this reading, is a figure without any stable identity, without *provenance* (nothing like incest to uproot the family tree). She's a figure of infinite regress – the fragile repository of others' meanings, herself her own child.

If the incest story is one travesty of the notion of woman-as-home, the infanticide story pushes the horrible logic yet further. *Beloved* starts with a haunted house ('124 was spiteful. Full of a baby's venom') that's a version of inner space, a place of safety which turns (as in the most frightening ghost stories) into a trap. It's a novel about possession: what you can possess, what possesses you, where the boundaries of self begin or end. Sethe and her living daughter live with the ghost of the daughter she murdered to make her safe, saving her from slavery and sacrificing her to the desperate possessive love that slavery engendered. Or that is one way of reading it. Morrison wants both to make the murder Sethe's act – her crime – and to see it as an act that comes out of history, so that Sethe is herself the victim, a suicide of sorts. Much of the book's complex time-shifting, the involuntary memories that visit Sethe, the feat of illusionism that materialises the ghost as a grown girl, have to do with blurring the distinction between material events and metaphysical propositions. This is how Sethe remembers the impulse to kill her children:

> Collected every bit of life she had made, all the parts of her that were precious and fine and beautiful, and carried, pushed, dragged them through the veil, out, away, over there where no one could hurt them . . . . (p. 163)

Paul D, a live survivor from the past who doesn't know her story, thinks to begin with that Sethe simply suffers the angry ghost in her house (a mere routine mystery and misery where 'Not a house in the country ain't packed to its rafters with some dead Negro's grief', p. 5), but he comes to revise his opinion:

> This here Sethe talked about love like any other woman . . . but what she meant could cleave the bone. This here Sethe talked about safety with a handsaw. This here new Sethe didn't know where the world stopped and she began. (p. 164)

Paul D's response is to call her act animal – '"You got two feet, Sethe, not four"' (p. 165) – echoing the slave-owner who drove them both to escape, who took a scientific interest in slave physiology. Morrison for her part takes a poet's interest, almost as shocking in its way. It's not obvious to her, either, that Sethe isn't a monster, or at any rate 'unnatural'.

The text's reflections on the meaning of barbarism recall the first western novel about slavery, Aphra Behn's *Oroonoko*, where the proud and princely slave of the title murders his pregnant wife, attempts suicide, and is preserved for a martyr's death at the hands of white-trash barbarians. Morrison's Sethe, of course, has to do it all herself – her husband Halle is missing, maddened, destroyed – and there is no martyrdom to atone for the murder. Unlike Oroonoko, she has been born into slavery, and her wild despair derives from the absence of possessions, of *self-possession*, that slavery engenders – 'men and women were moved about like checkers . . . . rented out, loaned out, bought up, brought back, stored up, mortgaged, won, stolen or seized' (p. 23).[6] The book's go-between and messenger, Stamp Paid, is given an elaborate and suggestive meditation on the way the whites have invented a new identity for blacks:

> Whitepeople believed that whatever the manners, under every dark skin was a jungle. Swift unnavigable rivers, swinging screaming baboons . . . . In a way, he thought, they were right. The more colouredpeople spent their strength trying to convince them how gentle they were . . . how human . . . the deeper the jungle grew inside. But it wasn't the jungle blacks brought with them to this place from the other (livable) place. It was the jungle white folks planted in them. And it grew. It spread. In, through and after life, it spread, until it invaded the whites who had made it. Touched them every one. Changed and altered them. Made them bloody, silly, worse than even they wanted to be, so scared were they of the jungle they had made . . . . (pp. 198–9)

This is the jungle Sethe inhabits ('you could hear its mumbling in places like 124', p. 199), and indeed it's inscribed on her skin, in the 'tree' of scars on her back – not a family tree, but the tangled sign of her owners' whips. Her savagery, her witchiness, her infanticide, her generation of ghosts are all jungle-bred, part of the slavery that is her history. So that her act is hers, and yet not hers. What she experiences is the nightmare of possession, in all the senses of that word except the self-reflexive one.

If you read *Beloved* this way, then the haunting and the magic have a terrible irony about them. Ghostly Beloved comes from 'the other side' (p. 213), but it's not some Africa of the spirit – or rather, it's impossible to distinguish what's vision and race-memory from the white folks' jungle. Beloved closes the house off from the world outside ('"This is the place I am"', p. 123), and offers Sethe an ecstasy of recognition and belonging: 'I am not separate from her   there is no place where I stop' (p. 210); 'my dark face is close to me   I am not dead   I am not   there is a house' (p. 213). The three-part choric dance of voices in which ahe, her sister and her mother come together, and the words arrange themselves unpunctuated on the page, has a key word – 'Mine':

> You are mine
> You are mine
> You are mine
>
> (p. 217)

But Beloved is also the enemy within, a vampire who grows obscenely fat as Sethe wastes away, who tempts her out of time to the only place that is truly timeless and safe, the place of death. And the narrative folds back on itself – Beloved this time is the possessive killer, Sethe shrinks to a child.

The threat is that you endlessly repeat the past (repetition as a vision of hell). Beloved is a cannibal ghost, not because (as the whitepeople would have it) cannibalism is natural to blacks; but because of the bottomless hunger engendered by slavery, which is perfectly, dreadfully, real though it's no longer natural. Perhaps the most disturbing effect of the text's uncanniness is the way it displaces the moral question about Sethe's humanity, and suggests that to be human is precisely to experience your self divided. Which of course (as Paul D discovers) makes Sethe's house not a home for the spirit, but a battleground. The novel's closing moves lay the ghost ('This is not a story to pass on', p. 275) and dissolve her into the landscape and weather:

> Down by the stream . . . her footprints come and go, come and go. They are so familiar. Should a child, an adult place his feet in them, they will fit. Take them out and they disappear again as though nobody walked there. (p. 275)

This ending draws attention to the text's powers of illusion: it's not a record, nor does its authority derive from bearing the message of continuity. In the end, it's about creating connections – a book as a meeting place.

Another way of putting it is to say that Morrison goes back into black history to find a line of dispossession. Far from writing as the matriarchal realist, she writes with the authority of someone who understands there's no safe place to write from. Mothers haunt her books all the same: Jade in *Tar Baby* is visited by a dream of 'night women', with 'sagging breats and folded stomachs' – 'they seemed somehow in agreement with each other about her, and were all out to get her, tie her, bind her' (p. 264). And Jade (who is brittle, cosmopolitan, fearful and greeedy) is by no means an exemplary figure, so that the guilty pull of the old unchosen role – 'fertility rather than originality, nurturing instead of building' (p. 271) – is real enough. Morrison specialises in naming the dangers. We still talk about black womem's writing at times as though its main impetus must come from the need to establish a separate place, but that's nastily close to assuming pastoral-fashion that the place in question will be a place of peace. Morrison implies something very different. I've been following through an 'existential' strand in the novels (about choosing yourself, in the context of unfreedom), and it's arguable that I'm importing this frame of reference from an alien culture, but I don't think so. Part of what the writing implies is that black culture has a right and a need to appropriate the ground of self-choice. Complete with its ironies. For example: back in the first of his existentialist fictions, *Nausea*, Sartre has his hero Roquentin fix on a black blues song, 'Some of these days', as a symbol of authenticity, a state of being purged of the sin of existing ('something precious and almost legendary').[7] Morrison's writing is not food as opposed to thought, not a refuge from complexity but a form of thinking in images. This, for me, explains in part the power of her writing: she has more urgent reasons than most white women novelists for insisting that the novel is about *inventing* a place to be, precisely because the notion of the black woman as bearing meaning (not making it) has been so pervasive. The result is that her fiction celebrates unnaturalness – humanity and fictionality – with outrageous conviction.

JOYCE CAROL OATES

> Twentieth-century literature is never far from parody, sensing
> itself anticipated, overdone, exhausted. But its power lies in
> the authenticity of its anger . . .
>
> (Joyce Carol Oates, *The Edge of Impossibility*, 1972)

Few contemporary writers have inhabited more styles than Joyce
Carol Oates. She is the author as picaresque character, the travelling
writer equally at home with Gothic, realism, romance and detection;
a writer who produces a campus novel one year (*Unholy Loves*, 1980),
a fantasy saga (*Bellefleur*, 1981) the next. At once chameleon and
prolific, she confuses 'high' modernism and 'low' genre-writing;
the very volume of her work mocks the notion of a stable canon,
that would put writing in its place, over against the promiscuity of
reading. In fact, she fits fairly exactly into the account Janice Doane
and Devon Hodges give of feminism's double destabilising impact:
not only 'exposing the strategies that are used to make sexual differences seem natural', but also simply 'writing, writing, writing'.[1]
Some of the novels are full-scale parodic acts of ventriloquism
(*Bellefleur*, *A Bloodsmoor Romance*, 1983, *Mysteries of Winterthurn*,
1984), all of them have an air of pastiche. This is particularly
disconcerting in a novel like *Marya: A Life* (1987), where the model
is the contemporary female *bildungsroman*. Marya's representative
status (a self-made woman of our time) is slewed by the book's
doubtful representational status. If you read it in the context of
Judith Rossner or Marilyn French it's a realist novel; but if you read
it in the context of the Oates oeuvre, it's trying on one more of the
available styles. These are not mutually exclusive ways of reading,
perhaps. However, the writing that accomodates them is *provisional*,
serial, not wedded to the notion of having the last word.

Or to put it another way: this is addicted writing – writing that
is generated by other writing (pastiche, parody) and self-generated
(by its own sense of incompleteness). Oates may be a self-conscious
writer, but – like Iris Murdoch, in this – she has profound theoretical
objections to the Great Novel that poses as terminal, to what Charles
Newman (for example) characterises as 'the strategy of dying, of
feigned exhaustion'.[2] Her early critical essays return again and again
to the argument that the notion of authorial subjectivity as a prison
is *itself* a prison. A 1973 essay on Sylvia Plath offers a sweeping
history of this 'pathology':

. . . the old corrupting hell of the Renaissance ideal and its "I"-ness, separate and distinct from all other fields of conscious-ness, which exist only to be conquered or to inflict pain upon the "I". Where at one point in civilization this very masculine, combative ideal of an "I" set against all other "I's" – and against nature as well – was necessary in order to wrench man from the hermetic contemplation of a God-centred universe and get him into action, it is no longer necessary, its health has become a pathology, and whoever clings to its outmoded concepts will die.[3]

Her own narratives from the 1970s turn the metaphysics of the adversarial 'I' back on itself, so that the separate spheres (active/passive, artist/others) are superimposed. *Do With Me What You Will* (1974) announces in its title the priority of 'other fields of consciousness': as it turns out, not the artist-as-hero, but the artist's model.

Do With Me . . . is a translation of a piece of legal Latin (*nolo contendere*). Lawyers are the active protagonists, rivals for passive heroine Elena, who like her namesake Helen of Troy is a prize, a vacant beauty – a one-time photographic model: 'She had never felt anything except through them, the intoxicating love of her own self, which hadn't really a body, but was an idea'.[4] The narrative strategy, however, involves getting the vacancies and absences onto the page, in the form of 'inner' voices, that interfere with the action so radically that at moments you almost expect other characters to overhear them:

> *There were two streams of words: one in the head, where you can feel them like stones . . . and one in the throat . . . .* (p. 40)

Such voices surface intermittently, in italics. Elena's in particular: otherwise, she is an object, a thing, an invention, the ideal reward for the men who create the court scenarios that dramatise the triumph of order. Both lawyers – her right-wing husband Howe, her lover Morrisey, working for civil rights – are caught up in an egotistical language of fiction-making. Thus Howe explains, putting together a murderer's defence – "'I'm constructing a very complicated story, a small novel'" (p. 178); or again, he's "'like a novelist writing a big crowded novel'" (p. 221). Morrisey, trying to persuade blacks in the South to testify in court, finds himself tormented by the necessity of having to listen to *them* speak – 'their own slow words . . . somehow *toylike* words. He liked this too. It was another language, this was a foreign country . . . . But to sit and listen!' (p. 242). The lawyers have one central trick in common, their *tour de force* involves establishing the guilt of the victim – Morrisey's triumphant defence of a black rapist, Howe's of many a murderer, including Morrisey's father. Finding the victim guilty becomes the book's metaphor for patriarchy, the 'masculine, combative ideal'.

But it is also the turning-point – a metaphor for the secret powers of passivity. This doubling-over is done through Elena who, increasingly, can't distinguish between herself and the women mangled in photographs and newspaper reports, the victims:

> "Elena? Are you listening? Are you still there?"
> *I was that woman found dead, strangled, in a riverside luxury hotel, twenty-eight years old, auburn hair and blue eyes and ex-model found strangled and alone . . . . when the police came they found no finger-prints "no clues" and they described themselves as "baffled" but when you read about it you thought*: SHE DESERVED TO DIE. THEY ALL DESERVE TO DIE. (p. 367)

'You' here ('when you read about it') could be either husband or lover, or then again (since she is so much their creature) herself. Elena comes to believe in the guilt of the victim, because it's a way of locating a kind of choice (all of this logic is strange, fugitive, a kind of whisper in the narrative babble); because she has lived all her life in a numb estrangement, 'innocent' of causing anything. But if the passive do cause things, then . . . . Her recognition of herself ('*I was that woman found dead*') wakes her up to the slow suicide of her life, and she recalls the original fiction which (almost like Original Sin) put her together the way she is. And here this immensely long, dense, illusionist narrative folds back on itself. Its opening sequence was about her father's abduction of her as a child, a 'doll', a sexless innocent. They drive franti-cally across the states, he crazed, she sick and starving, nearly dead when she's rescued. The plot replays that (a drive with her lover, the man still in the driver's seat), and replays and rewrites her sense of powerlessness and blamelessness, so that she finds herself at long last *incriminated*: that is, with the will to live –

All motion, all movement, was a kind of hell . . . . They had to possess you one way or another: ordinary loving maulings, or beatings and legal imprisonment . . . .

It was hellish, this realisation. And yet it excited her: the need to force something into existence, something that did not yet exist . . . . (p. 545)

She makes her own ending ('he appeared, exactly as she had imagined he would', p. 561) in which father and lover become figures in her story.

You could say Oates portrays Elena as the counsel for mystery ('In the end they hoped they might figure everyone out and solve them . . . . *She* would not be solved', p. 531). She speaks for the speechless, the dolls or dead bodies, the *things*. *Do With Me . . .* is a levelling book. The re-writing is aggressive and ironic at the same time, a re-description of the relations between the artist and the others. This helps to explain various metafictional moves – why, for example, Elena's father, rather improbably, is made to sound so like a romantic aesthete:

He thought: *Without the mind of man . . . what pleasure would exist in the universe? – what art?* (p. 5)

Indeed, these opening episodes with father at the wheel recall (oddly, but not so oddly when you think about it) Nabokov's Humbert Humbert on his drive with Lolita: a type of the artist as obsessive and prisoner. Nabokov is for Oates a curious kind of father-figure, and not only here. There may be many reasons why she parodies the arch-parodist, but among them Nabokov's lordly way with characters and readers figures large. Nabokov habitually, coyly, invites admiration of the author's lonely jokes. Here, for instance, is his devoted annotator Alfred Appel describing the effect: 'The "two plots" in Nabokov's puppet show are thus plainly made visible . . . in novel after novel his characters try to escape from Nabokov's prison of mirrors, struggling towards an awareness that only their creator has achieved by creating them – an involuted process which connects Nabokov's art with his life, and clearly indicates that the author himself is not in this prison. He is its creator, and is *above* it, in control of a book, as in one of those Saul Steinberg drawings . . . that show a man drawing the very line that gives him "life" . . . . '[5] Oates understands the meaning of mirrors very differently: they double up meanings, and breed possibilities (compare Angela Carter: 'mirrors offer alternatives, the mirrors had all turned into fissures or crannies . . . '). Re-writing wants to locate the 'things' that are routinely written out (mere images, 'inventions', creatures assumed to have no life of their own). Here is Oates in the preface to a volume of critical essays, celebrating the survival-powers of the absent, the creatures that have been living between the lines:

> The abyss will always open for us, though it begins as a pencil mark, the parody of a crack; the shapes of human beasts – centaurs, satyrs and their remarkable companions – will always be returning with nostalgia to our great cities.[6]

That 'pencil mark', I'm suggesting, is the parodist's signature.

Childwold (1977) is her most explicitly anti-Nabokov novel. Here the life in the cracks proliferates in the form not of random urban violence, but backwoods white trash. The 'I' of the narrative – middle-aged voyeur and author Kasch, returned to his family's picturesque home town – begins in good Humbertish style by picking up grubby, drunken 14-year-old Laney, whom he proceeds to invent:

> The girl with the heart-shaped face, the thin shoulders, gray eyes, bite-ridden legs . . . . Oh the grief of it, the nausea of triumph, the after hurt of pleasure squeezed from another's body . . . . My angel, my soiled angel, I reached up into your small tight body, didn't I, I jammed myself up into you . . . . Yawning and shivering she lay back against the car seat and I drove her miles and miles into the night, into the hills . . . .[7]

However, his lonely fantasies are cross-cut and intertwined with other voices. Laney's mother Arlene, handsome and horribly pro-lific, dreams in the third person – 'her lover had no name, no face, his body had flowed into hers, there was nothing left of him now but the baby inside her' (p. 74); and the horde of children are done in a frenetic collective gabble:

> . . . crawling, kicking, chortling, gurgling, ga-gaaing, whin-nying, wailing, chickie-chickie-chicking, slugs, slime, frogs, cocoons, daddy longlegs . . . . (p. 255)

Laney meanwhile has an enigmatic second person ('You'), in which she secretes her rebellion against both her mother's chaos and Kasch's timid advances.

'You' can live inside the unperson others address – 'you' can exit from the text almost, leaving Kasch ecstatically and disastrously entwined with mother, children, the whole smelly mulch of the fertile wasteland. Oates arranges a kind of death-by-smothering. He is dissolved into a burgeoning, random life that is (naturally) fatal for 'I-the-author':

> . . . shadows that scuttle with secret life, stairs that lead in all directions, corridors blocked off, rooms vacated and closed, the roof rotting, sagging . . . . Lips moist, parted in a sly smile, between her teeth a seed, is it? – a tiny seed – a yew seed – you step forward . . . . and it is over, it is done, your words are torn from you . . . . (p. 268)

The 'yew seed' is a promiscuous pun that makes Kasch pregnant with his own undoing. *Childwold* sacrifices the one to the many. There's an angry aside about class here too. In her Plath essay, Oates quotes Nabokov – "'Average reality begins to rot and stink as soon as the act of individual creation ceases to animate a subjectively perceived texture'" – and comments that this is work which 'cannot guarantee the existence of other human beings'.[8] The artist obsessed with 'the desire to *name* and to *place* and to *conquer*' (ibid.) not only constructs claustrophobia, he thrives on snobbish oppositions: he denies to others the monstrousness he claims for himself. He refuses, that is, to contemplate the possibility that his own involuted life-form is as much – or as little – 'natural' as any other.

Elena in *Do With Me What You Will* and Laney in *Childwold*, those second persons, have the strangeness of 'average reality'. One of Oates's points as a parodist is just this: her anger on behalf of *things*, among which are included various underclasses, along with slugs, slime, women (often) and children. I've been referring to 'voices' on the page, but the graphic devices in the texts (the italics, the blanks that mark off one narrative 'person' from another, the parentheses) are all open illusions. Her most memorable characters exist as patches of verbal bravura. In this, of course, they differ from no-one else's – except in their air of pastiche and provisionality. Which in turn depends on the reader's role. Oates makes life difficult for her readers, not mainly by virtue of density or hidden depth, but because she's hard to 'place':

> . . . That time twists and coils . . . that 'dialogue' is in some cases buried in the narrative . . . that the implausible is granted an authority and honoured with a complexity usually reserved for realistic fiction: the author has intended. *Bellefleur* is a region, a state of the soul, and it does exist . . . . [9]

This 'Author's Note' prefacing *Bellefleur* is characteristically sly. The 'author', it's fairly easy to decide, is a native of the same stylistic no-man's-land as the novel itself. Each book is a kind of *ad hoc* democracy where creatures with different degrees of likelihood struggle for space.

Mysteries of Winterthurn (1984) is perhaps the most compendious of Oates's compendia. Though it's a mock-Victorian detective trilogy, one can trace a cross-connection with *Childwold*, in the form of the revenge of the many. The children that ensnare Kasch – 'Many-armed. Many-limbed . . . . He is home at last . . . . Laughter, kisses, high shrill excited voices, angels' voices, angels crowding close' (p. 265) – reappear in gentleman-detective Xavier Kilgarvan's first case as full-fledged implausibilities. A chapter headed '*Trompe l'Oeil*' finds them disporting themselves in a mural painting, 'floating, and careening, and lurching about . . . . some recognisably, – and altogether shamelessly – male; some daintily feminine . . . and one or two of indeterminate gender. Ah, what a cornucopia of wings! . . . . feathered in silky black, or silver, or white; or feathered not at all, it seemed, so much as *scaled* . . . . '[10] Peeling them off the walls onto the page, where they live in italics ('*Impatient with waiting. With longing. So lonely. Hungry*', p. 9) is the sort of writerly task Oates relishes, and the result is a radically undecidable locked-room mystery. Her narrator suggests that 'while Mystery, satisfactorily *solved*, yields immense pleasure . . . that Mystery which cannot be solved . . . yields immense displeasure – nay, an actual sensation of physical sickness and dread' (p. 391. However, vertigo is an addictive drug. It's worth noting that the effect is produced not by a dearth of explanations, but by a gross over-supply of them, ranging from 'respectable' hauntings to schizoid sleep-walkings to banal atrocities. Oates adds mystification to mystery by a virtuoso display of digressive skill, and a fetishistic lushness of description, with clothes, furniture and settings all immaculately in period (down to the last tell-tale scars and stains) and all indefinably but unmistakeably fake. Characters, too, especially minor ones, are as 'round' as those of Balzac or Dickens – for instance, the Winterthurn ladies' doctor (aptly named 'Hatch') whose pompous discretion about unspeakable female problems repeatedly frustrates the police when they try to discover who bled onto whom.

In the manner of classic detectives, Xavier persists in imagining the likely culprit as male, solitary, vilely ingenious: in short, some kind of rival individualist. Whereas he might read a different message in the words of his elusive love, his cousin Perdita:

> *Woman is all that man is* not: *Woman is not all that man* is. Thus, dear Xavier, you must agree, 'tis impossible that you & I shall ever know each other, across this dread Abyss. (p. 219)

However, since these separate spheres fit his picture of things well enough, he contrives to ignore the dangerous suggestions that cluster round her *billet doux*. Every time Oates's hapless detective returns 'home', he encounters an obscene and insoluble mystery. He's a fish out of water, a hero in the wrong genre. Really what's happened is that behind his back the solid walls that separated off the different kinds of fiction have developed cracks. Interpretation, which used to be a safe game, has exceeded the rules. I am, of course, allegorising. Detective Xavier, puzzling over clues – especially written ones – finds himself faced with a tricky task of literary criticism:

> . . . the 'anonymous' letters . . . he read, and re-read . . . hearing a sinister voice in these rhythms:
> . . . . Such frailties can be attributed to the Moon's tide, tho' I (who know the wicked heart of Woman well) should attribute them to a volition *diseased & spiteful & mischievous & wanton* . . . . 'Whose voice? – *whose* voice do I hear?' the stricken man cried aloud. (p. 471)

The voice – some mad misogynist's, his own, his cousin Perdita's savage mimicry? – produces another attack of vertigo, and a merciful interval of amnesia. He's discovering that 'otherness' is not a separate shere; it proliferates, multiplies, and sows self-division *at home.* Joyce Carol Oates, who hardly seems to be one writer, and who writes enough to be several, may stand as a type of contemporary women's writing nonetheless. Who else, after all, could so exactly convey the subversive thought that there's *no end to it?*

Notes

Preface

1. Nathalie Sarraute, *Portrait of a Man Unknown* (*Portrait d'un Inconnu*, Paris: Editions Gallimard, 1948), tr. Maria Jolas, London: Calder and Boyars, 1959, pp. 68–9.
2. Roland Barthes, *The Pleasure of the Text*, (*Le Plaisir du Texte*, Paris: Editions du Seuil, 1973) tr. Richard Miller, New York: Hill and Wang 1975, pp. 28–9.
3. Marianne DeKoven, 'Male Signature, Female Aesthetic : The Gender Politics of Experimental Writing', in *Breaking the Sequence*, eds Ellen G. Friedman and Miriam Fuchs, Princeton University Press, 1989, pp. 72–81, p. 72.
4. Angela Carter, *The Infernal Desire Machines of Doctor Hoffman* (1972), reprinted as *The War of Dreams*, New York: Bard/Avon Books 1977, p. 2.

1.   AFTER THE WAR

Simone de Beauvoir

1. Simone de Beauvoir, *The Second Sex*, (*Le Deuxième Sexe*, Paris: Editions Gallimard, 1949) tr. H. M. Parshley, 1953, Harmondsworth: Penguin, 1972, p. 27.
2. Jean Leighton, *Simone de Beauvoir on Women*, London: Associated University Presses Inc., 1975, p. 184n. It's interesting that reluctant recognitions like this often appear in footnotes, rather than in the main body of the text. Not always: Germaine Greer in *The Change: Women, Ageing and the Menopause*, London: Hamish Hamilton, 1991, devotes a good deal of space to berating Beauvoir for the dismay with which she greeted middle age, and the prospect of a life without sexual intrigue, the latest in a long line of accusers who find her bleakness unbearable.
3. Quoted in Deirdre Bair, *Simone de Beauvoir, A Biography*, London: Jonathan Cape, 1990, p. 514. Boschetti is describing the division of editorial labour at *Les Temps Modernes*.
4. Leslie Dick, 'Feminism, Writing, Postmodernism' in *From my Guy to Sci-Fi* ed. Helen Carr, London: Pandora Press, 1989, pp. 204–14, p. 211.
5. Martha Noel Evans, *Masks of Tradition*, Cornell University Press, 1987, p. 101.

6. Simone de Beauvoir quoted in Dierdre Bair, *Simone de Beauvoir, A Biography*, p. 530.
7. Simone de Beauvoir, *Memoirs of a Dutiful Daughter*, (*Memoires d'une Jeune Fille Rangée*, Paris: Librairie Gallimard, 1958), tr. James Kirkup, 1959, Harmondsworth: Penguin, 1963, p. 345.
8. Simone de Beauvoir, *The Prime of Life*, (*La Force de l'Âge*, Paris: Librairie Gallimard, 1960), tr. Peter Green, 1962, Harmondsworth: Penguin, 1965, p. 25.
9. Iris Murdoch, *Sartre: Romantic Rationalist*, (1953), Fontana/Collins 1967, p. 47.
10. Beauvoir, *The Prime of Life*, p. 59.
11. *Ibid.,*, p. 62.
12. Simone de Beauvoir, *She Came to Stay*, (*L'Invitée*, Paris: Editions Gallimard, 1943), tr. Yvonne Moyse and Roger Senhouse, 1949, Fontana/Collins, 1975, p. 54.
13. Beauvoir, *The Prime of Life*, p. 128, p. 280.
14. Jean-Paul Sartre, *Being and Nothingness: An Essay on Phenomenological Ontology* (*L'Être et le Néant*, Paris: Editions Gallimard, 1943) tr. Hazel E. Barnes, 1958, London: Methuen, 1969, pp. 55–6.
15. Hazel E. Barnes, *The Literature of Possibility: A Study in Humanistic Existentialism* (University of Nebraska Press, 1959), London: Tavistock Publications, 1961, p. 52n.
16. 'Qu'est ce qu'un collaborateur?' in *La République Française*, September 1945, quoted in Barnes, *op. cit.*, p. 104.
17. Sartre, *Being and Nothingness*, p. 609.
18. Barnes, *op. cit.*, p. 297.
19. Beauvoir, *The Prime of Life*, p. 259, pp. 260–1, p. 340, p. 600.
20. *Ibid.*, p.342.
21. Beauvoir, *She Came to Stay*, p. 217.
22. Simone de Beauvoir, *The Mandarins*, (*Les Mandarins*, Paris: Librairie Gallimard, 1954) tr. Leonard M. Friedman 1957, Fontana/Collins 1960, p. 238, p. 240.
23. Beauvoir, *The Prime of Life*, p. 434.
24. Murdoch, *op. cit.*, p. 81n.
25. Simone de Beauvoir, *All Said and Done* (*Tout Compte Fait*, Paris: Editions Gallimard, 1972) tr. Patrick O'Brian, 1974, Harmondsworth: Penguin, 1977, p. 491.
26. *Ibid.*, p. 494.

Doris Lessing

1. Doris Lessing, *The Golden Notebook* (1962), Harmondsworth: Penguin, 1964, p. 237.
2. *Children of Violence* consists of the following novels: *Martha Quest* (1952), *A Proper Marriage* (1954), *A Ripple from the Storm* (1958), *Landlocked* (1965), and *The Four-Gated City* (1969).
3. Doris Lessing, *Martha Quest* (1952), St. Albans: Panther, 1966, p. 56.
4. Georg Lukács, *Studies in European Realism*, London: Merlin Press, 1950, p. 18.

5. Raymond Williams, *The Long Revolution* (1961), Harmondsworth: Penguin, 1965, p. 278. p. 287.

6. For a fuller treatment of this topic see Lorna Sage, *Doris Lessing*, London and New York: Methuen, 1983, especially pp. 30–48.

7. *A Ripple from the Storm* (1958), St. Albans: Panther, 1966, p. 193.

8. Iris Murdoch, *Sartre* (1953), Fontana/Collins 1967, p. 47, p. 51.

9. Nicole Ward Jouve, 'Of Mud and Other Matter: *The Children of Violence*', in Jenny Taylor (ed.), *Notebooks/ Memoirs/ Archives: Reading and Rereading Doris Lessing*, London: Routledge & Kegan Paul, 1982, pp. 75–134, p. 126.

10. Roland Barthes, *Writing Degree Zero* (1953), New York: Hill and Wang 1977, p. 37.

11. Florence Howe, 'A Conversation with Doris Lessing (1966)', *Contemporary Literature*, 14, 4, (1973), pp. 418–36, pp. 425–6.

12. Doris Lessing, 'The Small Personal Voice' (1957), *A Small Personal Voice*, ed. Paul Schlueter, New York: Knopf, 1974, pp. 3–21, 20–21.

13. *Ibid.*, p. 20.

14. Michel Foucault, 'What is an Author?' (1969), in J. V. Harari (ed.), *Textual Strategies*, London: Methuen, 1979, pp. 141–60, p. 144.

l5. Margaret Drabble, 'Doris Lessing: Cassandra in a World Under Siege', *Ramparts*, 10, 1972, pp. 50–4.

16. Doris Lessing, *The Four-Gated City* (1969), St. Albans: Panther, 1972, p. 528.

17. 'Doris Lessing at Stony Brook: An Interview' (with Jonathan Raskin), *New American Review*, 8 (1970), reprinted in *A Small Personal Voice*, p. 65.

18. Doris Lessing, *The Memoirs of a Survivor*, London: Octagon Press, 1974, p. 19.

19. See, for example, 'My Father' (1963); also Lessing's 1968 Afterword to Olive Schreiner, *The Story of an African Farm*, both reprinted in *A Small Personal Voice*.

20. Doris Lessing, *The Sentimental Agents in the Volyen Empire*, London: Jonathan Cape, 1983, p. 32. The *Canopus in Argos* series consists of the following novels: *Re: Colonized Planet 5, Shikasta* (1979), *The Marriages Between Zones Three, Four and Five* (1980), *The Sirian Experiments* (1981), *The Making of the Representative for Planet 8* (1982), and *The Sentimental Agents*.

21. *The Sentimental Agents*, p. 161.

22. Doris Lessing, *The Sirian Experiments* (1981), St. Albans: Panther, 1982, p. 80.

23. Doris Lessing, *The Making of the Representative for Planet 8* (1982), St. Albans: Panther, 1983, p. 80.

24. Doris Lessing, *Shikasta* (1979), St Albans: Panther, 1982, p. 101.

25. *The Sirian Experiments*, p. 11.

26. Michel Foucault, op. cit., p. 144. For a slightly fuller version of this reading of Lessing's 'science fiction' novels, see Lorna Sage, 'The Available Space' in Moira Monteith (ed.), *Women's Writing: A Challenge to Theory*, Sussex: Harvester Press, 1986, pp. 15–33.

Nathalie Sarraute

1. *La Quinzaine Littéraire*, No. 192, August 1974, p. 29.
2. Simone de Beauvoir, *The Force of Circumstance*, (*La Force des Choses*, Paris: Librairie Gallimard, 1963), tr. Richard Howard, 1965, Harmondsworth: Penguin, 1968, p. 27.
3. *Ibid.*, pp. 636–7.
4. *Ibid.*, p. 27.
5. Nathalie Sarraute, Foreword to *Tropisms and The Age of Suspicion*, (*Tropismes*, Paris: Denoel, 1939; *L'Ère du soupçon*, Paris: Librairie Gallimard, 1956), tr. Maria Jolas, London: Calder and Boyars 1963, p. 8.
6. Jean-Paul Sartre, Preface to Nathalie Sarraute, *Portrait of a Man Unknown* (*Portrait d'un Inconnu*, Paris: Editions Gallimard, 1948), tr. Maria Jolas, London: Calder and Boyars, 1959, p. xi.
7. *Ibid.*, p. xii.
8. *Ibid.*, p. vii.
9. Nathalie Sarraute, *Portrait of a Man Unknown*, ed. cit., p. 220.
10. Sartre, Preface to *Portrait of a Man Unknown*, p. viii.
11. Nathalie Sarraute, 'The Age of Suspicion', (1950) in *Tropisms and The Age of Suspicion*, p. 84.
12. Nathalie Sarraute, 'From Dostoievski to Kafka', (1947), in *Tropisms and The Age of Suspicion*, pp. 75–6.
13. Sartre, Preface to *Portrait of a Man Unknown*, p. xiv.
14. Beauvoir, *The Force of Circumstance*, pp. 636–7.
15. Susan M. Bell, in *Sarraute: 'Portrait d'un Inconnu' and 'Vous Les Entendez?'*, London: Grant and Cutler, 1988, p. 16, reports on just one such occasion, as late as 1971, a colloquium on the *nouveau roman*: 'her uneasy sense of not belonging was betrayed by her reluctance to attend and her departure at the end of [the] first day.'
16. Gretchen Rous Besser, *Nathalie Sarraute*, Boston: Hall/Twayne's World Authors Series, 1979, p. 170.
17. Sarraute, 'Les Deux Réalités', *Esprit*, No. 329, (July 1964), p. 74.
18. Sarraute, *Tropisms and The Age of Suspicion*, p. 118.
19. Nathalie Sarraute, *The Golden Fruits*, (*Les Fruits d'Or*, Paris: Editions Gallimard, 1963), tr. Maria Jolas, London: Calder and Boyars, 1965, pp. 140–1.
20. Nathalie Sarraute, *Between Life and Death*, (*Entre la Vie et la Mort*, Paris: Editions Gallimard, 1968), tr. Maria Jolas, London: Calder and Boyars, 1970, p. 172.
21. Murdoch, *Sartre*, p. 118.
22. Nathalie Sarraute, *Do You Hear Them?*, (*Vous les entendez?*, Paris: Editions Gallimard, 1972) tr. Maria Jolas, London: Calder and Boyars, 1975, p. 44.
23. Nathalie Sarraute, *Fools Say*, (*Disent les imbeciles*, Paris: Editions Gallimard, 1976), tr. Maria Jolas, London: Calder and Boyars, 1977, p. 105.
24. Bell, *op. cit.*, p. 43.

25. Nathalie Sarraute, *Childhood*, (*Enfance*, Paris: Editions Gallimard, 1983), tr. Barbara Wright, London: John Calder, 1984, pp. 5–6.
26. Sarraute, *The Golden Fruits*, p. 14.
27. Lessing, *The Golden Notebook*, pp. 67–8.

2. DISPLACED PERSONS

Christina Stead

1.   Stead quoted in Chris Williams, *Christina Stead : A Life of Letters*, London: Virago, 1990, p. 308.
2.   Mikhail Bakhtin's characterisation of *'carnivalised literature'* emphasises the 'multi-styled and heterogeneous nature' of all the genres infiltrated by a 'carnival sense of the world' (*Problems of Dostoevsky's Poetics*, edited and translated by Caryl Emerson, Manchester University Press, 1984, pp. 107–8). Bakhtin's materialist and utopian view of fiction was developed at around the same time as Stead was writing, and coincides splendidly with her practice.
3.   Stead quoted in R. G. Geering, *Christina Stead*, New York: Hall/Twayne World Authors, 1969, p. 44.
4.   Christina Stead, *Ocean of Story*, Viking, 1985, p. 498.
5.   Christina Stead, *The Saltzburg Tales* (1934), London: Virago, 1986, p. 98.
6.   Stead, *Ocean of Story*, p. 70.
7.   Stead quoted in Williams, *op. cit.*, p. 11.
8.   Stead, *Ocean of Story*, p. 10.
9.   Lorna Tracey picks up the same imagery, though she makes a distinction between artists and others I'd argue Stead doesn't: 'This continual passage of individuals strained up from oceanic darkness, examined under high magnification and then returned to oblivion . . . . she soon pours every individual into a text the size of Sydney Harbour . . . . ' 'The Virtue of the Story: *The Salzburg Tales*', *Stand*, Vol. 23, No. 4, 1982, pp. 48–53, pp. 52–3.
10. *New Yorker*, October 19th, 1940.
11. Stead quoted in Williams, *op. cit.*, p. 8.
12. Williams, *op. cit.*, p. 26.
13. *Ibid.*, p. 27.
14. Bakhtin, *op. cit.*, p. 107.
15. Quoted in Williams, *op. cit.*, p. 135.
16. Fadiman, *loc. cit.*
17. Christina Stead, *For Love Alone* (1944), London: Virago, 1978, pp. 192–193.
18. Ortega y Gasset, *On Love: Aspects of a Single Theme*, (*Estudios Sobre el Amor*) tr. Tony Talbot, London: Gollancz, 1959, p. 15.
19. There are several explicit allusions to the Ulysses story; see for example p. 222, or p. 348 ('the rigmarole of her buffoon Odyssey'). Stead would have been thinking of Joyce as well as Homer.

20. Randall Jarrell, 'An Unread Book', reprinted in Christina Stead, *The Man Who Loved Children*, Harmondsworth: Penguin, 1970, pp. 5–38, p. 36.
21. Stead quoted in Williams, *op. cit.*, p. 235.
22. Ellen Rooney, *Seductive Reasoning*, Cornell University Press, 1989, p. 27.
23. Terry Eagleton,'The end of English', *Textual Practice*, Vol. 1, No. 1, 1987, pp. 1–9, p. 4.
24. Christina Stead, *I'm Dying Laughing*, edited and with a Preface by R. G. Geering, London: Virago, 1986, p. 122.

Jean Rhys

1. Carole Angier, *Jean Rhys*, Harmondsworth: Penguin/Viking, 1985, p. 15.
2. Jean Rhys, *Wide Sargasso Sea*, London: André Deutsch, 1966, introduction by Francis Wyndham, p. 10.
3. *The Madwoman in the Attic*, New Haven: Yale University Press, 1979.
4. Angier, *op. cit.*, p. 120.
5. Jean Rhys, *Smile Please : An Unfinished Autobiography*, London: André Deutsch 1979, p. 21.
6. *Ibid.*, p. 168.
7. Ford Madox Ford, Preface to Jean Rhys, *The Left Bank* (1927), reprinted in *Tigers are Better-Looking*, New York: Popular Library, 1976, p. 160.
8. David Plante, *Difficult Women. A Memoir of Three: Jean Rhys, Sonia Orwell, Germaine Greer*, London: Gollancz, 1983, p. 25.
9. *Jean Rhys: Letters 1931–1966*, edited by Francis Wyndham and Diana Melly, London: André Deutsch, 1984, p. 280.
10. Jean Rhys, *The Left Bank* (1927), reprinted in *Tigers are Better-Looking*, New York: Popular Library, 1976, p. 233.
11. Rhys's 1930s novels were *Quartet* (1928), *After Leaving Mr Mackenzie* (1930), *Voyage in the Dark* (1934) and *Good Morning, Midnight* (1939). In 1927 Rhys had met Leslie Tilden Smith, her second husband (whom she married in 1934); he was a literary agent, and seems to have been a major help in getting the books written and published. He died in 1945.
12. 'Outside the Machine', *Tigers are Better-Looking* (1968), New York: Popular Library, 1976, pp. 92–3. Subsequent references in this paragraph to the short stories are to this edition.
13. *Jean Rhys: Letters 1931–1966*, p. 31.
14. Jean Rhys, *Wide Sargasso Sea*, London: André Deutsch, p. 70.
15. Jean Rhys, *Smile Please*, London: André Deutsch 1979, p. 161.
16. Endings notoriously troubled her, see *Letters, passim*; the manuscript of *Good Morning, Midnight* was, she said, sent off while she was asleep. Its 'man in the dressing gown' supplies one of her most despairing denouements.

17. Ellen G. Friedman calls this an act of 'audacious grafting' – 'Rhys determined to write Brontë into modernity.' 'Breaking the Master Narrative: Jean Rhys's *Wide Sargasso Sea*', in *Breaking the Sequence: Women's Experimental Fiction*, eds Ellen G. Friedman and Miriam Fuchs, Princeton University Press, 1989, pp. 117–28, p. 118, p. 127. My reading emphasises the tragic or displaced (or 'Bohemian') meaning of modernity for Rhys.

18. *Wide Sargasso Sea* won the W. H. Smith prize for fiction, and Rhys and her work achieved prominence, and a canonical status, with (ironical) rapidity.

19. 'The Insect World', *Sleep it Off Lady* (1976), Harmondsworth: Penguin, 1979, p. 126.

20. *Jean Rhys : Letters 1931–1966*, p. 235.

Elizabeth Smart

1. Elizabeth Smart, *By Grand Central Station I Sat Down and Wept* (1945), Londom: Polytantric Press, 1977, p. 7; p. 98.

2. See Chapters 4 and 5; both Millett and Carter are writing about sexual moments when the metaphysical version of conjoined opposites (*discordia concors*) fails to apply. They are also, of course, both writing as women brought up on the metaphysical poets, part of the post-war canon, thanks to Eliot and Leavis. Elizabeth Smart, like her lover George Barker and like Dylan Thomas, was absorbing this particular modernist legacy a stage earlier. Donne's power to symbolise sexual mystique is undiminished. See, for example Kathy Acker – 'the realm of sex is holy. Silent. Identity is lost at the point of orgasm.' She goes on to quote Donne's *Epithalamium*. ('Desire and Power', *Marxism Today*, August 1990, p. 21.)

3. For the opposite reading of the poetical heritage, in particular of Wordsworth, see the remarks on Margaret Drabble, Chapter 3 below.

4. The origin of this transference of procreative meanings to metaphor is Plato's *Symposium*, where immortality is the name of the game, and those who simply have children are convicted of literal-mindedness. Smart's Journals for the period leading up to the affair with George Barker have now been edited by Alice Van Wart (*Necessary Secrets*, London: Grafton 1991). The final section (1939–1941) covers the ground of *By Grand Central Station*: the 'ardent boy', for example, is identified as John Finch. Smart writes (April 4th, 1940): 'I know that perhaps tonight his mouth like the centre of a rose closes over John's mouth burning with apologies of love like a baby at the breast' (p. 281).

5. Elizabeth Smart, *The Assumption of the Rogues and Rascals*, London: Granada, 1978, p. 108.

6. Sandra Gilbert and Susan Gubar, *The Madwoman in the Attic*, New Haven: Yale University Press, 1979. They write that 'the text's author is a father, a progenitor, an aesthetic patriarch whose pen is an instrument of generative power like his penis' (p. 7), paraphrasing

Harold Bloom on 'the anxiety of influence' (where being original involves an Oedipal conflict with a literary father-figure). Women writers, according to Gilbert and Gubar, undergo a more fundamental ordeal, since they are excluded from the patrilinear tradition.

7.   Christine Brooke-Rose, 'Illiterations' in *Breaking the Sequence: Women's Experimental Fiction*, eds Ellen G. Friedman and Miriam Fuchs, Princeton University Press, 1989, pp. 55–71, p. 59.
8.   *Ibid.*, p. 61.

Tillie Olsen

1.   Tillie Olsen, *Silences*, (1979), London: Virago, 1980, p. 19.
2.   See the story 'Yes, Yes' in Tillie Olsen, *Tell Me A Riddle* (1962), London: Virago, 1980.
3.   Tillie Olsen, *Yonnondio* (1974), London: Virago, pp. 190–1.
4.   *Silences*, ed. cit., p. 117.
5.   *Tell Me A Riddle*, ed. cit., p. 121.
6.   *Ibid.*, Introduction.
7.   *The Assumption of the Rogues and Rascals*, London: Granada, 1978, p. 63.
8.   *Silences*, ed. cit., p. 202.
9.   *Breaking the Sequence*, eds Ellen G. Friedman and Miriam Fuchs, Princeton University Press, 1989, pp. 72–81, p. 72; my italics.
10.   Mary Jacobus, quoted by DeKoven, *loc. cit.*, p. 77.
11.   Christine Brooke-Rose, 'Illiterations' in *Breaking the Sequence*, ed. cit., pp. 55–71, p. 61.
12.   *The Golden Fruits* (1963), tr. Maria Jolas, London: Calder and Boyars, 1970, p. 14.
13.   *Silences*, ed. cit., p. 27.
14.   *Tigers are Better-Looking* (1968), New York: Popular Library, 1976, p. 115.
15.   *Sexchanges*, Yale University Press, 1989, pp. 332–41: 'For ultimately Eliot yearns with Joyce and Lawrence . . . to bring a thoroughly male Ulysses home from the sea to his soft-skirted, definitively female Penelope' (p. 341).
16.   *Silences*, ed. cit., p. 262.

Françoise Sagan

1.   Françoise Sagan, *Réponses: The Autobiography of Françoise Sagan* (Societé Nouvelle des Editions Pauvert, 1974), tr. David Macey, Black Sheep Books, Godalming: The Ram Publishing Company, 1979, p. 12.
2.   Françoise Sagan, *Bonjour Tristesse* (Paris: René Julliard, 1954) tr. Irene Ash, Harmondsworth: Penguin 1958, pp. 46–7.
3.   Though both novels share the irony that 'freedom' involves rivalry for the favours of a lover/mentor. Sagan is barefaced about this, defying Freud in order to grab father.

4. Françoise Sagan, *A Certain Smile*, (*Un Certain Sourire*, Paris: René Julliard 1956) tr. Irene Ash, Harmondsworth: Penguin 1960, p. 28.
5. *Réponses*, ed. cit., p. 51.
6. Françoise Sagan, *Wonderful Clouds* (*Les Merveilleux Nuages*, Paris: René Julliard 1961) tr. Anne Green, Harmondsworth: Penguin 1963. p. 60.
7. Shari Benstock, in *Women of the Left Bank: Paris 1900–1940*, Austin: University of Texas Press, 1986, is concerned – understandably enough – to emphasise the resilience and survival-powers of the women writers she discusses, and to rescue them from the image of ragged Bohemianism. They belong largely to an earlier generation, of course; and to a more coherent Anglo-American expatriate world.
8. Michel Foucault, 'What is an Author?', (1969), reprinted in Josué Harari ed., *Textual Strategies* (1979) London: Methuen, 1980, pp. 141–60, p. 141.
9. Foucault (*ibid*), ends on this characteristically *atopian* note, as does Toril Moi (quoting Derrida) in *Sexual/Textual Politics* (London: Methuen 1985). The desire for a placeless writing (see Preface p. ix) ends up privileging the traditional male *avant garde*.

3. THE MIDDLE GROUND

Iris Murdoch

1. Whether writing as philosopher or as novelist, Murdoch deliberately uses 'ordinary' language ('jumble', 'muddle', 'stuff') to measure her distance from abstract hypothesising, which needs jargon. 'Contingency' is perhaps her major concession.
2. Iris Murdoch, *The Fire and the Sun*, Oxford University Press, 1977, p. 89.
3. Iris Murdoch, *Sartre* (1953), London: Collins Fontana Library, 1967, p. 94.
4. Iris Murdoch, 'The Sublime and the Beautiful Revisited', *Yale Review* XLIX, 1959, pp. 242–71, p. 270.
5. *The Fire and the Sun*, p. 86.
6. J. P. Stern, *On Realism*, London: Routledge & Kegan Paul, 1973, p. 54.
7. Murdoch reads Plato as an anti-formalist and an iconoclast. More lately, in *The Book and the Brotherhood*, 1987, her characters see analogies between radical deconstruction and the pre-Socratics, and Plato becomes (relatively) a good thing: '"Plato did a good job when he threw out the preSocratics." "Yes, but they're back!"' (Harmondsworth: Penguin, 1988, p. 126).
8. For a rather more detailed demonstration of this textual tic, see my essay 'Female Fictions' in Malcolm Bradbury ed., *Contemporary British Fiction*, London 1979, pp. 67–87.
9. *Sartre*, p. 43.

10. Iris Murdoch, *Under the Net* (1954), Harmondsworth: Penguin, p. 20.

11. *Sartre*, p. 97. The footnote in question reads: 'The striking symbol of the petrifying Medusa is interpreted by Freud as a castration fear . . . . Sartre of course regards as its basic sense our general fear of being observed . . . . '

12. Iris Murdoch, *The Red and the Green*, London: Chatto & Windus, 1965, p. 50.

13. See above; and Murdoch, *Sartre*, p. 19, where she paraphrases with humourous relish: 'These evocations of the viscous, the fluid, the paste-like sometimes achieve a kind of horrid poetry . . . . '

14. Iris Murdoch, *An Accidental Man* (1971), Harmondsworth: Penguin 1973, p. 250.

15. Iris Murdoch. *The Nice and the Good* (1968), Harmondsworth: Penguin 1969, p. 107.

16. Iris Murdoch, *A Fairly Honourable Defeat* (1970), Harmondsworth: Penguin 1972, p. 214.

17. Ed. cit., p. 395.

18. Iris Murdoch, *Nuns and Soldiers* (1980), Harmondsworth: Penguin 1981, p. 328.

19. In this she is in the gender-blurring (or more accurately, gender-multiplying) tradition of James, Forster and Woolf, like her contemporary Angus Wilson.

20. Ed. cit., p. 250.

21. Iris Murdoch, *The Sea, the Sea*, London: Chatto & Windus, 1978, p. 126.

22. Iris Murdoch, *The Black Prince*, London: Chatto & Windus, 1973, p. 57.

23. There is a good case for arguing indeed that Murdoch is a *Neo-Platonist* herself. See my article 'The Pursuit of Imperfection', *Critical Quarterly*, xix, 2 (Summer 1977) 67–87. Also the discussion in Peter Conradi, *Iris Murdoch: The Saint and the Artist*, London: Macmillan, 1986.

24. *The Book and the Brotherhood* (1987), Harmondsworth: Penguin 1988, p. 23.

25. Socrates' term in *The Republic*. Murdoch has been very interested in the question of the relation between eros and academe, love and learning: see her own Platonic dialogues in *Acastos*, and *The Fire and The Sun*, where '"Falling in love", a violent process which Plato more than once vividly describes (love is abnegation, abjection, slavery) is for many people the most extraordinary and most revealing experience of their lives, whereby the centre of significance is suddenly ripped out of the self, and the dreamy ego is shocked into an awareness of an entirely separate reality' (p. 36).

Edna O'Brien

1. Edna O'Brien, *Zee and Co* (1971) Harmondsworth: Penguin, 1971, p. 87.

2.   Edna O'Brien, *The Country Girls*, London: Hutchinson, 1960, p. 190.
3.   Edna O'Brien, *Some Irish Loving* (1979), Harmondsworth: Penguin, 1981, pp. 148–9.
4.   Edna O'Brien. *Girl with Green Eyes* (*The Lonely Girl*, London: Cape, 1962) Harmondsworth: Penguin, 1964, p. 149.
5.   Edan O'Brien, *Night* (1972), Harmondsworth: Penguin, 1974, p. 27.
6.   Edna O'Brien, *Mother Ireland* (1976), Harmondsworth: Penguin, 1978, pp. 56–7.
7.   Edna O'Brien, *The Love Object* (1968), Harmondsworth: Penguin, 1970, p. 151.
8.   Edna O'Brien, *Johnny I Hardly Knew You*, London: Weidenfeld & Nicolson, 1977, p. 59.
9.   Edan O'Brien, *Mrs Reinhardt & Other Stories*, London: Weidenfeld & Nicolson, 1978, p. 207.
10. *Ibid.*, pp. 129–30.
11. Edna O'Brien, *Returning*, London: Weidenfeld & Nicolson, 1982, p. 72.

Margaret Drabble

1.   Margaret Drabble, *The Middle Ground*, London: Weidenfeld & Nicolson, 1980, p. 19.
2.   Margaret Drabble, *The Garrick Year* (1965), Harmondsworth: Penguin, 1966, p. 170.
3.   Margaret Drabble, *A Summer Birdcage* (1963), Harmondsworth: Penguin, 1967, p. 71.
4.   Margaret Drabble, *Jerusalem the Golden* (1967), Harmondsworth: Penguin, 1969, p. 131.
5.   Margaret Drabble, *The Needle's Eye* (1972), Harmondsworth: Penguin, 1973. p. 45.
6.   Margaret Drabble, *The Waterfall* (1969), Harmondsworth: Penguin, 1971, p. 84.
7.   Margaret Drabble, *The Realms of Gold*, Weidenfeld & Nicolson, 1975, pp. 181–2.
8.   Margaret Drabble, *The Ice Age* (1977), Harmondsworth: Penguin, 1978, p. 286.
9.   *The Realms of Gold*, ed. cit., p. 324.
10. *The Midddle Ground*, ed. cit., p. 163.
11. Middle-distance focus is vitally important to the maintenance of her poise. Cf. J. P. Stern (*On Realism*, London: Routledge & Kegan Paul, 1973), p. 55: ' . . . realism must stand back . . . at a certain distance – neither too far away nor too close by . . . . This middle distance varies from age to age. Indeed, what else is an age . . . than a bundle of experiences whose affinities are seen from a more or less common vantage point? But though it varies from age to age, this middle ground is at all times the determining condition of the realist artist's choices and thus his real and relative freedom.' One way of describing Drabble's 1980s dilemma is that she finds herself

describing a world of arbitrary, devalued freedoms, and her vantage point becomes (relatively, very relatively) vagrant itself.

12.   Margaret Drabble, *A Natural Curiosity*, London: Viking, 1989, p. 243.
13.   Drabble's characteristically catholic 1986 Booklist for the British Council and Book Trust, *Twentieth Century Classics*, rather pointedly omitted Lessing – an example perhaps of Drabble the woman of letters policing the boundaries of the 'classic' in the way that her novels have charted the bounds of the real, waving goodbye to characters who don't fit. In the final volume of her present trilogy, *The Gates of Ivory* (1991) however, the form is 'shot to hell' very much in Lessing's fashion. The book models itself on a grisly bundle of relics which are all that is left of a British loner who has disppeared in Cambodia (very much the sort of character she used routinely to exclude).

Mary McCarthy

1.   Mary McCarthy, *The Company She Keeps* (New York: Harcourt Brace & Company, 1942), Harmondsworth: Penguin, 1965, p. 191.
2.   Mary McCarthy, *On the Contrary*, London: Heinemann, 1962, p. 267.
3.   'The Case Against McCarthy: A Review of *The Group*' in Norman Mailer, *Cannibals and Christians* (1966); reprinted in Patricia Spacks ed., *Contemporary Women Novelists: A Collection of Critical Essays*, Engelwood Cliffs, N.J.: Prentice Hall, 1977, pp. 75–84, p. 75.
4.   Mary McCarthy, 'My Confession' (1955); *On the Contrary*, London: Heinemann 1962, p. 77.
5.   Mary McCarthy, 'No News, or, What Killed the Dog' (1952); *On the Contrary*, p. 39.
6.   *On the Contrary*, p. 50.
7.   Mary McCarthy, *The Groves of Academe* (1953), St Albans: Panther, 1964, p. 76.
8.   Mary McCarthy, 'The Character in Fiction' (1961); *On the Contrary*, pp. 271–92, p. 287.
9.   Norman Mailer, *Cannibals and Christians* (1966), London: André Deutsch, 1967, p. 201.
10. Simone de Beauvoir, *The Prime of Life* (1960), tr. Peter Green, 1962, Harmondsworth: Penguin, 1965, p. 133.
11. *On the Contrary*, ed. cit., p. 200.
12. Mary McCarthy, *Cast a Cold Eye*, New York: Harcourt Brace & Company, 1950, p. 61.
13. Mary McCarthy, *A Source of Embarrassment* (1950), St Albans: Panther, 1964, pp. 126–7.
14. *On the Contrary*, p. 271; p. 292.
15. Mary McCarthy, *The Group* (1963), Marmondsworth: Penguin, 1964, p. 12.
16. A much later essay, 'Novel, Tale, Romance' (1981–2), collected in *Occasional Prose*, London: Weidenfeld & Nicolson, 1985, pp. 127–52, returns to the same point. 'The novel, after all, is the literary form

dedicated to the representation of our common world, i.e., not merely the common ordinary world, but the world we have in common . . . . Common sense, also known as the reality principle, rules the novel . . . . ' (p. 143).

17. Mary McCarthy, *Memoirs of a Catholic Girlhood* (1957), Harmondsworth: Penguin, 1963, p. 192.

18. Or perhaps not. Anne Tyler's novels, set firmly in Baltimore, are an exception in this sense. Tyler represents a particular cunning transformation of the matriarchal/realist model, with her motherly men, extended families and plots strung across generations. Like Margaret Drabble – the Drabble of the 1960s and 1970s, that is – she has her own 'parish'. Characters who leave Baltimore fall off the edge of her world.

19. Alison Lurie, *Foreign Affairs* (1984), London; Michael Joseph, 1985, p. 206.

4. THE MOVEMENT

1. Erica Jong, *Fear of Flying* (1973) St Albans: Panther, 1974, p. 30.
2. Stephen Heath, *The Sexual Fix*, London: Macmillan, 1982, p. 119.
3. Andrea Dworkin, *Intercourse*, London: Secker & Warburg, 1987, p. 47.
4. Andrea Dworkin, *Letters From a War Zone*, London: Secker & Warburg, 1988, p. 30.
5. *Intercourse*, ed. cit., p. 63.
6. *Letters From a War Zone*, ed. cit., p. 36.
7. Kate Millett, *Flying*, London: Hart Davis, MacGibbon, 1975, p. 14.
8. Stephen Heath, *The Sexual Fix*, ed. cit., p. 135.
9. See the discussion of the terrain of the *avant garde* in Chapter 3 above, particularly on Olsen. Sandra Gilbert and Susan Gubar in *Sexchanges* (Yale University Press, 1989) explore ways in which modernist transvestism reasserts gender definitions.

Joyce Johnson

1. Joyce Johnson, *Minor Characters*, Boston: Houghton Mifflin Company, 1983, pp. 261–2.
2. James Baldwin, *Nobody Knows My Name* (1961) New York: Dell Publishing, 1963, p. 183.
3. *Ibid.*, p. 182.

Kate Millet

1. *Flying*, London: Hart Davis, MacGibbon, 1975, pp. 148–9.
2. Foucault's 'What is an Author?' (1969) I have already referred to in the discussion of Lessing in Chapter 1. Roland Barthes (*The Pleasure*

of the Text (1973), New York: Hill and Wang, 1975) and Umberto Eco (*The Role of the Reader* (1979), London: Hutchinson, 1983) both celebrated the reader's creativity, Eco with more circumspection. For him 'open' texts – like Joyce's *Ulysses* – turn out to be 'closed' in the sense that they programme and pre-empt readerly 'play': 'those texts that according to Barthes (1973) are able to produce the "jouissance" of the unexhausted virtuality of their expressive plane succeed in this effect just because they have been planned to invite their Model Readers to reproduce their own processes of deconstruction by a plurality of free interpretive choices,' p. 40). Eco's monster novel *Foucault's Pendulum* (1988, tr. William Weaver 1989) provides a sceptical commentary on the prison of 'limitless' interpretation: the heroine, interestingly enough, is the one who inscribes limits, and re-roots meanings.

3.   This was truer than one knew. In *The Loony Bin Trip*, London: Virago, 1991, Millett tells the story of her 'madness': of the refusal and inability to police her own boundaries which led in 1973 to her being diagnosed as manic-depressive, and to two episodes of forced hospitalisation (1973, 1980). Her lover and the 'apprentices' who were supposed to make up an Amazon utopia turned, for her, into agents of the medical establishment, thought-police. The group grammar, in short, exacted a terrible price.

Erica Jong

1.   Erica Jong, *Fear of Flying* (1973), St Albans: Panther, 1974, p. 75.
2.   Henry Fielding, *Shamela* (1741), *Joesph Andrews* and *Shamela* ed. Martin C. Battestin, London: Methuen, 1965, p. 336.
3.   Sandra Gilbert and Susan Gubar, *The Madwoman in the Attic*, Yale University Press, 1979.
4.   *Intercourse*, London: Secker & Warburg, 1987, p. 124.
5.   Vladimir Nabokov, *Lolita* (1955); *The Annotated Lolita* ed. Alfred Appel, London: Weidenfeld & Nicolson, 1970, p. 20. Nabokov's first person is parodied and 'analysed' with a great deal more panache by Joyce Carol Oates (see Chapter 5). The re-emergence of the character-as-author (an eighteenth-century commonplace) is one consequence of the so-called death of the author – not a death at all, but a demystification and exposure of the processes of fiction (the 'author-function'). In *Fear of Flying* the 'I' is demystificatory by default: the Nabokov tricks don't work with genders reversed. In other words the author-function, when foregrounded, reveals fault-lines that had been concealed by both realist and modernist conventions.
6.   *Intercourse*, ed. cit., p. 127.
7.   Erica Jong, *How to Save Your Own Life*, London: Secker & Warburg, 1977, p. 170.
8.   Toril Moi, *Sexual/Textual Politics: Feminist Literary Theory*, London: Methuen, 1985, p. 148.

9.   Shere Hite, *Women and Love*, London: Viking, 1988, pp. 14–15.

Diane Johnson

1.   Diane Johnson, *The Shadow Knows* (1974), London: The Bodley Head, 1975. p. 75. 'Only the shadow knows' is a catchphrase from a 1940s US radio show starring Lamont Cranston as the ubiquitous 'detective' shadow; Johnson's title also wittily alludes to the shadowed identity of her heroine, who takes over the detective role. The female 'I' uncovers things (including the slipperiness of 'I') which are occluded in classic detective fiction: this 'I'/eye adapts to the dark, and becomes familiar with the kinds of routine violence that are invisible to Famous Inspectors.
2.   Joyce Carol Oates, *The Mysteries of Winterthurn*, London: Jonathan Cape, 1984, p. 354.
3.   Hélène Cixous, 'The Character of "Character"', *New Literary History* 5, ii, 1974, pp. 383–402.
4.   Compare Iris Murdoch's argument with Plato, in *The Fire and the Sun*, discussed above; also Margaret Atwood's self-revision in her dystopian *The Handmaid's Tale*, discussed in Chapter 5 below.
5.   Muriel Spark, *The Driver's Seat* (1970), Harmondsworth: Penguin, 1974, p. 25.
6.   Joyce Carol Oates, *Do With Me What You Will*, London: Gollancz, 1973, p. 280.
7.   Judith Rossner, *Looking for Mr Goodbar* (1975), New York: Pocket Books, 1976, p. 390.

Marilyn French

1.   Marilyn French, *The Women's Room* (1977), London: Sphere Books, 1978, pp. 14–15.
2.   Kate Millett, *Flying* (1974), London: Hart-Davis, MacGibbon, 1975, p. 148.
3.   Nicci Gerrard, *Into the Mainstream*, London: Pandora Press, 1989, p. 136.
4.   Marilyn French, *Her Mother's Daughter* (1987), London: Pan Books, 1988, p. 768.
5.   Marilyn French, *Beyond Power: Women, Men and Morals*, London: Jonathan Cape, 1985, p. 545.
6.   Stephen Heath, *The Sexual Fix*, London: Macmillan, 1982, p. 67.
7.   Janice Doane and Devon Hodges, *Nostalgia and Sexual Difference*, London: Methuen, 1987, p. 10.
8.   Angela Carter, *The Infernal Desire Machines of Doctor Hoffman* (1972); reprinted as *The War of Dreams*, New York: Bard/Avon Books, 1977, p. 2. This novel has of course been reprinted since under its original title: my attachment to my grubby, down-market paperback version reflects my sense of the importance of Carter's association with 'genre' fiction; and in general, her penchant for 'transformations'

of all sorts. Her career has been an interesting demonstration of the shifting demarcations of textual 'space'. Currently, for instance, her work figures on lists of required reading in many British schools.

5. DIVIDED AMONGST OURSELVES

Fay Weldon

1. Fay Weldon, *Praxis* (1978), London: Coronet, 1980, p. 163. Weldon the 'woman of letters' judges literary prizes, joins in polemics about the Rushdie affair (in the Chatto *Counterblasts* series), writes *Letters to Alice on First Reading Jane Austen* (London: Coronet 1984) and is – in general – prolific, available, opinionated.
2. Fay Weldon, *Female Friends*, London; Heinemann, 1975, p. 249.
3. Fay Weldon, *Down Among the Women* (1971), Harmondsworth: Penguin, 1973, p. 83.
4. Fay Weldon, *Female Friends*, ed. cit., p. 9.
5. *Ibid.*, p. 159.
6. Fay Weldon, *Remember Me* (1976), London: Coronet, 1979, pp. 76–7.
7. Fay Weldon, *Watching Me, Watching You* (1981), London: Coronet, 1982, p. 171.
8. Fay Weldon, *The Life and Loves of a She-Devil* (1983), London: Coronet, 1984, p. 56.
9. Fay Weldon, *The Cloning of Joanna May*, London: Hodder & Stoughton, 1989, p. 202.
10. *Ibid.*, p. 202.

Margaret Atwood

1. Margaret Atwood, *Lady Oracle* (1976), London: Virago, 1982, p. 313.
2. Margaret Atwood, *Surfacing* (1973), London: Virago, 1977, Introduction by Francine du Plessis Grey p. 3; p. 6.
3. Coral Ann Howells, *Private and Fictional Words*, London: Methuen, 1987, p. 4; p. 55.
4. Margaret Atwood, *Cat's Eye*, London: Bloomsbury, 1989, p. 411.
5. Margaret Atwood, *Bluebeard's Egg* (1987), London: Virago, 1988, pp. 231–2.
6. Margaret Atwood, *Surfacing* (1973), London: Virago, 1979, p. 176.
7. Margaret Atwood, *The Handmaid's Tale* (1985), London: Virago, 1987, pp. 83–4.
8. There's an ongoing argument with Plato in several of the texts discussed in this book: explicitly in Iris Murdoch, slyly in Diane Johnson's *The Shadow Knows*, and again here in Atwood. The central issue is the Philosopher-Ruler's claim (cf. the Commanders in *The Handmaid's Tale*) to proprietorship of the real, and dismissal of the world of shadows, reflections, imitations. In *Surfacing*

Atwood behaved like a good essentialist, disclaiming imitations and opposing nature to culture; in *The Handmaid's Tale* she explores the cultural production of notions about people's natures, and the value of imitations as destabilising devices, offering alternatives and enabling definitions to wander. Atwood has taken to sowing scepticism about universalising discourses – cf. 'universal readers'.

9.   Margaret Atwood, *Life Before Man*, London: Jonathan Cape, 1980, p. 48.
10. Margaret Atwood, *Bodily Harm* (1982), London; Virago 1983, p. 300.
11. Margaret Atwood, 'An end to audience?' in *Second Words*, Toronto: Annansi, 1982, pp. 334–57.
12. *Cat's Eye*, London: Bloomsbury, 1989, p. 244.

Angela Carter

1.   John Berger, *Ways of Seeing*, London: BBC/Penguin, 1972, p. 47.
2.   Angela Carter, *The Magic Toyshop* (1967), London: Virago, 1981, p. 33.
3.   Angela Carter, *Heroes and Villains* (1969), Harmondsworth: King Penguin, 1982, p. 137.
4.   Angela Carter, *Love* (1971), revised edition London: Chatto & Windus, 1987, p. 2.
5.   Angela Carter, *Love*, London: Hart-Davis, 1971, p. 84.
6.   Angela Carter, *Love*, 1987 ed. cit., p. 22.
7.   Angela Carter, *The Passion of New Eve*, London: Gollancz, 1977, p. 75.
8.   Michel Foucault, *The History of Sexuality* (*La Volonté de Savoir*, Paris; Editions Gallimard, 1976), Volume One: An Introduction, tr. Robert Hurley, Harmondsworth: Penguin, 1981, p. 93.
9.   Angela Carter, *The Sadeian Woman*, London: Virago, 1979, p. 11. The passage continues: ' . . . so does the repression and taboo that governs our experience of flesh. The nature of actual modes of sexual intercourse is determined by historical changes in less intimate human relations, just as the actual nature of men and women is capable of infinite modulations as social structures change . . . . '
10. Angela Carter, 'Notes From the Front Line' in *Gender and Writing*, ed. Michelene Wandor, London: Pandora Press, 1983, pp. 69–77, p. 71, p. 76.
11. Angela Carter, *The Passion of New Eve*, London: Gollancz, 1977, p. 191.
12. Carter's contribution to a 1990 conference on 'Strangeness' imagines 'The Curious Room' in which the sixteenth century Archduke Rudolph kept his collection of marvels and monsters (mandrakes, mermaids and so on). One passage in particular comes close to describing this room as a type of the 'matrix of transformations': 'Perhaps, in the beginning, there was a curious room, a room like this one, crammed with wonders; and now the room and all it contains are forbidden you, although it was made just for you, had been prepared for you since time began, and you will spend all

your life trying to remember it.' 'The Curious Room', *Swiss Papers in English Language and Literature*, Vol. 5, 1990, pp. 215–32, p. 223.

13.   Angela Carter, *Nights at the Circus*, London: Chatto & Windus, 1984, p. 25.

14.   'On to the female body have been projected the fantasies and longings and terrors of generations of men and through them of women . . . a constant exchange takes place between images and reality.' Marina Warner, *Monuments and Maidens* (1985), London: Picador, 1987, p. 37.

15.   Carter's most recent novel, *Wise Children* (1991), makes its story-line out of a family tree: a theatrical dynasty in which the men belong to the legitimate stage, the women to vaudeville (though it turns out that it's a wise child that knows its own father, on either side of the blanket). *Wise Children* is a carnivalesque uprooting of the 'line', and fittingly enough one of its central settings is a Hollywood forest, where they're making *A Midsummer Night's Dream* (Shakespeare as literary 'father' is being reclaimed for the illegitimate 'branch').

Toni Morrison

1.   Toni Morrison, *Beloved* (1987), London: Picador, 1988, pp. 272–3.

2.   Toni Morrison, *Tar Baby* (1981), London; Triad Panther, 1983, p. 166; p. 168.

3.   Toni Morrison *Song of Solomon* (1977), New York: Signet/New American Library, 1978, p. 224.

4.   Toni Morrison, *Sula* (1974), London: Triad Grafton, 1982, p. 78.

5.   Ed. cit., p. 17.

6.   Behn, however, does suggest one of the most sinister and far-reaching consequences of slavery's 'progress'. Though the narrator, and various other sympathetic characters, promise Oroonoko that he will be able to return to Africa, it's clear that the way back is blocked. The white man's narrative of slavery (as opposed to 'classic' old-world slavery stories, in which masters and slaves change places, depending on the fortunes of battle) is a one-way traffic which seeks permanently to rename and reclassify black Africans.

7.   Jean-Paul Sartre, *Nausea* (*La Nausée*, 1938), Harmondsworth: Penguin 1963, p. 252.

Joyce Carol Oates

1.   Janice Doane and Devon Hodges, *Nostalgia and Sexual Difference*, London: Methuen, 1987, pp. 9–10.

2.   Charles Newman, 'The Post-Modern Aura', *Salmagundi*, Nos 63–4, 1984, pp. 3–199, p. 99.

3.   Joyce Carol Oates, *New Heaven, New Earth*, London: Gollancz, 1976, pp. 118–19.

4.   Joyce Carol Oates, *Do With Me What You Will* (1973), London: Gollancz, 1974, p. 373.

5. Vladimir Nabokov, *The Annotated Lolita*, London: Weidenfeld & Nicolson, 1970, p. xxxii.
6. Joyce Carol Oates, *The Edge of Impossibility* (1972), London: Gollancz, 1976, p. 8.
7. Joyce Carol Oates, *Childwold*, London: Gollancz, 1977, p. 60.
8. Joyce Carol Oates, *New Heaven, New Earth*, London: Gollancz, 1976, pp. 126–7.
9. Joyce Carol Oates, *Bellefleur*, London: Jonathan Cape, 1981.
10. Joyce Carol Oates, *Mysteries of Winterthurn*, London: Jonathan Cape 1984, p. 25.

Index

Bold references indicate the main treatment of the writer in question